THE AMERICAN DREAM

THE
AMERICAN DREAM

Walking in the Shoes of
CARNIES, ARMS DEALERS,
IMMIGRANT DREAMERS,
POT FARMERS, *and*
CHRISTIAN BELIEVERS

Harmon Leon

NATION
BOOKS

NEW YORK

Published by
Nation Books, A Member of the Perseus Books Group
116 East 16th Street, 8th Floor
New York, NY 10003

Nation Books is a co-publishing venture of the Nation
Institute and the Perseus Books Group.

Books published by Nation Books are available at
special discounts for bulk purchases in the United States
by corporations, institutions, and other organizations.
For more information, please contact the Special
Markets Department at the Perseus Books Group, 2300
Chestnut Street, Suite 200, Philadelphia, PA 19103, or
call (800) 255-1514, ext. 5000, or e-mail
special.markets@perseusbooks.com.

Designed by Timm Bryson

Library of Congress Cataloging-in-Publication Data
Leon, Harmon.
  The American Dream : walking in the shoes of carnies,
arms dealers, immigrant dreamers, pot farmers, and
Christian believers / Harmon Leon.
      p. cm.
  ISBN 978-1-56858-352-5 (alk. paper)
  1. United States—Civilization—1970- 2. Popular
culture—United States. 3. United States—Social
conditions—1980- I. Title.
  E169.12.L447 2008
  306.0973'090511—dc22
                              2008023160

10 9 8 7 6 5 4 3 2 1

Not everybody knows how I killed old Phillip Mathers, smashing his jaw in with my spade; but first it is better to speak of my friendship with John Divney because it was he who first knocked old Mathers down by giving him a great blow in the neck with a special bicycle pump which he manufactured himself out of a hollow iron bar.

—FLANN O'BRIEN

CONTENTS

CONTENTS

INTRODUCTION

When I was a child, my active imagination told me that the American Dream was to become a doctor who drove a garbage truck (I liked the way you could hang on to the sides of the vehicle while it was in operation). Ask a room full of any other seven-year-olds, and they'd each have a completely different take on the question. Just imagine if all those children's American Dreams had been fulfilled; we could have a world made up entirely of ballerinas, superheroes, and rappers.

What is the American Dream? Every proud citizen has their own unique, different idea on what it might entail. The definition is broader than Rosie O'Donnell's hips. Does the American Dream truly exist? Or is the whole myth a shame? Can the American Dream be achieved, or is it a pimp-slapped whore?

We live in a country of immigrants—dreamers, pragmatists, and everyone else in between—who have come to the United States in search of a better life. This conceptual American Dream ideal dates as far back as the sixteenth century, when Englishmen were persuaded to move to the colonies, thinking naïvely that the land of plenty, opportunity, destiny, and of personal and religious freedom awaited them. We now find ourselves in a country filled with twenty-four-hour waffle houses, gun-toting astronauts, topless doughnut shops, and carnies—all beautiful in their own individualistic way.

The American Dream is an idea so simple and yet so complex that it's difficult to define. The concept changes depending on ethnic heritage, economic, social, or political background. One component seems fairly consistent: the obsessive quest for money. Americans living in a society dedicated to capitalism are intently focused on the almighty dollar. To an older generation it's the old rags-to-riches tale, wealth sought after in the traditional way: through thrift and backbreaking hard work. For the scratch-card generation, it's been replaced by a get-rich-quick notion: achieving it without having to lift a finger, while eating a tub of pudding on your couch and watching *Dr. Phil* with the sound cranked up—becoming fatter and richer than your neighbor. Remember, the grass is always greener on the other side of the American Dream fence!

Americans have the right to be alive, free, and to pursue fulfillment in whatever way suits them, so long as that pursuit does not interfere with the freedom of their neighbor. In the words of powdered-wig-wearing Thomas Jefferson, every man and woman has a constitutional right to the "pursuit of happiness." But how does one encapsulate this concept in such a diverse nation? Think about how vastly different this "pursuit of happiness" is to a southern Bible-banger as compared to a Californian wife-swapping swinger.

That's why I'm going to set out on a cross-country quest for the American Dream. Yes, in order to better understand the elusive definition behind these words, I'll infiltrate and live the lives of vastly different people: I'll experience their perception of the American Dream by walking in their shoes. By posing as a legitimate member of each subculture—through cunning preparation and disguises—I'll see the world through their eyes. By acting as one of them, attempting to understand their ideology and American Dream, I plan to learn firsthand how the term is broadly perceived. Is the American attainable by everyone—no matter what their background—or is it, as one turn-of-the-century immigrant put it, "I arrived in America thinking the streets were paved with gold. I learned three things: (1) The streets were not paved with gold; (2) The streets were not paved at all; and (3) I was expected to pave them!"

As a jumping-off point for each excursion, threaded through the book will be an array of testimonials from actual people within that subculture, telling in their own words what the American Dream means to them. All facets of the culture will be examined, from liberal to conservative, rich to poor, religious fanatics to sexual deviants, as well as those who've come freshly over our borders. Oh, yeah, also celebrity impersonators—the more diverse the cross section, the better.

Yes, it's a dangerous job, but I'm up for the challenge. Think of me just like Indiana Jones, but without the bullwhip and leather jacket or direction from Steven Spielberg. Or impending danger from Nazis. On second thought, think of me nothing like Indiana Jones, though I will attempt to discover the highs and lows of the American Dream. Let's go!

IMMIGRANT AMERICAN DREAM

THE AMERICAN DREAM:
IN THEIR OWN WORDS
Jose Mota Cisneros, formerly of
Apozol, Zacatecas, now a U.S. citizen

What are my thoughts on the American Dream?

When I was a little kid, I didn't really think about those sorts of things. I came to the United States because there was no way to make a living in Mexico—not even to feed ourselves. So that was the main reason: opportunity.

I came across the border three times. The first was in 1971 when I was fourteen. There were about four guys my age. We went first to Tijuana and found a coyote, who are everywhere. They're out on the streets. They approach you. They're looking for you. They charged three hundred dollars.

We walked all day and all night. He had no idea where we were. It was scary. It was dark. I was never comfortable. We went over hills, overnight, all night and all the next day. The whole twenty-four hours, nothing but walking. We got picked up in a van filled with twelve people, and they asked us where we wanted to go, and they took us all the way to

1

Hamilton, California, where my big brother was. The walk was really hard but it was safe and easy.

I ended up staying for three years, until I was seventeen.

I worked picking and cleaning beets. Then I started working on a ranch in an almond field. That was easier work, but still long days. I found out that opportunity in the United States was less than I thought there was. I made no money, the kind of work I was doing was awful, and it was for such low pay. I did nothing but work day and night. Then I felt that that the American Dream was impossible, because without a green card, there's really not much opportunity other than survival.

When I went back to Mexico, I still couldn't even afford food doing any kind of work I could. That's how bad it was!

Then I came back a second time when I was nineteen. The coyotes charged me four hundred dollars. I was going with a group of guys, but this time we were robbed with knives at our stomachs. I get really sad to remember this because I want to forget these details.

They robbed us for everything we had: all of our money, food, and such. And that was after we walked all day and night. You don't pay a coyote until he gets to your destination. No one wants to carry that much money around, because you could get robbed. We had no money, no food. That was the worst nightmare.

We ended up in a trailer in San Diego packed completely with people to drive us further north. People had their asses in my belly and were passing out around me. When the truck was moving we were fine. But then we started suffocating was because the driver saw immigration at a checkpoint on Highway 5, and so the truck turned around. They left us in a parking lot, in the back of the trailer, and it became very hot. We couldn't breathe. My friend had a knife and started cutting through the back of the truck. We took turns breathing through the hole. Finally the person with the truck took us to his home and opened the door there, so we could breathe. You can't even imagine how hard it was.

Since we couldn't go across farther than the checkpoint, we had to go all the way back to the border. I got caught and ended up in jail for seventeen days, then was sent back to Mexico before I could try and get over again.

Then my dream changed, because that's when I started getting better work, and things turned to my favor. I thought I could attain the American Dream and eventually become legal. I realized there was opportunity. Coming over that time, the main thing was opportunity to work and feed my family back in Mexico and to save money to buy a home and then to eventually return.

The third time I came over I was twenty-two years old. We were near the airport, and there was this little wire, and we just walked over it. Maybe it was so patrolled there that they didn't assume you're going to cross. There was this station wagon that picked us up and that station wagon was air-conditioned.

I don't know why I walked those other times for so long. All the torture I went through before, and I didn't understand why this time it was so easy. All I know it was comfortable, and it was fast. It's just luck. One guy will take a bunch of people and stuff them in the back of a truck, or another guy will pick you up and take you in a station wagon. I'm very confused about that.

On the third time, I met my wife, and we fell in love and got married. So my dream changed again: to stay here in the United States and raise a family but maintain our Mexican customs, traditions, and language and not lose that. My dream kept changing from when I was fourteen and we could just barely feed ourselves, to the second time where I was trying to help my family, to finally when I ended up staying in the United States, falling in love, raising a family, and giving my daughters the opportunity to educate themselves.

Nobody ever plans to stay here. The dream is to come, set yourself up, create an opportunity, create a setup to help you to stay, and then go back. That's always everybody's dream: my dream, all my friends', their dads' dream. That's all we hear, "We're going to go back!" But we ended up doing so well, we can't really go back; we'll never go back. It's just impossible to make money there.

Have I reached my dream? Yes, I have. The only thing I miss is not being able to see my mother. . . . But I want to remain in the United States. It's a pretty short answer about the American Dream, but it's simple.

Illegal Alien Tourist Attraction

Running through the Mexican wilderness, I hear the sound of gunshots. The guy behind me slips on a rock and falls. Holding out my hand, I help him up. More gunshots. The sound of border-patrol sirens cuts through the air. We keep running as we're told to stick close to the group, and most important, to keep quiet. There's still a long, long way to go before we reach the border. . . .

Throughout our nation's history, immigrants have come to America to make a better life for themselves. Their dream simply involves being able to work in America. Remember that poem engraved on the Statue of Liberty?

> Give me your tired, your poor, / Your huddled masses
> yearning to breathe free, and so on and so forth . . .

Well, the "golden door" has slammed shut. Our borders have closed; it has become increasingly difficult to immigrate legally, thus the surge of numbers who now illegally cross into America. In 1980, there were an estimated 2 million illegal aliens, while now there are roughly 12 million working in the United States, who constitute 5 percent of our country's workforce—especially those jobs no one else wants to do.

Living illegally in America is incredibly difficult and involves working in fear, always hiding, and not being able to go back to your home country to visit your family. Because mostly young men make the trek across the border, the impact on the countries they leave behind—children raised by grandparents, ghost villages depleted of working-age men who've left to work across the border—is lasting and negative. Yet until economic conditions improve in these countries, the stream of people in search of work will continue.

In order to better understand this quest for the American Dream, I shall become an illegal alien.

First, I need to sneak over the border. Where else does the richest country in the world collide head on with an emerging nation than at the U.S.-Mexican border? By one estimate, 850,000 illegal immigrants arrive in the United States each year. In 2005, five hundred people died trying to journey across the desert, a number that has doubled since 1995. Risking death seems a little too dangerous for a humor writer.

Fortunately, there's a tourist attraction deep in the heart of Mexico where every Saturday night people can pay roughly twenty dollars to simulate what it would be like to be an illegal immigrant sneaking over the U.S. border while being chased by fake border guards who fire fake bullets at you. Sign me up. Yes, I shall sneak across the fake U.S. border in order to live the true American Dream.

PSEUDONYM: Chad Polochuk
PERSONA: Canadian illegal. Because he prefers a
challenge, Chad shall sneak into the United States
via the Mexican border.

Just like the multitude of new immigrants trying to make sense of American culture, the locale around me overwhelms my

senses. In Mexico City, I'm a foreigner in a new land trying to figure out how things work, harvesting no command of the language, heavily utilizing the art of French mime to communicate.
I hold out handfuls of money when paying for things with blind,
panicking faith, hoping people will grab the correct amount, as
if to say with utter innocence, "Take what is needed. I trust you
won't rip me off. Go on, take it!" Money is grabbed from my hand
from snickering cab drivers. This transaction takes place several
times. Soon I realize it would be wise to actually figure out
how the currency works.

The Journey Begins

Parque Eco Alberto is a nature reserve near the town of Ixmiquil-
pan in Hildago, roughly seven hundred miles from the U.S. border—the site of my make-believe, nighttime illegal alien border
crossing experience. I need to drive three hours from Mexico
City (add a few more hours when unable to read road signs) to
the three-thousand-acre eco-park communally owned by the
Hñahñu Indians (of whom now fifteen hundred live in Nevada,
mostly working as laborers).

Driving out of Mexico City is one of the scariest experiences
I've had—ever! Given the choice, I'd rather be an untrained
lion tamer then drive completely lost in a severely dented eight-
dollar-a-day rental car with no air-conditioning in the middle of
thick Mexico City traffic.

Vehicles seem to merge, at random, perpendicularly into un-
marked lanes. Sweat pours down my forehead. All signs are in
Spanish. Suddenly I find myself in a part of town where carts
are being pulled by donkeys. This can't be right. God, why

aren't the police pulling me over by now? Why won't they take me out of my lost misery!? I hope my eight-dollar little rental car doesn't get crushed by a truck. Will sneaking over the fake border be as hard as trying to get to the place to sneak over the fake border?

Not knowing how, but very thankful, I finally make it to Hildago. Still the clock ticks away. The sun goes down, and the rural landscape turns to darkness. I drive frantically through the darkened Mexican countryside on twisty one-lane roads. "No *inglés*! No *inglés*!" people exclaim when asked directions, pointing vaguely towards the mountainside for the benefit of the manic, fast-talking foreign man who's sweating profusely. Will I have to return to the United States without getting a chance to cross the fake United States border? Following a road sign that says *ALBERTO* and is emblazoned with the international symbol for swimming, I take my chances and veer down an isolated road in Mexico into pitch black.

Time to Sneak

"I'm here! I'm here!' I scream, sprinting through the gravel parking lot from my dented rental car with my arms thrashing, toward a gathering of people speaking loudly in Spanish, illuminated outside a small, lit cabana. I cry, "Don't cross that border without me! I'm here!"

A poster, which reads *CAMINATA NOCTURNA* ("nighttime hike") and shows the silhouette of several people standing by a cactus and a pickup truck under a moonlit sky, confirms I'm at the right locale. It's not exactly an illegal-alien theme park. By day, families come here for the waterslides and swimming.

Funded by the Mexican government, the fake-border-crossing experience has been Parque Eco Alberto's main moneymaking attraction since 2004, drawing in mostly tourists from Mexico City.

"I'm so happy to be here!" I exclaim to Yuri, attractive and clad in khakis—one of the three *coyotes* on our evening's journey. She's also the first person I've met today who is fluent in English (she worked as a nanny for a year in Connecticut).

"Do I need to fill out any forms?" I question, wondering if being chased in the dark in the Mexican wilderness by fake border guards requires a heavy insurance waiver.

The answer: no insurance waiver needed, just two hundred pesos, payable in cash (a bargain compared to the thousands people pay coyotes to sneak over the "actual" border).

Among the forty jubilant people gathered for tonight's border crossing are a good mix of young and old people, some little kids, and a pregnant woman (is she planning to have her baby across the fake U.S. border to mooch off our fake Social Security system?). I ask, "Is this a fun Saturday night out for people?"

"Most come from Mexico City," Yuri explains about the middle-class tourists in attendance. "But a good amount are locals."

The border-crossing experience has even attracted those as far reaching as Russia and the Netherlands, who come to Mexico to get a U.S. border crossing experience—seven hundred miles from the real, *actual* border.

"How close is this to the real thing?" I ask handing Yuri my two hundred pesos.

"This *is* the real thing!" she exclaims.

"Will we get chased?" I gleam with enthusiasm.

"Yes!"

"What if they catch us? Do we get deported from the park?"

"We won't get caught, because we're smart. If we do, we'll walk away," she assures, once again restating, "Cuz we're smart."

"Maybe I should change my clothes," I say, gesturing towards my shorts (I, too, am smart).

"That would be a good idea," she replies, knowing we'll soon be traversing desert, hills, brambles, and riverbeds in our faux crossing of the Rio Grande from Mexico into the U.S.

CHECKLIST FOR CROSSING SIMULATED
BORDER IN SIMULATED MANNER:
1. Don't wear shorts.
2. Bring a jacket.
3. In regard to shoes, make sure they're tied!

After changing into proper attire, I make it back for border-crossing roll call. Big smiles and anticipation are plastered on everyone's faces. Though everyone is speaking Spanish, a distinct female voice with an L.A. twang, proclaims, "This is going to be weird!"

Suddenly, a video camera is shoved in my face. Putting my hand up like a border crossing Paris Hilton, I blurt to the woman, "No pictures!"

"But you are in a public space," she protests like we're in America.

"Yeah, but this is a different country," I respond, acknowledging a large, girthy man with military buzz cut standing next to her.

"I have a show on Fox News Radio in L.A.," the girthy man interjects, gesturing to his young, hot assistant who is fluent in Spanish. Who would have thought deep in the heart of Mexico, the only other Americans for a simulated U.S. border crossing would be from Fox News!

"So what do you think is going to go on?" I ask.

"I'm just going to tell about my experience," he explains with a gleam in his eye for what is to follow.

Not the first time Mr. Fox News has done a story involving border issues, he also covered the Minutemen Project—the elderly vigilantes who took to patrolling the U.S.-Mexico border while sitting in lawn chairs, in order to prevent the feared onslaught of illegal aliens entering our country.

"I was impressed how they really had their stuff together," he says with admiration about the vigilante group who take to hunting down illegal aliens like angry villagers chasing the Frankenstein monster. Now the Fox News guy is here in Mexico to make sure the rumors aren't true that this is an illegal-alien training ground for those gearing up for the real thing.

Let the Games Begin

On instruction, my border-crossing compadres and I pile into four pickup trucks. We're driven down a darkened road into the unknown.

"If it's about anything, it's about our culture," Yuri explains, as we squat in the back of the moving vehicle under the clear star-filled night.

"What do people think of the experience?" I ask, adjusting my cramped, crouched position.

"We don't tell them anything," Yuri says, staring in my eyes. "We want them to discover it for themselves!"

The pickup trucks park in front of a small isolated church. Upon arrival everyone mills about in the dark not knowing what to expect. Will this be like an illegal alien Renaissance Faire where instead of a children's theater group adopting bad English accents, they portray coyotes and fake border guards? Already, the paunchy Fox News guy is in front of the church filming his hot assistant, who provides on-camera commentary for a documentary he is also producing.

"What everyone is doing, waiting for the church service to begin, preparing for what is to come, praying . . . ," she recites, flubbing the line. "People are gathered in front of this church to pray for safe passage. . . ." She flubs the line again: "What are they praying for? Safe passage."

"We can't do that many takes," the Fox News guy snaps. (How will we ever make it across the fake border if members of our group keep up this *Lord of the Flies* animosity?) Looking at the collective participants, the Fox News guy adds with snide smirk, "It's probably easier to sneak across the U.S. border."

"I came across the U.S. border," interjects a man who manages a motel in town, now acting as the Fox News Radio's hired guide, holding their camera equipment (probably being paid much less than an American camera assistant and doing twice the work).

"Why didn't you tell us that?" Fox News Radio replies.

"I came across in 1995," he confirms in broken English, as brownish moths dart about in the air. "We were fifteen guys. For two to three hours we run. Two trucks were waiting for us. Then we waited for twelve hours in a house. Finally we said, 'Let's go!'"

"Why did you do it?" Fox News questions.

"Work!" he replies, the obvious answer. "I find work in Dallas, Texas, painting houses." The local motel manager only returned to Mexico when his mother passed away. "It's harder to work in the U.S. than now," he confesses. "It's the same thing everyday. You have to wait for work all day." (Pause.) "I don't want to cross again. It's too dangerous. I have friends who've died there."

Suddenly, all the lights go off. Silhouetted by the moonlight, the church steeple now resembles an ominous giant at the gateway to the new land. When the lights come back on, three men in black ski masks appear. (I hope they're part of this.) The leader, wearing a straw hat on top of his black ski mask, commands the group in Spanish.

"What's he saying?" I ask Yuri, as we gather in a circle under a tree dripping moss. She leans in close and puts her hand on my shoulder.

"He crossed the border twenty-five years ago, cuz he had no home, no family, no food. There were no cars, no roads, no schools. But now things are better! You can work here; there's a lot of things you can do here." Unlike those who think this is a training camp for illegal aliens, the main purpose is to pay homage to the path immigrants have beaten across the desert. Yuri continues to translate, "The desert has claimed many lives, but tonight we will make it across the border!"

In the star-filled night, she rubs my shoulder and asks, "Are you scared?"

"I'm not sure."

"He could lead you, but he could fall down too." My coyote touches my shoulder at every translating opportunity (does my coyote have a mild border-crossing crush on me?), whispering in my ear while grabbing my arm. The sound of a dog barking grows in the distance.

"When they think of us they think of Speedy Gonzalez," I see the ski-masked man act out the character, seeing they cast him in his role. "This is how they know us! We are no aliens, we are humans too. We are good workers!"

People look ready to go. A little kid starts crying. Let's get on with the action. Damn it, I have a fake U.S. border to cross to begin my life in the American Dream!

"Where are the Mexicans?"

Ninety-seven percent of the people raise their hands.

The ski-masked man questions the Fox News posse, "Where do you come from?"

"We're from L.A.!"

"Heaven," the ski-masked man responses. (Has he been to L.A. lately?)

We're then given twenty seconds to think about why we want to cross the fake American border. Closing our eyes and holding hands, I imagine living in the land of Tom Cruise, coked-up Lindsey Lohan, and Mountain Dew—my American Dream.

A flag is unfolded. The Mexican National Anthem is sung. Then, "Stylistos, ready?"

"*Si!*"

My coyote squeezes my hand real tight. "Remember, run!" (Am I getting signals from my coyote?) "Are your shoes tied?" (See, shoe tying is an essential part of border-crossing protocol.)

"Yes!" I say with confidence. "My shoes are tied!" Then, noting my jacket, I confess, "Perhaps wearing a bright yellow soccer top isn't the best idea for sneaking across the border!"

Onward to the Border!

There're shouts of *"rapido!"* There're shouts of *"vamos!"* We take off running, directed to first circle the church. "Be real quiet and stay close." Within five minutes, the sirens start. They are onto us! More shouts of *"vamos!"* and *"rapido!"* A speeding vehicle with police lights careens in our direction. All forty of us are running. I'm running while laughing. (Who doesn't enjoy being chased in the dark!)

"Shut off the light; they're coming. Fast! Fast!"

The headlights draw near. *"Rapido! Rapido!"* We're directed to duck into a building site. Red police lights dot the dark, barren landscape. This is purely mental. I'm now crouched behind a building wall with forty others, giggling like a schoolgirl. The simulated border patrol truck stops in front of the building site with its searchlight traversing the landscape in our direction. Simulated tension is in the air.

"Get down. Get down," someone warns me in English.

We huddle in a corner. "Turn it off! Turn it off!" someone sternly says to the Fox News assistant, who annoyingly has her camera light on. Can the simulated border patrol officer hear my schoolgirl giggling? One question though, if we're still in simulated Mexico (*real* Mexico, actually), then why are we running? Technically, on simulated-legal paper, we really haven't done anything wrong other than a public display of nighttime running.

For some reason the fake border patrol didn't detect us (or hear my schoolgirl giggling). They drive off. There's a collective sigh of relief. If that's all it takes to ward off the border patrol, then so far sneaking into the United States is pretty easy. In fact, it's kind of fun. It's like capture the flag. Is it wrong that it's fun?

Like an irate high school gym teacher, as soon as the fake border patrol departs, the ski-masked leader instructs us to run and run fast (no slackers in border crossing).

"Rapido! Rapido!"

In groups of four we're again made to run down the darkened, deserted road. Women and children go first. Yes, forty people running as if it were a nocturnal *Running of the Bulls*. I soon find myself in a full sprint, still laughing my head off. Is the girthy Fox News guy able to keep this pace? He's nowhere to be seen, though his assistant runs alongside the man who manages the local motel, who's now holding her camera. Is it going to be all sprinting from here on out?! My lungs puff like a six-packs-a-day smoker. My sides ache. My muscles are stiff from driving all day in a dented rental car. Fortunately, we slow to a trot and follow a muddy path near a beautiful rushing-river gorge lit by the moon and stars and surrounded by mountains dotted with cactus and sharp, rocky bluffs.

"Rapido! Rapido!"

Apparently we didn't give the actors portraying fake border guards the slip. Just as we catch our breath, they're back with sirens blasting, parked on the roadway right above the canyon. Made to huddle bunched together in the thick, thorny bushes, the flashing red lights illuminate the mountains. Searchlights traverse across the foliage, hitting all areas but ours.

This time the uniformed fake-border-patrol actors stretch their thespian prowess. They send a message via bullhorn, taunting us in both English and Spanish, echoing throughout the wilderness, "Don't try and cross the border; you have family here. You have a life here. Don't trust the coyote; he will take your money and desert you!"

The searchlight steers toward our general, thicket-hiding direction. We're signaled to crouch lower. A thorny bush goes up my ass. A little kid starts crying. "Will you shut that damn child up!" I feel like screaming. "Do you want to ruin this for us!"

Then gunshots. *Blam! Blam!* Shots are fired out. I'm pretty sure the fake border guards are only firing fake bullets (then again, we didn't sign an insurance waiver). Regardless, I'm being shot at in my quest for the American Dream!

"We know where you're going. Give up now!"

Question: where the hell is the Fox News guy? He's nowhere to be found. Did they shoot the girthy right-wing radio presenter, or is he leading the charge? (Trying to prevent fake jobs being taken once we cross the fake U.S. border!) Unlike last time, the fake border guards exit their white pickup trucks and set out on foot with flashlights in hand, roaming the bushes, still taunting us in both Spanish and English.

"Don't trust the coyote; he will take your money and desert you!"

There're only three of them and there're forty of us. I think we can take them. I'm pretty damn sure they're only firing blanks as well.

The Journey Continues

A bonding camaraderie develops among the border-crossing participants. Someone lifts a fence for me to duck under. Another holds a branch out of my way. We form a line and traverse a narrow rock ledge, where improper footing would land one from the elevated bluff into the rushing river. (Good thing we didn't sign an insurance waiver.) I hold on to the shoulder of the person in front of me. The person behind me does the same to my shoulder.

Like it is a haunted house in the wilderness, one of the ski-masked assistants hides in a bush, grabbing people's feet as they pass while making monster noises. Someone loses a shoe in the mud. Another child starts crying. Then, there's a body. Lying in the path, one of the guides is face down on the ground, unmoved.

"Man down! Man down!" I cry, stepping around him as the group keeps moving.

Is he really hurt, or through the art of *acting*, simulating being a dead person?

"He got drunk," someone shares with a laugh.

Regardless, we walk by, assuming the latter. There's nothing we can do anyway. The fake border patrol is hot on our ass—he'll have to be left behind! A tree branch hits me in the face.

Down by the River

By the river, at a picturesque clearing, rumors fly that we have crossed the border. Have we crossed the border? Is that it? Are we now in the fake United States? That wasn't hard.

"The stars are really bright tonight," says Yuri as the rush of the water reverberates in the air.

We're told to hold hands, as the leader gives what I assume is a congratulation speech. (If there's hand holding, surely we must be in the fake U.S.A.?) Our ski-masked leader instructs everyone to throw a rock into the rushing river. We pick up stones and toss them. A series of splashes. We're throwing rocks in celebration, right, cuz that's what one does when they cross a fake border?

"Now we climb," whispers Yuri.

"Climb? What? Didn't we just cross the border?"

"No!"

"Then why the rock throwing?"

Before she can explain, the Fox News assistant completely ruins the mood and loudly explains to her camera. "We throw a stone into the river to symbolically expel evil spirits, so we can continue our journey." (Continue?!) She demonstrates by tossing a rock (which involves three takes). Emerging from behind a tree, the Fox News guy makes a return appearance. (Strange, you never see him and the fake border patrol at the same time—coincidence or something more?)

"Now we climb," Yuri says again with a smile. No longer do I have time for our budding border-crossing romance; I must climb!

There's a Tunnel Ahead

And climb we do. We scale up the mountain bluff. Loose rocks slip from under my tired feet. More effort is needed not to fall down. I grab a tree branch for support. *"Aaaaah!"* It turns out to be a prickly cactus. I'm starving from not eating dinner. We've been hiking for three hours, let alone for days on end across a desert with no water, and I've already had enough.

"We need to go into the tunnel," Yuri says, gesturing to a tiny entrance underneath a roadway.

"Really?!"

"You have to trust the leader. Otherwise, what do you do if you're left on your own?"

The group walks tightly together through a small, echoing, dark tunnel. Suddenly, the border patrol resurfaces on the road directly above us. (They're really starting to get on my tits!) Swirling red lights greatly contrast the still darkness, from our cavernous tunnel vantage point.

"Mas poquito! Mas poquito!" quietly, but firmly stresses the leader (I know from seven Spanish lessons on CD that it translates to *"more smaller")*. Hellishly claustrophobic, I'm stuck directly in the middle, as we're made to move tightly packed together inside the tunnel.

"Are you okay?" asks Yuri, noting the momentary panic-stricken expression across my face.

"Um . . . sure," I say, contemplating turning myself in and surrendering to the fake border patrol, except I'm unable to move.

"We know where you're going. You have a life here," once again taunts the border patrol actors with their bullhorn. And then, "Forget about the American Dream!"

Shit, I've come this far, there's no way I'm going to forget about *my* American Dream.

As claustrophobia increases, the border patrol sticks around much longer than the previous time. My schoolgirl giggling has permanently ceased. This isn't as funny as before, as my mind now thinks about all those immigrants who pack themselves in the back of trailer trucks, in brutal, desperate, inhumane conditions. For those who think this is an illegal-alien training course, think again. It's more like *Scared Straight.* After they depart, more running, more loose rocks, more tripping, more branches in the face, etc. . . .

The Promised Land

It's well past midnight. Arrests have been made. For some reason, four teenage boys jump out from the bushes when they hear the patrol sirens and futilely try to make a run for it down the middle of the road. They don't make it very far. Caught directly in the vehicle searchlights, the culprits are frisked by the fake border guards, slightly manhandled, handcuffed, and then thrown in the back of their pickup trucks. They then speed off, satisfied with their catch. The rest of the group watches from a bluff a safe distance away (at least I'm given a chance to momentarily sit down), as the border guards scream, "Stop right there!' with their (hopefully) fake guns drawn.

Something is slightly fishy, though. Those who are arrested weren't with the rest of the group prior to the point of being arrested. I think they are also merely "actors." If so, this demonstration has somehow become like the *Illegal Alien Batman Forever Stunt Show* at 6 Flags Magic Mountain. The Fox News crew stands directly on the side of the road filming the apprehension without any interruption or questioning—I knew they were in cahoots with the fake border patrol!

Once again, the group is instructed to get in the back of one of four waiting pickup trucks.

"Put this on!"

Blindfolds are handed out. Instructions are made not to peek. Too tired to disagree, I wrap the piece of cloth around my eyes. The pickup trucks take off. Around hilly terrain and windy roads we drive in complete, utter silence and darkness. Is this a trap? Will our fake border-crossing end with us getting faux executed by drug lord impersonators? I should have listened to the fake border patrol's stern warning and not trusted the coyotes.

Coming to a stop, we're guided from the vehicles to a grassy area, once again made to hold hands. Surely we must be across the fake U.S. border. As the ski-masked leader lectures the group in Spanish, I'm left imagining what the fake U.S.A. looks like. Will we take off our blindfolds to find our leader now drinking a Coca-Cola while wearing an Uncle Sam outfit as firecrackers shoot out of his ass to the tune of *"God Bless America"*?

A countdown begins.

". . . 4-3-2-1!"

Slowly the cloth is removed from my eyes. I can see. We're welcomed to the Promised Land. The entire mountainside is lit up. Thousands and thousands of candles placed on the large bluff and are logistically situated to form the outline of the country of Mexico. Faces glow from the light. A random guy hugs me. I hug him back. It's an amazing site, though I feel slightly lonely, unable to verbally communicate to everyone here; for the first time this evening, feeling very, very foreign.

"We've made it!" exclaims Yuri, with a huge, brightly illuminated smile.

"Yes, we made it," I reply. "We truly are here."

Now I Get a Green Card

After making my way across the fake U.S. border, Canadian illegal alien Chad Polochuk decides to journey across the *real* U.S. border (via airplane, minus the fake border guards chasing me, etc.).

Upon arrival, I kiss the soil—United States soil! Not only am I in the land of the free, but also the home of the brave, water-board torture, and celebrities leaving limos without panties! Lady Liberty smiles down on me in this land of golden opportunity.

One small problem: as a fake illegal alien, in order to fulfill my American Dream, I need to obtain a green card. Issued by the INS, green cards are essential documents needed to verify immigrants as resident aliens with the legal right to work in the United States. With an estimated 11 million illegal immigrants nationwide, a green card is gold for those questing the American Dream—and often unobtainable.

So what am I to do? How am I to obtain a job in this rich country? How will I support my fictional family!? I could wait around for years to win the green card lottery (they make it sound like this can be done with a scratch-and-win card). I could claim political asylum. Maybe I could marry a complete stranger in order to get this prized piece of work-permitting documentation?

To hell with that! I want my American Dream *now!* I want a green card by midafternoon, no later! In order to reap the fruits of prosperity in this land of plenty, the process shall be greatly sped up. That's right, I'm going straight to the black market!

Black Market Clash

The counterfeit-green-card boom kicked off in 1986 when the federal law began to require all employers to verify legal status before hiring an employee. Putting a crimp in the size of the illegal workforce, the law said that if an immigrant couldn't present a green card, that equaled no job! Under the 1986 law, employers aren't required to verify the validity of immigration documents, and many chose not to, as they want to exploit the cheap labor force.

My quest for finding a work permit to fulfill my American Dream has taken me to the Mission District of San Francisco. I'm wearing a Toronto Maple Leafs hockey jersey, adding to my Canadian-illegal-alien persona. On a sunny Saturday afternoon, there's a myriad of activity with its ninety-nine-cent stores, churro vendors, check-cashing places, and plentiful taquerias. As long as there is a demand to become a working American, there will be those who sell black-market green cards. The busy season is late spring and early fall due to the fact that a lot of immigrant work is in agriculture. San Francisco, like most major cities, has a steady demand, being that here it's mostly restaurant jobs.

A Las Vegas–based syndicate recently tried to muscle in on the San Francisco and New York markets, creating the same gang dynamics of the drug trade, only with the fake-green-card industry. Thus, I'm weirdly nervous. Will this be hard? Is there an "initiation," or "test"? Will I get a *beatdown* before I'm allowed to buy a fake green card? Am I going to be *the patsy* in an elaborate police sting operation? Am I going to have to use karate at some point?

I've recruited a Mexican friend of mine to help with the translation process, and to give validity to my honky-cracker-gringo green card pursuit (Canadians aren't usually seen waiting at Home Depot with the other day laborers). A friend of hers just came over from Guadalajara and went right to the Latino neighborhood. He tipped her off that in front of photo and passport stores are where you go to get fake green cards.

"He's a *fresa* [strawberry]," she says, describing her wispy friend. "He's not going to do heavy labor; he's a wheeler or dealer," she adds, explaining his goal is to find a business to take back to Mexico or vice versa. "He wants to buy clothes in bulk and then mark up the price and sell it on the black market." In the meantime, *Fresa's* going to use his new phony green card in order to find temporary work on a fishing boat.

Sauntering towards Twenty-first and Mission, a Latino guy wearing a down jacket and baseball cap stands in front of a music store two doors down from the passport-photo place, suspiciously hanging out with a very serious expression on his mug. We glance over, but he doesn't make eye contact. Not thinking much of it, my friend suddenly hears him say to a passing Latino man, *"Micas? Micas?"* (Street slang for *"green card."*)

As my friend turns, he finally initiates eye contact. After a brief exchange in Spanish, the guy breaks into a friendly grin; he knows he has a customer.

"My friend is from Canada," she tells him.

"You betcha, eh!" I throw out with convincing Canuck twang.

"He's looking for a green card."

"Okay," the guy says. Not questioning whether I might be an undercover cop, he shows no fear of being busted, and immediately escorts us inside the passport-photo place so I can get a picture taken for my phony green card.

My black-market ambassador gives a familiar nod to the store's proprietor, who seems to know what's going on; after all, he brings in a fresh supply of regular, steady customers. (Some businesses will even give a small percentage for that.)

Taking my place in line behind a little kid with glasses, I learn the black market prices go as such:

- Twenty-five dollars: fake green card
- Twenty-five dollars: fake social security card
- Ten dollars: real passport photo (for a fake green card)

"Is it okay to get just the green card, eh?" I ask in fabricated Canadian accent.

"No business!" my black-market ambassador coldly snaps. Due to the risk, it must all be a package deal; you can't just buy one fake government identification card.

Agreeing to both, I say, "I need to work, eh!" My black-market ambassador nods his head sympathetically, clearly understanding what I mean.

"Why are you smiling so much?" asks the photographer, before snapping the photo that will grace the front of my work-permitting fake green card.

"Because I'm soon going to become an American!" I boast with pride. "U.S.A.! U.S.A.!" I chant.

Upon green-card photo-session completion, my black-market ambassador hands me a white envelope. "Sign your name and write your birthday," he requests. "It's for the green card."

This is exciting. I'm wheeling and dealing on the black market for phony government documents! I bet within these circles I could easily buy someone's kidney! I boldly jot, "*Chad Polochuk.*"

With the transaction finalized, a real name is finally given: "I'm Roberto. Here's my cell-phone number," he says, scribbling the info into my notebook. "Come back at two PM," he adds in a really friendly manner as if this were a Sunday-school picnic. Roberto clarifies, "I don't make the cards; I send them off to be made."

"You betcha, Roberto," I say, extending my hand in a fair black-market transaction handshake (mildly disappointed I won't be taken to a shady building to see the whole operation with the slight fear of being robbed). Making it even easier for me, he doesn't want any money up front!

Excellent! The ability to work and make minimum wage in the United States is a dream for many immigrants. This dream will come true with a two-hour turnaround time.

Uncut, blank, phony document stock smuggled in from Mexico; a scanner; typewriter; laminator; and cutting board are the tools of the document forger. A phony Social Security card's foundation paper, with light-blue marbling over a white background, can be bought at almost any art-supply store. Each eight-and-a-half-by-eleven-inch sheet of light blue paper makes eight fake Social Security cards. The result provides any new immigrant (or terrorist) the documentation needed (though I doubt Al Qaeda searches for guys in front of a photo place).

Going the forged-green-card route surely beats standing on Cesar Chavez Street vying with dozens of others for a day-labor gig. Added to that is the amount of money one can make in America. Even an unskilled worker making eight dollars an hour still earns substantially more than many back home, where wages can be as low as two dollars per hour. In addition, landing a job even with illegal documentation can lead to eventual permanent status if the employer files a petition. Thus it's sometimes worth the risk of being deported just to get your foot in the door.

With time to kill, I venture on my own. Strolling down Mission Street, I now notice that in front of every damn passport or photo place two guys occasionally throw out, *"Micas? Micas?"* How can police not catch on? It becomes apparent when you know what to look for. I'm no Columbo, yet I'm aware of this.

When I return at two PM, Roberto is standing in front of *Fashion Emporium.* There's a bustle of activity: four others now encircle the passport-photo place. Roberto seems to be taking direction from a guy clad in a silver baseball cap adorned with dollar signs.

"Five minutes! Five minutes!" he shouts, seeing me from across the street, making exaggerated hand signals to stay where I am.

My faux government-issued documents are still not ready; my American Dream is taking longer than I thought it would. Two well-dressed Chinese gentlemen are waiting as well, anxiously shifting their weight from foot to foot. Their attention is also focused on Roberto. All the morning green-card orders have to be done at one time.

I post up by a parking meter two doors down from a portrait studio, where yet another guy in front exclaims, *"Micas? Micas?"* like it's the most natural thing in the world. (Mission Street has more fake-green-card guys than churro vendors!)

Roberto gets on his cell phone and frantically paces up and down the block, adamantly talking, while the guy with the silver dollar-sign hat—slightly scarier than friendly Roberto—ventures across the street. He stands behind us, muttering *"Micas? Micas?"* as people continually pass, working the crowd.

Twenty minutes later, still no black-market green card. Impatient, the two Chinese gentlemen look mildly concerned.

Many paranoid questions race through my mind. Can the police arrest us for this? Will the judge make an example out of me? Does Roberto think I'm an undercover cop? Will zombies walk the earth and drink the blood of the living? Did I leave the iron on in my house?

Roberto still paces the street, periodically stopping to gesture "five minutes," extending his hand to emphasize this time increment, making a mockery of the expediency of my American-Dream quest.

The big cheese finally arrives dressed in casual business attire, with the sides of his head shaved and a long rat tail in back. He confers with Roberto. Suddenly a large red pickup truck pulls into a parking spot across the street from the photo place, igniting a flurry of activity. Like it were a covert military operation, Roberto runs toward the vehicle and sticks his head into the truck's driver's-side window. After a few minutes he runs back across the street and into the passport-photo place. Emerging several minutes later, Roberto makes his way over and quickly hands me the envelope with my signature on it, which contains two pieces of newly constructed government identification. His partner with the dollar-sign baseball cap does the same to the two Chinese gentlemen. (I think Roberto actually got the card laminated at the photo shop.)

"Do I give you the money here?" I ask.

"Yes!" he says with a sense of urgency.

"Can I open a bank account with this or get a driver's license?"

"No, it's just for work!"

"How about a Blockbuster membership?"

"No!"

Not one for chit-chat while making a black market transaction in open, broad daylight, Roberto then walks away very fast, disappearing in the Saturday afternoon crowd.

My green card reads, RESIDENT ALIEN, and boasts on the back, PERSON IDENTIFIED BY THIS CARD IS ENTITLED TO RESIDE PERMANENTLY AND WORK IN THE U.S.," is adorned with some person's smudged fingerprint, my forged signature, and has sort of cloudy blotches within the lamination. My Social Security card is cut at an irregular angle. I guess this would work, if I applied for a job in a poorly lit room or cave.

Regardless, I now possess the passable ID that separates immigrants around the world from working in the land of Air Jordans. What people in other countries dream of, I just obtained effortlessly for fifty dollars (plus ten for the passport photo).

The two Chinese gentlemen look at their cards with big smiles. Nodding, they seem very pleased. Together we swiftly walk in the same direction down Mission Street.

"Let the American Dream begin, eh!" I share with them. They shoot me a paranoid look, also walking away very quickly. No time for small talk; we're now all behind a façade of being legal U.S. citizens. Smiling towards Lady Liberty in the east, I'm now legal to work in America! I just hope I don't get deported.

I Land an Illegal Job!

With my fake green and spanking-brand-new phony Social Security card, it's time to go to work—literally. Canadian illegal alien Chad Polochuk will now get a job like any good U.S. citizen (except with fake documents). Welcome to America!

To test the validity of my sixty-dollar investment, I'm going to try and land a job not usually sought by illegals. Like my friend explained, most illegal work done in San Francisco is in restaurants and construction. Unlike applying for a dishwashing job—where phony documentation wouldn't be questioned—I go off the curve.

An ad in the weekly paper states the San Francisco Ballet is looking for a crack team of telemarketers. Chad Polochuk calls the provided number.

"Bring two forms of ID," a woman named Clarissa tells me after scheduling an interview, stressing that theirs is a *fun workplace.*

Eyeing my two forms of fake identification, I quickly proclaim, "Yes, I got two forms of ID!" I add, "I just became a resident alien, and I'm very proud of them!"

Friday at 2:30 I enter a second floor office on Market Street, where I'm lead to a round table with five potential San Francisco Ballet telemarketers who fill out job applications. The collective anxiety of complete strangers vying for the same job hangs in the air. One bearded man resembling a well-to-do magician, wears a suit. Why? Telemarketing is a job all about interrupting people while eating dinner. Who cares what you look like? That's why I'm wearing a toque and T-shirt that says, CANADIAN GIRLS KICK ASS, which also stresses my foreign-origin status.

Clarissa, an attractive, perky woman, informs our table-encircling group, "This is a fun place to work! We share food. We listen to music. This is the first job I've had where I don't wake up in the morning and say, 'Oh, god, I don't want to go to work!'"

Everyone nods their heads. All I see is sterile cubicles and signs posted on the walls, encouraging people to get their sales numbers up. Clarissa makes it sound like the San Francisco Ballet telemarketing office might partake in boss-initiated *Hawaiian Shirt Friday.*

In ten- to fifteen-minute durations, individuals go into Clarissa's private office for a personal interview. Rolling up my sleeves, I jot on my application all my previous job experience from Moosejaw, Canada:

- *Telemarketing/Moosejaw Hockey News*
- *Sales Associate/Carl's Curling Supplies*
- *Tim Horton Donuts*

To help seal Chad Polochuk's first job in America, under the question, "Do you have an interest in the arts?" I write, "Yes. I was a member of *Back-Bacon Breakers*, Moosejaw's third largest interpretive dance troupe."

"Why do you think you're qualified to work for the San Francisco Ballet?" Clarissa asks during my turn behind the closed office door.

"Because I follow the ABCs: *A*lways *B*e *C*losing!" I say, leaning forward in my chair, then giving her a Canadian wink.

"That's what I like to hear!" Clarissa remarks with a smile. "Wow, that was easy." I'm welcomed to the San Francisco Ballet telemarketing team—a mere one minute into my interview.

"Sweet! I just *snuck over,* I mean *moved,* here from Canada, and that would be great, eh!" I blurt, wondering why all people don't simply tell perspective employers exactly what they want to hear to please them.

Clarissa then hands me an *Employment Eligibility Verification* sheet and tells me to fill it out back at the round table with the magician and the others. Like a Chinese menu, it allows me to choose from three columns of federally approved identification that states I'm legal to work in the U.S.A.

The top of the page reads:

> *I am aware that federal law provides for imprison-*
> *ment and/or fine for false statements or fake docu-*
> *ments in connection with the completion of this form.*

(Good thing my phony federal identification cards don't contain my real name!) Everyone else has their two forms of identification already on the table: driver's licenses, Social Security cards, or passports. Slapping my cards down, I'm the only one presenting themselves as a *resident alien.* The man resembling a magician's Social Security card is of a much different color than my faux version. Clarissa goes around the table inspecting everyone's identification documents, the fine line that separates millions from earning a living in this country.

Leaving some of my *Employment Eligibility Verification* info blank forces Clarissa to closely examine each fake ID (discolored Social Security card, cloudy laminated green card), as we dance the tango of legal-illegal, what is good and what is bad, criminal and noncriminal. She gives a good, hard look. After a few moments she fills in "Issued by U.S. Justice Department" where I neglected to, on the line for resident alien card. Clarissa then tells me to report for training tomorrow morning at 9:30 AM.

"This is the first job I've had outside of Canada," I beam.

Clarissa smiles, then tells our country's newest citizen, "Welcome to America."

The fruits of this land will soon be mine!

Illegal Reality

Using the hoe in my hands, I'm digging hard at the dirt. Man, there's a lot of weeds. Sweat pours down my back. I've been at this since seven AM. For the next eight hours, this hoe will be in my hands. Tomorrow, if I return, I'll have this hoe in my hands again. We start work early because in the afternoon the sun gets much too hot. Despite a fake green card, it's highly doubtful that many illegal aliens would end up working a cushy job at the San Francisco Symphony with the potential option of zany *Hawaiian Shirt Fridays.*

Most of the work found within the American Dream is done where I now stand—in the middle of a large field, and it's heavy physical labor for $8.25 an hour. A few other workers hoe nearby. Another works a forklift. The sound of Spanish fills the air. Two small dogs bite at my heel as I work my way down the field in a never-ending row of chard, celery, artichokes, garlic, and cabbage, deep in the heart of rolling hills in Steinbeck's *Of Mice and Men* country. Blisters are on my hands. I have trouble deciphering chard from weeds, tearing up all vegetation in my path. The sprinklers around me go, *"Fft-fft-fft."*

Close by, day laborers stand in packs of two and three along the side of the road and wait for construction jobs, where they can make fifteen dollars an hour. They don't even want to work on the farm, despite that those here are grateful to have the job. But it could be worse: I could be working the strawberry fields, bloodying my hands harvesting one of the most back-breaking, labor-intensive crops. About once a year, the Department of Immigration makes a sweep of the farms in the area and fines twenty-five hundred dollars if someone is caught working illegally.

"Hablas español?" a worker named Juan, who wears a cowboy hat, asks me while tinkering with a tractor by the barn, while chickens do their thing.

"Uh, no," I respond, *"Hablas inglés."*—I'm considered the foreigner when it comes to agricultural work. Juan has worked here on and off since the seventies, even bringing over relatives from Mexico to work. Although he has made enough money to buy a house back home, he likes the farm and chooses to live on the property in a small trailer by the barn, where clothes hang on a line.

"Who did you talk to about working out here?" questions the son of the woman who runs the farm, surprised to see a gringo doing migrant-labor work. It's reverse prejudice. I'm looked at like some crazy homeless guy who talked his way into working for the day to make spare crack money, now up to his ankles in chard.

I get back to my hoeing. *"Fft-fft-fft,"* go the sprinklers. More blisters on my hands. Juan laughs with a friend as they tinker with an engine. The tractor near the barn starts casting long shadows across my feet. Soon the sun will go down on us workers out here in the field, and it will be the end of another day in the United States of America, and the day after will be another day as well for everyone here, on the farm living the American Dream.

Once again the sprinklers go *"Fft-fft-fft."*

CHAPTER TWO

CARNY AMERICAN DREAM

THE AMERICAN DREAM: IN THEIR OWN WORDS
Tom Hoey, American carny 1992–2002

Being a carny and electing to travel year-round, which many do, is very different than living in one place, as I do now. First, you have the freedom of selecting your "route," or the carnival ride companies you will play with, and because of that your "neighbors" can change constantly, which exposes you to different outlooks and styles of living.

The carny code is pretty simple. You mind your own business. It is up to you how you and your children elect to live. Excluding abuse of hard drugs or pedophilia, most carnies could care less how you live your life, what religion you believe in, or what your politics are. Carnies are mostly libertarians in nature and resent the interference of the government and most authoritarian figures. You could be gay or lesbian, rich or poor, religious or atheist, and no one in our community will voice any disapproval or try to convert you or change your mind. Most believe that we must choose our own paths and make our own rules, as long as they do not affect others around us.

As a rule, most carnies can be generous to folks who are down and out, and we take care of our own. There is no such thing as an official retirement age. You work as long as your health permits, and most carnies die "on the job," so to speak. If you have some hard times or if your business is not going well due to something out of your control, we will take up a "carny collection" to help you out.

What is unique to our trade is that each day is normally quite different. We tend to be facing new entertainments and new challenges every day. We never know what the next "date" or "spot" will bring.

I can recall many moments that have been frozen in my memory. The parts of my time as a carny that were joyful could not have been experienced in any other industry. What stays with me is the joy in a child's face when he or she rides on the Carousel or wins a cheap twenty-five-cent prize. This is a moment—one that you have shared with them—that you know will remain in their memory forever.

As in any industry, the most permanent memories tend to be negative. Muddy, flooded lots, successive days of rain, and the waiting, since life in the carny is similar to life in the army. But . . . there are exciting memories also, of Thanksgivings around a huge picnic table, where you and all your carny friends group together, experiencing love and companionship that you cannot enjoy in any other industry.

Our work is our life and work is, most times, when we are having the most fun. Who wouldn't like a job that is exciting, dramatic, and fun . . . every day, every hour, every minute.

I, CARNY

NO DRUNKS OR DRUGGIES! reads a hand-scrawled flyer trumpeting carny work, posted on the Showtown Bar's bulletin board in Gibsonton, Florida (hometown of "Lobster Boy" Grady Styles).

I stare slack-jawed at the poster, wondering whether *only* drunks or druggies apply for this type of work; I'm fixated by the offer.

I call the number.

"I'm not a drunk! I'm not a druggie!" I holler to a woman named Phyllis—the very first time I've *ever* mentioned these facts during a job interview.

"Well, get on out here! We need you!" Phyllis replies without hesitation.

Next thing I know, I'm packing my bags, then driving, en route to rural Indiana and . . . the American Dream!

When one thinks of carnies, what springs to mind is missing teeth, crystal meth, small hands, and the smell of cabbage. These are stereotypes. Like Old West outlaws, their freewheeling, nomadic lifestyle—moving from town to town—lends itself to a life wholly outside of mainstream society, speaking a language entirely their own, in a world filled with hardened, scary, scary people. And I want to learn their secrets. Yes, it's time to run away with the carnival!

The night before my weeklong carny tour of duty began, I couldn't sleep. Plagued with the same haunting feeling one would have the night before going to prison, questions raced through my mind: Will carnies steal my shoes? Should I sleep with my money in my sock?! Is there a carny initiation involving feces and a piñata?!?

That's why, in order to fit in, I decided to adopt the adequate carny persona:

PSEUDONYM: Ajax (no last name).
DISGUISE: American flag bandana. Black T-shirt with cut-off sleeves (or simply no shirt at all). Big

scorpion belt buckle. Cowboy boots, long jeans.
Mirror aviator shades. One tooth blacked out.
DIETARY HABITS: Anything skewered on a stick.

Arriving in the southwest corner of Indiana—the kind of town where people pull up to convenience stores and leave their pickup trucks running while going inside—I walk onto the lot of the 162nd Annual Gibson County Fair grounds. Dozens of shirtless, tattooed carnies, with large, soft, doughy bodies from months of carnival-food eating (corn dogs and fried Twinkies aren't exactly the Atkin's diet), bustle to set up the Midway in the two-hundred-degree summer humidity, under a large banner that boasts:

BURTON BROS AMUSEMENT
FIRST IN FAMILY FUN.
QUALITY IN MOTION

Stuffed-animal prizes are being hung inside *joints* (booths), R keys put in place, while *ride jockeys* tighten bolts on rides with visibly questionable safety standards.

What could be more American than a small-town county fair deep in the heartland, where the smell of carnies and cotton candy wallow in the humid, midwestern summer-night air like a whirling kaleidoscope viewed from on top of the Ferris wheel—backed, of course, by heavy metal music?

The carnies have just done a *circus jump*: three hours of tear-down immediately followed by a three-hundred-mile drive from a small town in Illinois, then setting up the entire carnival mid-way by the five PM opening. (Perhaps that's where the fabled carny crystal meth comes into play?)

Looking around at the cavalcade of precarnival activity, I settle into the fact that this will be my temporary new home, and
these are my soon-to-be peers.

"Ajax has come to work," I state (referring to my fictional self
in the third person) to a round woman with frizzy poodle hair.
Supervising the situation while riding a four-wheeler is Phyllis,
who, for some reason, now goes by *Miss* Phyllis.

"I'm straightforward. If you see me not talking to you, that
means you pissed me off," Phyllis says. (Should I mention that's
passive-aggressive rather than straightforward?)

"Ajax has got to get his shit together." I mutter, swearing to my
boss mere sentences into our introduction.

Though downright mean (leery of outsiders?) in a dysfunctional motherly sort of way, Phyllis takes me in—a guy wan-
dering off a rural Indiana street in a black sleeveless T-shirt and
big scorpion belt buckle. No W2 forms to fill out, no ID required, no real name needed. The only carnie requirement is to
work the joint, tear it down (*slough*) when necessary, then set
it up again in the next town. Anyone who does that can find a
home with the carnies.

"You'll share a trailer with Jared," Miss Phyllis mumbles as I
jump on the back of her four-wheeler and ride to the *backlot*,
where, set up behind the Tilt-A-Whirl, on the fringe of the fairground, lay rows of long, white trailers.

The first thing I learn is the whole carny-teeth thing is true;
they all have fucked-up teeth—the tooth fairy would have a
field day here.

"I got my shit thrown around everywhere," remarks Jared, my
new roommate—a gangly kid with teeth jutting out at all angles.

"That's okay," I somehow hear myself saying.

"I got a TV," he boasts.

"I like TV," I reply.

Jared leads me to the end of a long trailer—the new-guy sleeping quarters. He opens the door to a dark crevasse, with just enough room to fit two stacked mattresses situated like bunk beds and an assortment of garbage. It smells like a ferret cage. The odor from the hot, stuffy cubbyhole literally makes me start gagging. Seriously! I can't stop. This is where I'll be sleeping for the next week. Yes, hello, scabies!

"Don't let any ride jockeys into your trailer," Jared warns in a hushed voice.

"Why?" I ask as my eyes water.

"Cuz we can smoke weed, and they can't," he explains, then asks, "Do you spark up?" quickly adding, "You'll get kicked out if you have any of the locals in your trailer." Jared nudges with a wink, "You probably won't ever see me. Last night, after we got to town, I hooked up with one of the girls who works at the gas station!" Peaking my curiosity, Jared blurts, "Skittles is the biggest asshole."

"Why?"

"He told Miss Phyllis the girl from the gas station was only fifteen."

(Pause.) "Okay."

"He got me in trouble."

(Pause) "Yeah, what an asshole."

Jared takes me under his wing, talking a mile a minute. He seems to be, as the kids put it, "tweaking." "I had four yellow jackets today," he spits out, while we stand inside his Fish Till You Win joint. "I haven't slept in two days."

"When Ajax sleeps, the nightmares come," I contribute.

Like bad-movie expository writing, Jared gives a rapid lowdown on some of the other carny characters. "That's Wayne-o," he says, pointing to a thirty-year carny vet; a rail-thin, shirtless, mustached man with reptilian movements traversing across the fairgrounds. "He's the biggest crackhead there is, but he's really smart."

"Okay." (Pause.) "Heroin makes Ajax smart!"

> **CARNY TIP:** In the Basketball game, the balls are overinflated, and neither the ball nor the hoop is regulation size. Forget shooting off the backboard or rim; the key is to drop the ball straight down in an alley-oop shot.

I'm recruited to help a few carnies set up flags on poles on the oven-hot metal roof of the water-squirt joint (you squirt water into a clown's mouth in order to blow up a balloon); all the while the veteran carnies size me up—if I show weakness they'll exploit it.

"I'm going to call you Hyde. You look like that guy from *That '70s Show*," says a large, ten-year vet with shaggy hair, who then keeps calling me by a different nickname every time he sees me. Later, he stares at my police regulation mirrored sunglasses. "No, I think I'm going to call you Chips."

Is he calling me Chips cuz he thinks I'm an undercover cop? Am I going to be put down in the middle of the night and taught a lesson?! Will they duct tape me to the Scrambler until I puke my guts out?!! Is that what carnies do?

"I'm going to call you Chips!" he once again stresses. (So goodbye, Ajax; hello, Chips!)

"You can call him Skittles," sarcastically pipes in Jared to his nemesis, the *legendary* Skittles!

"Don't call me that," Skittles replies.

My plan is to work really hard the first day so the carnies will warm to my presence (and stop thinking I'm an undercover cop). At least my disguise is so good the other carnies think I'm actually from Princeton, Indiana!

Then the interrogation begins.

"Hey, Chips, have you worked as a carny before?" Skittles asks, eyeballing me with suspicion.

"Oh, yeah, all over," I reply with a grunt, wincing in pain with the final heave of my body upward, onto the roof.

"Where?"

"Northern California."

"Did you work for the Garcia brothers?"

"Yeah." (Pause.) "Them. The Garcia brothers!"

Skittles shoots me a funny look. (It must be a trick question.) "What's your specialty?"

"I'm good at talking the talk," I stutter. "Yup, talking the talk!"

"No, I mean what *joint* did you work?"

"Um, the one where you shoot out the red star with a BB gun."

"You mean Shoot out the Star," Skittles corrects, rolling his eyes.

"Yeah, that's the one." I quickly go back to inserting flags on poles. Clearly, I didn't pass the veteran-carny test. (Mental note to self: next time infiltrating carnies, memorize the names of games!)

Then: "Do you spark up?" questions Skittles. (They keep asking me this.)

CARNY TIP: A hose and some ziplock bags make for
an ideal carny bath when showers aren't available.

"Doesn't that fuck up the rat?" I ask John, a balding carny with
some sort of dent in his forehead, setting up his joint the Mouse
Game, which involves a live rat spun around on a roulette wheel,
but instead of a ball landing on a number, people wager on
where the live rat will stop.

"A little bit," John says.

A huge part of being a carny is mastering the art of catcalls and
insults, otherwise known as the crack. Since carnies don't work
on salary and get paid a percentage of what they swindle from
fairgoers (*marks*), they must learn how to reel them in. "You in-
sult them. Don't look at no one in particular, but they know who
you're talking about," advises John (who, in Joseph Campbell
terms, would be my mentor at the gateway, that I meet right before crossing into the new land). John's a carny lifer: a childhood
in foster homes, got a girl pregnant at seventeen, divorced after
finding his brother's car in the driveway and the two coked out
of their heads in a romantic tryst, then three years in the military, and after that, a carny ever since. "Like, say to a skinny guy,
'Hey, buddy, if you stood sideways, I wouldn't be able to see
you!' It gets their attention."

"What if I said to a fat guy, 'Hey, buddy, when's the last time
you've seen your dick in the shower? Was it February 1994?" I ask.

After a moment of thought, it's not recommended.

With other carnies, I have interactions where I'll say hi and
they don't even acknowledge my presence.

"You know, I just don't give a fuck!" exclaims a hefty woman named Sheila, a four-year carny vet who used to work with a traveling petting zoo (who, unlike other carnies, is only missing one tooth). She is extremely stressed about hanging stuffed animals in her *punk joint*, Duck Pond. (Kids pick a toy duck out of a water tub. The number on the bottom corresponds to a prize.)

Volunteering to help Sheila, I inquire, "Where do you hang the Little Mermaids?"

"Hang that son of a bitch over there!"

Sheila's having a bad day, continually using the phrase *son of a bitch* as an adjective, wallowing, pissed off, in a sea of stuffed animals, which need to be hung by the time fair gates open.

"I'm very straightforward. If you piss me off, I'll tell you!" she says (that's not passive-aggressive), adding, "People don't respect me, because I'm a woman!"

Our girl's-choir meeting is interrupted by a large man with a limp. "I don't see your stuffed animals hung up yet!" he screams about stuffed-animal-hanging punctuality.

"I'm ready to quit," Sheila says when the man limps away. "I hate him!" (The man is also her husband.) "He's an '*agent*,'" she angrily remarks, making quote fingers. "He thinks he can boss people around cuz if we don't make money, he still makes money!"

Sheila's little daughter suddenly comes running over. She starts drinking out of the tub where the fake fish are floating.

"Baby, don't drink out of there," the carny woman says with motherly concern. "Goldfish were in there yesterday."

The boss man, Monty, pulls up in a golf cart. He's a gruff, crusty old man with a harsh, weathered face and a lifetime of

carnivals under his belt. Monty is married to Miss Phyllis. Monty
is also very mean.

"What the hell is going on with your hair?" he barks like I just
puked in the punchbowl. "Come here!" Monty commands. "Let
me see that hair!"

"Sure thing, chief!" I say, calling him "chief" to let him know
he's the man in charge. If Monty started screaming, "Don't eye-
ball me, boy!" I wouldn't be surprised.

Though formally in full disguise, I was scolded earlier by an
older, big-haired woman, with southern attitude right out of a
William Faulkner novel. "You need to wear a show shirt. And no
bandanas!" she had said, referring to my outfit, which would—
intentionally—scare children.

Throwing me a yellow show shirt that stank of thick cigarette
smoke and said BURTON BROS, she arrogantly added, to let me
know where the cards laid, "I'm Mrs. Burton, and it's nice to
meet you!" If this were the TV show *Dynasty*, she'd be one of the
Carrington family. But it's not, and she merely runs the carnival
with Monty and Miss Phyllis, the ones who work directly beneath her in the hierarchy.

Without my bandana, my San Francisco dreadlocks are now
fully exposed. That's why Monty is yelling at me and my hair.
"Don't mess with Monty," Sheila advises, as he drives off in his
golf cart. "He carries a *piece*."

"Has he ever used it?" I enthusiastically ask, *sooooo* wanting
him to pull it out and start waving it around near the corndog
stand.

"No one wants to find out," she replies as AC/DC's "You Shook
Me All Night Long," blares from the midway. "And, don't piss off

the Burtons. Show them some respect." (Too late. I've already pissed off a Burton.)

> **CARNY TIP:** The key to knocking over the milk jugs
> with a baseball is to try and hit it at the base of the bot-
> tom two, and not where the three jugs intersect.

"Jake Owen will be playing tonight, including his hit, 'Yee Haw'!" comes trumpeting over the loudspeaker, mixed with the sweet music of carnies trying to lure townies toward their joints, backed by the midway's heavy metal hits of the eighties. It's Friday night at the carnival. The gates open, the lights flicker on, and the air is filled with carnival smells and the anticipation of the crowds.

Despondent small-town Goth kids clad in metal-band T-shirts are the first to meander sullenly onto the fairground—wanting to break out of their little Indiana world. They mingled among a hearty mix of hefty farm-fed folks with Bible Belt values, rural baby-moms pushing strollers, and mullets, mullets, mullets.

Miss Phyllis assigns me to work at the new-guy joint, the Goldfish Game, right by the fun house with the sign that reads RAIDERS and has a large painting of a man who could vaguely pass for Indiana Jones.

A sign in the Goldfish Game joint reads:

8 BALLS $1.00
20 BALLS $2.00
BALL IN BOWL WINS
NO LEANING

Carnies are paid a percentage of what they take in, thus, the job purely exemplifies the American Dream: the harder you work, the more money you can make. Those who pay their dues move up the ranks to the cushier carnival games. The more rubes you can get to try and knock over weighted-down milk bottles, the more money you're going to pocket. That's why no one really wants me to work alongside them because that's less money for them.

"What do you do?" I ask my new carny sidekick Shane, adjusting my green money vest in hopes of job training.

Shane—half of whose face is horrifically scarred—sarcastically snaps, "I'll stand here and steal people's money!" He then asks, "Do you spark up?" (Why do they keep asking me this?)

There's no real strategy to the Goldfish Game; it's all pretty much blind luck. The deal is, if a mark tosses a ping-pong ball into one of the small lower bowls, they win a thirty-cent goldfish swimming in a water-filled plastic bag. It's all theirs to carry around with them for the rest of the evening.

Shane then gestures toward Wayne-o the crackhead, working the knock-over-milk-bottles-with-a-baseball joint. Shane says with admiration, "Wayne-o takes their money before they even know it. He reels them in with lines like, 'You haven't given me a chance to steal your money yet.'"

Yes, that's what I need, an attention-getting line. So I try my hand at the crack.

"Hey, get over here, fuckface!" I scream at a man in a baseball hat who gives me a double-take. *"Let's see how bad you are!"* And then, *"Step right up, shit-for-brains!"*

"I don't think you should be cussin'," Shane suggests.

"Hey, you, wearing the panties. Are you man enough to play?!"

Scary-looking farm folk, who'd normally frighten me, their little fat farm kids—who look like tiny, serious adults with fried-food smiles—and people so fat they waddle now encircle us, tossing ping-pong balls.

"We're swamped!" I cry to Shane, freaking out for no reason, when two more marks approach the Goldfish Game. A local with candy-corn teeth insults the integrity of our joint. "I saw a show on this. There's no skill involved!"

"Get out of here *now!*" I scream. "Don't piss me off! I'm a carny!" I scream while widely bugging out my eyes.

I soon learn working the Goldfish Game is a job a really smart chimp could easily do. It involves running around in sort of a crouched position, chasing bouncing ping-pong balls to and fro, as dozens of little kids scream, "Can I have some balls? Can I have some balls?"

Some kids cry when they lose. *"You stop crying!"* screams a mom, providing a true life lesson. "Not everyone wins!"

"Come on. You're throwing like a girl" scorns the dad to his two-foot-high son.

Miss Phyllis pays a visit in her golf cart. I hope Miss Phyllis starts liking me. (And why is Monty so mean?!) She catches two leaners—a clear violation of Goldfish Game bylaw number four. "If you do that again, you're kicked out!" she angrily warns the small children. She then drives off, leaving behind her thirteen-year-old daughter to supervise and scream at us when we're not doing things right.

"The girl in the hat is giving me the eye." Shane says in between scooping up ping-pong balls. He gives her a complimentary goldfish in hopes it will be exchanged for sexual favors.

How did Shane become a carny? "I was being kicked out of my house and I didn't have anywhere else to go. I was in the right place at the right time!" Fortunately the carnival came to Shane's small town with the offer to chase ping-pong balls for a cash percentage. Shane jumped on board. "I have a warrant out for my arrest in my town," he adds. "And I don't want to go back to jail!"

"What's the warrant for?"

"Public intoxication."

"How much do you have to pay?"

"$345." (Pause.) "I don't want to go back to jail."

Taking a ping-pong ball break, I go to a food joint and savor in the culinary delight of a deep-fried Twinkie and watch a local band of long-haired, pudgy farm brothers playing heavy metal. Teenage girls congregate in front of the stage, screaming like they're seeing the Beatles in 1964—it's simply beautiful.

Indiana carnivals aren't all about carnies with questionable pasts taking your money.

"We're going to start with the sixteen-year-old girls!" the announcer bellows from the loudspeakers.

Along the perimeter of a mud pit, teams of teenage girls dressed in matching uniform (short shorts, knee-high socks), stand in front of a grandstand full of fairgoers. As a team they must dive into the mud-pit, wrestle a pig, then lift it onto a pedestal.

"They have one minute to catch that pig," declares the announcer.

First up is the *Hottie Hogsters*. Six teenage girls jump into mud and grasp at a loudly squealing pig. The result is something not unlike a wet T-shirt contest, mixed with mud wrestling and, say, bestiality porn. Many questions run through my head. Do I like this? Is it wrong to like this?! Have I always been into this?! Has a door been opened in my life that should have remained shut?!! Why is this sport not everywhere?

"Time! 34:50."

Afterward, groups of people caked in mud walk around the small-town carnival. I wish life weren't like stereotypes, but sometimes it is.

Strolling leisurely back from my extended break, I find Shane elbow deep in ping-pong balls. It's *prime time*. Little kids and their parents are yelling at Shane. He's swamped!

"I don't know how much longer I'm going to do this," Shane confides in a moment between scooping up ping-pong balls. "I haven't been paid yet." At the end of the night, carnies can take out a *draw*; money deducted from their weekly wages. (Other carnies get cash advances by simply pocketing cash.) Then, like Ratso Rizzo in *Midnight Cowboy*, Shane asks, "What's Florida like?"

I give a brief synopsis of the state of Florida.

"Florida!" Shane repeats with a dreamy look of piña coladas and beaches, while Steve Miller Band's "The Joker" blares from the rides and the smell of corn dogs and cheese curds permeates the night air. Across the way, small cars go round and round in a tiny circle, giving the impression that the child rider is actually driving the vehicle, but in reality it's operated by a pot-bellied, chain-smoking ride jockey. Round and round go the cars. "Florida." Shane repeats.

The carnival gets real ugly towards the eleven PM closing time. Two portly teen farm kids dry hump on a bench behind the

Pony Corral Ride. Like mindless animals in heat, they're oblivious to the carnival world around them.

"Hey, chill out there!" screams an adult. "That's how babies start!" They keep dry humping. "No, I'm serious!"

The portly teens keep moving to other openly public locales, staying until other adults sternly tell them to stop. (So that explains all the local baby-mamas.)

After the joints shut down and the multicolored lights are flipped off, the closed carnival feels like something out of *Mad Max*; the townies have left, and it's carnies only! The darkened rides are silhouetted against the moon like sleeping dinosaurs. Walking toward the backlot trailers, I smell like a cross between goldfish, sweat, and despair. What lies ahead for the *new guy*? A carny blanket party, where I'll be hit with extra-large corn dogs!?

The fun has already begun. Two drunken carnies are having a contest to see who can pull off more of the other's beard. It's like something straight out of the movie *Gummo*.

"Come on, is that the best you can do?!" one says, as the other emerges with a handful of his facial hair. If I ever wanted someone killed for $100 or less, I'd know where to go, and these guys would be my two best candidates.

Four other carnies stand in a circle drinking from a whiskey bottle, sharing stories of townies who'd exchange sexual favors for free stuffed animals.

"You got to be careful, there's a lot of teenyboppers running around," a carny wisely advises.

"Let's put it this way, she's old enough to know better, and young enough to enjoy it!" his compadre philosophizes.

Besides the indoctrination of Chips, there's another new carny in the mix.

"She's one hit away from giving me a blowjob," a carny whispers to his buddy as he stumbles behind a tree to pee. "We met her off the Internet. She said she was really into carnies."

Yes, a carny groupie!

"Are you the new guy?" the groupie slurs with whiskey breath and a voice like a raspy transvestite, who looks worn like the title character in the movie *Monster*. "I'm the new girl." (Unlike the other new carnie, I won't be giving out blowjobs tonight.)

The groupie then starts hitting on Ed—a quiet carny with a very low monobrow, built like a circus strongman, kind of a gentle giant who I'd peg as the most normal-looking of the whole carny bunch.

"Look how strong you are," she says, feeling Ed's muscles.

"He's one of us," pipes in Skittles. "Look at his teeth."

Sure enough, silent Ed has really fucked-up teeth.

"You were in the military for a while, weren't ya?" Skittles asks in a manner like he's revealing a tragic secret.

After an uncomfortable pause, Ed quickly blurts, "The army." He then looks down and falls silent.

"I'm going back to my trailer," the carny groupie proclaims. "Anyone want to go?" The question is open to anyone within earshot.

"I'll join ya, baby," replies a swaying pot-bellied ride jockey.

There's reason to celebrate—it's payday. Outside the window of Miss Phyllis's trailer, carnies are still lined up, being handed bills for their weekly take, counting the cash, making sure they didn't get swindled on the money they swindled. I get my fifteen dollars draw for the evening, which will be taken out of the roughly eighty dollars I made. I'm ready to party!

John wears a dirty T-shirt that has the hand spray-painted words, Snapz da Clown and Juggler 4 Life. Offering me a beer back at his trailer, he explains, "I worked as a clown in a dunk tank for fifteen years."

"That's a long time," I say. He's referring to the large tank of water, over which a seat is suspended—when a target is struck with a baseball, the seat tips into the tank of water, thus "dunking" Snapz da Clown.

"I sat in a dunk tank for fifteen years."

(Pause.) "Okay."

John shares a tale of a dunk-tank worker who was so fat he couldn't lift himself out of the water and ended up shitting in the dunk tank! (How would Monty react to that?!) John points to the large indent in his skull, from hitting a metal bar inside the dunk tank, which turned the water blood red.

"The boss bandaged it up and said, 'Get out there. You need to make money.' So I did." John only parted with his previous carnival vocation last year. "I left with $2,500 still on the books," he says, emitting really strong body odor, and quit after a confrontation with his boss at a carnival gig in Mississippi.

"He was terrified of clowns," John gives as a reason for his dismissal. "And he accused me of sleeping with his wife. He pulled a knife on me. My reflex action was to grab the first thing I could and hit him over the head with it," he says, referring to an ambiguous blunt object. With intense eye contact John adds, "I'm bipolar. There was blood everywhere!"

The next thing John did was walk thirty-five miles to the nearest bus station. He got out of town, and joined up with Burton Bros Amusement to work the Mouse Game.

He opens his trailer door; inside, rat cages are everywhere.

"These are my friends," John says, dangling a rat by the tail.

While other carnies pull at each other's beards, Shane and I are supposed to bag goldfish for tomorrow. Since carnies are on percentage-only pay, this entails working an extra two to three unpaid hours.

"If you go buy some beer, I'll do the fish bagging," Shane says, not really seeming to mind. The next thing I know, I'm in a pickup truck driving to the twenty-four-hour Wal-Mart with Sheila, John, Ed, Jared, and Ryan, who wears a basketball tank top and looks vaguely like a short Eminem (if Eminem were missing a considerable amount of his upper teeth).

"What did you do before this?" Ed the gentle giant asks.

"This and that," I say, looking forward like I'm harvesting terrible secrets. "I had to hit the road and disappear for a while— if you know what I mean!"

"I hear ya, I hear ya," Ed says. Though Ed looks the most normal, he adds, "If I weren't here, I'd either be homeless or in jail." (How come no matter how hard I try freaking out the carnies, they always end up freaking me out more?)

"You can't wear your show shirt in public!" Sheila angrily informs me, noting that I'm still draped in my dirty yellow Burton Brothers chemise, as other carnies also descend upon Wal-Mart.

It's odd seeing the carnies mingle among normal society. They dart around WalMart like little kids buying toys of the future: cell phones, shoes, DVD players. Like a man-child, John can't stop talking excitedly about the latest Transformer toys he just saw. I'm less excited: no beer for sale at the twenty-four-hour Wal-Mart. In fact, no beer for sale in this county.

I overhear a townie tell her friend, "We went to the fair, and it was really lame. There wasn't even any good rides!" I take offense—that's *my* fair they're talking about.

"If you come by tomorrow," I say, licking my lips in carny fashion, "I'll make sure you win the big teddy bear, sweetheart!"

Blank stares.

"I just spent my whole paycheck," a smiling ride jockey exclaims, carrying a DVD player in a slow trot. Other carnies run through the parking lot with their new purchases like they just looted the place.

Back in the truck, Jared once again talks a mile a minute, playing with his newly purchased cell phone like it were a futuristic sci-fi device. Ryan keeps going on about a thirty-one-year-old stripper he met at the Fish Till You Win joint.

"I'm going to smoke a blunt and sit on the couch, and she's going to give me a lap dance!" Ryan keeps repeating this information over and over again. He and Jared have plans to meet her over at the gas-station girl's house. Then, once more, "I'm going to smoke a blunt and sit on the couch, and she's going to give me a lap dance!"

Ryan looks up from his lap dancing daydream as a car drives by with a loud sound system blasting big-bass hip-hop.

"I use to have a sound system like that," he remarks as the music trails off into the distance. "But the police confiscated it."

"How come?" I inquire.

"They confiscated it when I went to prison."

Ryan goes back to talk of blunt smoking and the lap dancing that will follow.

On our way back to carny camp, we stop for gas and run into Shane walking toward us with one of the ride jockeys. Strangely, he looks surprised to see us.

"I couldn't find any beer," I inform him.

"That's okay," he mumbles.

Unable to find the gas-station girl's house, we leave Ryan and Jared to scout it on foot in a low-rent neighborhood by the train tracks—the 'hood (or the kind of place that girls who date carnies live). Random shit seems to be thrown in people's yards.

On returning to carny camp, a drunken, lanky, shirtless ride jockey confronts me. He pulls my dreadlocks and declares, "I'm going to cut that off in the next couple of days, and it will be mine!"

"Sure thing, chief!" Quickly, I change the subject to the gas-station-girl rendezvous.

Excited, the lanky ride jockey shows me he, too, has the gas-station girl's number plugged into his cell phone. In fact, everyone else seems to have the number as well.

Unable to fall asleep in my ferret-cage-smelling trailer, I opt for snoozing in my car, falling asleep with dreams of the tooth fairy, goldfish, boulder-size ping-pong balls, men pulling each other's beards, and Monty screaming from his golf cart and waving around *his piece*.

CARNY TIP: How hard could it be to pop a balloon with a dart? The darts are dull and the balloons are so limp they barely holding their shape. Arc the dart so that it hits the board on a steep downward trajectory, thus using the weight of the dart to pop the balloon.

The next morning, while Jared sets up his Fish Till You Win joint, I ask, "How did it work out?"

Jared makes an unhappy face. "Not so good. Ryan cock-blocked me!"

"Really? How!?"

"He passed out once we got there."

How surprising. It seemed Ryan was dead-set on the whole blunt-smoking, lap-dancing scenario (or so I heard). I tell Jared I hooked up with a girl who works at the *other* gas station in town. But no time to chitchat about the details, I'm late for setting up my Goldfish joint—but surely carnie buddy Shane has watched my back.

On arrival, my joint remains untouched.

"Shane split!" Miss Phyllis's annoying seventeen-year-old niece informs me.

"What?!" I exclaim. My best friend in the carny world has bailed!

"We thought it was a setup. We thought you weren't showing up, too!"

Since I slept in my car and they couldn't find me, rumors flew that I drove Shane to the bus station. That's the reason they don't allow carnies to have their own cars: they're afraid they'll try and escape.

"I do remember him asking, 'Do you think there's a bus station in town?'" I mention as part of the investigation.

Shorty (a ride jockey called Shorty cuz he's short) fills me in. "Shane left with his lady and a ride jockey in the middle of the night."

"Which ride jockey?"

"LJ who ran the Ponies."

Shorty refers to the ride similar to the cars going in a circle, except it's fake ponies going in a circle. "I didn't care for him too much," Shorty professes. "He was always running his mouth off, telling people what to do. And it was only his first week!" Then with resentment, "If someone quits like that and gets seen around, they'll end up getting their asses kicked *big time!*"

Looking down, I mumble, "Whenever someone gets close to me they always leave."

Guilt flows through me. If only I would have done goldfish bagging with Shane. Maybe then I could've provided an intervention. I should've seen the warning signs: Shane's comments about Florida. His comments about splitting if he didn't get all of his money in this week's wages. His inquiries on the locale of the bus station.

"Do you have a driver's license?" Miss Phyllis's annoying niece asks, since now another driver is needed when they pack up and travel to the next town.

"Do many of the other carnies have licenses?" I curiously inquire.

"*Noooooooooo!*"

Yes, I've just moved up the carny hierarchy! No longer am I "the new guy." They need me! Regardless, the fifteen-year-plus carny gang still scares the beejeebes out of me; they're constantly sizing me up, looking for a crack in my veneer (I'm *not* an undercover cop!). Lined up with arms folded in front of the Basketball joint, their laughing and joking stops when they see me approaching.

"Hey, Chips! Turn around," Wayne-o interjects, trying to tear down my confidence. "I think you've got shit on your pants!" (Laughs.)

"Hey, Chief, did you hear Shane split?" I respond, trying to create common ground.

Skittles seems unfazed. "I know he wasn't real happy with the goldfish," adding, "That means everything in your vest is all yours, and that's what it's all about, Chips."

> **CARNY FUN FACT:** The highly insular nature of carny society has fostered popular suspicions of inbreeding, supposedly manifested by a tendency toward small hands or thumbs.

Now I'm on my own; the loudspeaker incessantly reminding me that Jake Owen is in concert with his hit, "Yee Haw"! I look at my joint and find sentimental reminders of Shane: his bag of Doritos, his sunglasses, his empty pack of chain-smoked Marlboros, his discarded cigarette butts. I'll miss Shane's laugh. I'll miss Shane's interest in Florida. Like a slow, melancholy Miles Davis ballad, these are "Traces of Shane"—memories of the way we were!

To make up for the loneliness, my joint is now filled with the cages of hermit crabs, I guess compensating for live bunnies (illegal in Indiana).

"Step right up, and you ladies can get crabs!" I scream (because I'm so very witty!), taunting people with my crack (literally—my pants now ride intentionally low like a refrigerator repairman). Then I repeat seven other variations of the same witty and obvious joke. To Shorty, I bellow, *"Come on over, and get a case of crabs!"*

"That's good," laughs Shorty while bumming a smoke off of a townie. "That's good!"

I explain, "Crabs in this case could apply to both a crustacean or a venereal disease—thus the humor." (Blank stares from Shorty.)

"Shorty bit the head off a live frog in Danville!" the merry-go-round guy informs me.

Completely confused, I question, "Was it on a dare?"

"No. I just did it," Shorty replies with a shit-eating grin. "I felt it jumping around in my stomach, then it stopped!"

We're interrupted by a local, stroller-pushing baby-mama, presenting the perfect straight-man setup, "How do I get crabs?"

"Sleep with a carny," I remark with a snort, high-fiving Shorty.

A voice of reason pops into the baby-mama's head, "If I win a crab, then I'd have to care for it." (She should have thought of that in other circumstances! High-five, Shorty!)

"If I want crabs, I'll look down my pants," shares a man whose belly rolls out from under his shirt. (Somehow I believe him.)

"Can I just buy a crab?" asks a smart-aleck kid in a baseball cap.

"We're not a pet store!" I state, laying down the law.

"What do you do with them later?"

"We make a good crab soup," I lick my lips, for I've taken the opportunity to become the "creepy carny," the kind that permanently embeds kids' memories. Alone in my joint, I start doing kung fu kicks (complete with sounds) for the benefit of those passing by, pondering if I could actually get a hummer by giving away free hermit crabs.

The hermit crabs move less and less as the hot day wears on. Monty takes to hovering over me, making sure I'm not pocketing cash (I'd be the *only* carny not pocketing cash). "You haven't been giving away the crabs have you?" he barks, as I cease my kung fu kicks.

"Only thirty or forty," I reply. Veins pop out on Monty's neck. Screaming follows. Now I see how being a complete asshole controls these vulnerable people; the rest of the carnies will try pleasing their bosses just to get them to be nice for once. Noting the nonmovement from their cages, I add, "I think the hermit crabs are kind of, um, dying."

"No, they are not!" Monty snarls, then drives off in his golf cart. Yes, I'm glad bunnies are illegal in Indiana.

Then I'm back to being a grown man chasing around ping-pong balls, surrounded by little kids and their parents, yelling at me ("Can I get some balls? Can I get some balls?")—feeling like an indentured servant, working ten hours in my sweaty joint while being told I'm not doing things right by a thirteen-year-old.

> **CARNY TIP:** To win at the Ring Toss game, snap your
> wrist as you throw the ring to achieve the most spin
> possible; this will stabilize the ring, making it easier to
> land cleanly on your target.

Silhouetted against the darkened rides on the outskirts of the backlot, Wayne-o startles the hell out of me, jumping out from behind a tree while eating a corn dog. "Hey! They're waiting for you!"

(Pause.) "Okay."

Who's waiting for me? Why are they waiting for me?! Is this where the after-hours feces-filled piñata initiation carny ritual begins?!

Wayne-o and I walk momentarily in silence. Then he turns to me. "Do you want a corn dog?"

"What?!"

I'm stunned. Is this a trick to steal my shoes? Thirty-year carnie vet Wayne-o is offering me, *me*, a corn dog. I think I've officially been accepted as a fellow carny! We all want acceptance, and maybe that's the allure of the carny life—no matter how big of a freak you are in the outside world, if you work hard enough, you can be accepted as a carny.

My smile gleams from ear to ear. "Yes, Wayne-o, I'll have a corn dog!"

Outside the trailer where we get paid, about two dozen carnies are all gathered around Monty, exhausted, smelling of caked, dried sweat and food served on a stick. Like a carny General Patton, Monty conducts a general assembly meeting. Sitting in a lawn chair with beer in hand, Monty is in the midst of his State of the Union address, critiquing our performance at the 162nd Annual Gibson County Fair. Chewing on my corn dog, I file in next to silent Ed; the meeting is already in progress.

"When it's prime time, you are there to make money!" Monty tells the crew, who listens with a combination of fear and respect. "If you have to piss, learn to hold it!" He then stresses the carny equivalent of ABC (Always Be Closing), providing evaluation for improving our crack. "The more you talk, the less they listen."

"We're showmen," Skittles pipes in. "We're here to put on a show!" Then insight: "When I first started out, I'd give half my vest to learn the secrets of how to approach your mark. We'll give it to you for free!" As an example, he adds the crack gem, "Have you been robbed today? Here's your chance!"

Big Jimmy (unlike Shorty, he's big) follows up with the classic, "The carny's sauced. He's getting there. Step right up and win a teddy bear!"

Resting her hand on her chin, under the starlit night, Miss Phyllis looks on from the open window of her trailer. Other important carny rules are stressed, "Always wear a shirt on the midway!"

"Wayne-o got into trouble for that," Big Jimmy blurts with a laugh.

"They snapped a picture of me for the local paper," cackles Wayne-o, still nibbling on his corn-dog stick. "They had a caption that said, 'Do you want these people coming to your town?' (Pause.) I got kicked off the show for that!"

"You want to find a more relaxed job than this," Skittles mentions to the newer carnies. "Sure, why don't you go work nine to five in an office cubicle?" He scans the group. "Ryan, tell me another job where you walk away with a g in your pocket every Wednesday?" Prison alumnus Ryan's blank face takes in the information.

"I've tried to get out many times," interjects Big Jimmy. "Then the season rolls around and I can feel my suitcase start shaking and the sawdust in my shoes, and I come back again!"

Raising his voice like an angry, dysfunctional father figure, Monty singles out Fish Till You Win's Jared. "You got to get the money out there faster. That's all there is to it. I see you out there talking to people, but I don't see you taking their money!"

Berated in front of his carny peers, Jared lowers his head with every harsh word. It's tough love, but for his own good. In the end, Jared will be a much better carny because of it. Yes, Jared's carny Richard Gere will one day thank Monty's carny Lou Gossett Jr. (if this were a carny *An Officer and a Gentlemen*).

"Hey, Monty, any advice on how I can get more marks into my joint?" I ask, becoming a complete carny kiss ass (amazed I've formed a sentence almost entirely in carny-speak).

"It's a walk-up game. All you have to do is stand there and let them come to you," he grunts, swigging his can of beer, confirming to me that any complete moron could easily do my job.

> **CARNY TIP:** The object of the Coin Toss game is to toss a coin onto a plate without it bouncing off. Use a very high arc, with as little spin as possible. If that doesn't work, covertly cover the coin with spit before tossing it.

"Same day, different shit," Wayne-o blurts, the morning after Monty's big powwow.

"You have to get the sludge off the shower with a blowtorch," he mentions, about the one hygiene option for all the carnies (those who don't want the old-fashioned hose-and-ziplock carny bath), as he emerges from the facility inside one of the trailers. Pulling up a lawn chair outside of Wayne-o's trailer, this is what being in the inner circle must feel like! The carny community finally accepts me—and I like it! Maybe being a carnie isn't all that bad. Maybe deep down I'm really just a carny at heart?

"Hey, Chips, do you want a wake-up pill?" offers Wayne-o, emerging from his trailer.

"Shhhh," interrupts Skittles, not wanting others (outside the inner circle) to hear.

"When Wayne-o waves his arms in the air, he looks like one of those dinosaurs in *Jurassic Park*," jests Big Jimmy.

Wayne-o interjects with self-deprecating humor, "Smells like cabbage. Tiny fingers."

"Monty said the vets should lead by example," quips Skittles, letting down his guard (for the inner-circle benefit). "We should come out wearing suits and ties, holding briefcases!"

I sit back and smile. Things are beginning to look up! It's starting to feel like one big, happy, toothless family! That is, with the exception of Jared. He's nowhere to be found. His Fish Till You Win joint remains untouched. Shorty again plays the role of the messenger. "Jared jumped!" he informs me. "That's six in the last two days. Three of our workers and three ride jockeys." Wow, that *was* some pretty harsh *tough love*!

"Whenever someone gets close to me, they always leave!"

Shorty recites the entire list of carnies who've escaped in the middle of the night, "Shane, Jared, LJ, Jill, Tommy—all left! It's crazy!" He reasons, "People are tired of the bullshit. Monty and Phyllis drive around and see people pulling out their own money and think they are pocketing cash."

Freaking out at Jared's disappearance, I reassure Miss Phyllis's annoying seventeen-year old niece with my *jealous-gas-station-girl-boyfriend* rumor: "Jared might have had a run in with *Mr. Smith and Mr. Weston!*" I state, while using the expression "his lady" a lot.

"That's why Monty doesn't want us going to locals' houses!" she exclaims with concern.

Other carnies feel differently. Sheila, now working the water-squirt joint, knows the true lowdown. "Jared called me earlier and said, 'I'm not coming back!'" Once again, he was, as the kids say, tweakin'!" "He sounded all incoherent like he'd been up all night. He had to take a second to think about what he was saying."

"He's going to get *sloughe*d," John blurts with fire in his eyes. "In carny, *sloughed* has two meanings." He elaborates, "The first is 'to tear down'!"

"Steve is going over there right now, and Jared doesn't know it!" Sheila smirks. "He's going to get slammed against the side of the van!"

I feel bad for Jared. He's going to get the living shit kicked out of him simply because he didn't want to be a carny anymore. Then again, I also imagine the scenario has the makings of . . . *the best episode of* Cops *ever!* Think of it: two carnies fighting it out in the front yard of a gas-station girl's house—most likely without shirts on.

John, meanwhile, continues to get worked up. "Jared's joining the military next month. If he doesn't show up, you know what happens?"

"He'll have to eat his own weight in cheese?"

John's eyes widen for angry emphasis, tilting his head with each word. "He's AWOL. He'll get court-martialed! Or executed! Cuz, need I remind you, *we are at war!*"

I expect Jared to be dragged back like Paul Newman in *Cool Hand Luke*, made to spend a night in the box, but instead of the box he would spend the night duct-taped to the spinning Tilt-A-Whirl. I look over at the empty Fish Till You Win booth and think of all the good times we had. I'll miss Jared's laugh; I'll miss the way Jared kept asking me if I sparked up—memories of the way we were!

"I get his TV," John says, finally breaking a grin.

The Last Night at the Fair

Once again, I've moved up the carny hierarchy. The bosses have become slightly nicer (or less mean), in fear of losing me in the middle of the night as though I were trying to escape communist East Germany.

Prime-time rush hits fast. The fair is *live*! Motley Crue's "Girls Girls Girls" loudly blasts from the midway. Sweat drips down my brow, soaking my shirt. My vest has fallen down to my ankles. Money is dropping. Ping-pong balls fly everywhere. There's Wayne-o the crackhead, interacting with small children. I wave at Wayne-o. He waves back.

With sounds of the Demolition Derby reverberating like background music, I'm hunched over, running around like a dancing monkey boy, secretly hating the ride jockey operating the cars that go round and round, chain-smoking, and bumming cigarettes off of locals, as little kids endlessly scream.

"Here, have a fish anyway," I say to a disappointed little girl near tears. (I'm a goddamn saint!) The goldfish is dead. She freaks out. In fact, thee-quarters of my goldfish are dead in the summer heat, floating in their tiny bags like water-filled plastic coffins. Dumping out the stench-filled water tub of dead goldfish in the trash behind the cotton candy booth, I assume this is some sort of allegory for carny life; again, glad bunnies are illegal in Indiana!

Sheila comes over to my joint with a sinister smile. "Is any of your stuff in the trailer or is it all Jared's?"

"No, why?"

"I'll tell you later!"

Did the carnies kill Jared? Are they now getting rid of all traces of evidence?

Momentarily, there's another new guy working the Fish Till You Win joint. Except I really don't get a chance to meet him cuz he quits after a mere two hours, mysteriously disappearing. Pissed off, Monty asks, "Did he leave his vest? Are the big bills still in there?!"

Miss Phyllis makes an unhappy face, "Not a lot of them!"

I take the opportunity to show Miss Phyllis blueprints I sketched on an Icee cup how we could make the Goldfish Game more efficient. "Can we take a meeting to discuss this?" I inquire. Stony silence follows.

Smells of ping-pong balls, dead fish, sweat, and several days of not bathing emit from my body at the end of the long evening. Eating nothing but carnival food for days on end has made me delirious, as I walk unfazed past an angry carny confrontation. A gruff, bearded man who looks like a motorcycle outlaw flicks his cigarette at a fellow ride jockey. "You're giving me attitude!"

His pudgy little carny son hands him a large wooden stick. "Here, Dad, use this!"

"Not impressed by this spot!" utters Skittles, almost pouting, sitting in a lawn chair, summing up our time spent at the 162nd Annual Gibson County Fair. "Not impressed!"

"Did you hear Jared jumped?" I inform Wayne-o.

He nonchalantly shrugs it off. "In the next ten years, you'll see them come and go."

"You're not going to leave are ya, Chips?" inquires Ryan with a touching sense of concern.

"Hell, no!" I proclaim. "I'm a carny for life!"

"Do you want to spark up?" Ryan asks.

I'm hesitant. I've been hearing for days about this fabled "sparking up." Now I'll actually find out what it entails. Is it heroin? Is it crystal meth? Is it some new carny hybrid-drug that's only found on the Ferris wheel circuit?!? Ryan pulls out some marijuana and a cigar. This whole time it was harmless, old-school weed.

"Sure, I'll spark up," I say. "Let's spark up!"

Smoking a blunt with a guy just out of prison truly adds to my street cred (right up there with a pair-of-lesbians threesome). Tonight, Ryan's promised to train me on fish bagging. Completely stoned, we sit alone in the back of a trailer, where dozens of haphazardly dangling electric cords hang over several goldfish aquariums.

"I'm going to be straightforward with you," Ryan warns. "If I see you not doing it right, I'm going to tell ya!" Like a meticulous machine, every ten fish Ryan bags, I bag one. (This is pointed out several times.) Only three hundred more bags to go (and two to three hours of unpaid work).

"When did you get out of prison?" I ask, making small talk, grasping for another fish.

"April."

"How long where you in for?

"Three years."

"Why did you go to prison?"

"Stacked-up charges." (Something's mumbled about burglary and weapons.)

"What was prison like?"

Ryan turns towards me. "You sure ask a lot of questions!" The low hum of the air conditioner fills the trailer. Awkward silence follows. His strong eye contact says, "We won't be talking about prison anymore!"

In a reflective moment, Ryan summarizes his carny experience, "Only a couple of guys make good money; the rest don't or waste it on crack." Regardless, he's happy to be here, mentioning, "I don't want to go back to prison!"

Ryan abruptly says he'll be right back. He doesn't return. Tomorrow is a circus jump to Indianapolis. That means at the end of the ten-hour work day, three more unpaid hours will be spent on the slough, then four hours will be spent driving, and then the carnival will immediately be set up again in the next town. I think it's a hell of a good time for a *Harmon jump* and get the hell out of this American Dream.

Penning my carny swan song—a farewell note heavily quoting Shakespeare—I tape it to the largely unfinished pile of plastic goldfish bags, in a place were Monty will surely see it:

> *If we do meet again, why, we shall smile;*
> *if not, why then, this parting was well made.*
> —*Julius Caesar, act v, scene i*

Following in the footsteps of Shane, Jared, Jill, and LJ, I escape the carny camp like it is the Turkish prison in *Midnight Ex-*

press. "Chips jumped!" I imagine Shorty saying, filling people in, knowing from here on out I'll have to watch my back every time I go to a carnival. In fact, I keep nervously looking over my shoulder while speeding out of town.

Glancing into the rearview mirror of my rental car, I smile. My teeth, my teeth, my precious, precious teeth!

CHAPTER THREE

CULT OF CELEBRITY
AMERICAN DREAM

THE AMERICAN DREAM:
IN THEIR OWN WORDS
Don Wrege (www.ozzylookalike.com),
from his as-yet unpublished *My Year as Ozzy*

The first time I took notice of a celebrity look-alike with curiosity was at Denver's National Western Stock Show in 2000.
My deejay girlfriend was manning the radio station's promo-
tional booth, and they had hired a Willie Nelson clone and a
Dolly Parton double (so to speak) to stand and smile while
people had their pictures taken with them. I thought it was a
bit strange that folks would line up and wait for over half an
hour to be photographed with fakes. It seemed silly, but
people seemed to enjoy it. I didn't think much more about
celebrity look-alikes until MTV gave aging rocker Ozzy Osbourne and his bizarre family a television series. His physical
appearance at this stage of his career seemed to mirror my
own, or at least vast numbers of people thought so.

I wasn't a Black Sabbath or Ozzy fan—In my opinion, I just
look like an everyday garden-variety middle-aged hippie with
long hair and wire-rimmed glasses, living in Boulder, Col-
orado, among a bunch of other aging hippies in this strange

little town. Even before the Osbournes had their television show, people would occasionally come up to me and ask if I was Ozzy. I didn't think much of it at the time, as it happened mainly in crowds, especially at concerts, and most of the questioners were drunk. Once the television series hit—and it hit big—I was harassed everywhere nonstop.

When it got to the point that I couldn't go a couple of days without some stranger calling me Ozzy, just for fun, I asked a friend to take a couple of photos of me with my hair down. I tinted a pair of old round glasses blue with RIT dye, put on a black T-shirt and sweatpants, hung some gold chains around my neck, and tried to strike a suitable Ozzy pose for the camera. Just three weeks after I posted the photos on my personal website, all hell broke loose. I found myself in Las Vegas onstage at the Imperial Palace and partying with other fake celebrities. I was waved through the VIP entrance of the House of Blues by an unsuspecting security staff, then was asked politely by management if I might step onstage and say a few words to the screaming crowd that was none the wiser.

Two weeks after my Vegas debut, I was flown to New York by ABC to appear on Live with Regis and Kelly, then on to Chicago to appear on the first of two Jenny Jones Show episodes. I fooled thousands of Kentucky Derby visitors into believing they were cheering for the real Ozzy, was driven in a stretch limo around Denver for three hours during a live radio broadcast confronting confused "fans" and causing a near riot at an Ozzfest concert. I appeared in the 2002 MTV Video Music Awards program being ridden like a pony by a fake Britney Spears, made the front page of my hometown newspaper, appeared in a series of Oklahoma car dealership commercials, and was paid handsomely to show up at industrial "meet & greet" receptions in costume. I appeared in an AMC documentary, was interviewed on coast-to-coast radio New Year's Eve, and damn near slept with Sandra Bullock. (Okay, a Sandra look-alike, but hey, sometimes close is good enough.) I was given flights, drivers, limos, a suite on Times Square I could never have afforded myself.

By the time I finally hung up my rubber bat at the end of 2003, amazing things had happened to me. It was an overdose of the kind of attention I spent a lifetime dreaming about. It was more fun than I have ever had in my life, but at times I came dangerously close to losing my own identity in the craziness of the moment.

Along the way I learned a lot about the celebrity look-alike business and those who participate in it. I got a rare glimpse at how "fame" looked from the other side—from the perspective of the famous. Fame is something the outside world lends to an individual. It takes the cooperation of the public to create the phenomenon. I was lifted to a position afforded famous people simply by virtue of my appearance, in spite of my earnest attempts in Los Angeles through the years to earn it on my own.

Is fake fame no less satisfying than the real deal? All the sweetness and none of the calories? What did it feel like when my limo was surrounded by young co-eds, thrusting pens, pencils, and pads through the window for my "autograph"? I felt like a rock star. In that moment it didn't matter to me that I wasn't who they thought I was. I was in my dream of dreams. While a dream isn't reality, it is when you're asleep. My take on it is, if someone thinks you're famous—then you are.

In a society that elevates individuals to celebrity status sometimes for simply being who they are (Paris Hilton, Anna Nicole Smith, et al), is there a "real" famous (Ozzy earned it over a thirty-plus year career) versus "fake" fame (I was a poser)? I think so. Do they feel different? At times I think not.

Does an audience require "the real thing" in order to be entertained? Obviously not—something else was going on. The people who actually thought I was the real Ozzy, I can understand. The people who knew I wasn't and still participated in the illusion by behaving like the real Ozzy was in their presence interested me greatly. A friend of mine summed it up for me by suggesting that this emotional response was simply a reptilian brain reaction to past pleasure. He explained it to me thusly.

Upon seeing Ozzy (or in my case, his likeness), Ozzy fans' brains release certain soothing chemicals that cause a feeling of happiness. Happiness learned through multiple pleasurable experiences that went before, like attending one of his concerts or watching his television show. Therefore, even though they are gazing upon a known replica, there are still squirts of happy juice flowing into their gray matter, and they react in a primal way as if they are experiencing the real deal. At first I thought my friend was nuts, but I found myself in more and more situations where I witnessed first hand what he had described.

What, if anything, did I learn from my Ozzy experiences, other than people are easily fooled when they want to be? I learned that fame can be largely false, because it can be based as much on an illusion as on talent or accomplishments. I learned that people love to be entertained so much that they will suspend their disbelief to an astonishing degree. I learned that if five people in a crowd of a thousand believe in something, they can cause the others to "see" it as real too. I even began to better understand how religion works.

At some point in the Ozzy look-alike madness it became clear to me that, as sad as it might sound, what I had experienced during that year was "it" for me. That it was as close as I was going to get to being a rich and famous rock star—as close as I was going to get to achieving my lifelong dream. This thought was potentially devastating but actually amused me upon greater reflection. Fate had handed me, at the very last possible moment, I might add—in my fifties—a first-class ticket on a roller coaster ride showing me, from the inside, what it could have been like.

My dilemma, my potential nightmare, in fact, came down to how I was going to internalize the experience. Should I allow myself to feel like I had reached my goal of achieving fame? Was the attention I received as a fake celebrity worthy of this? Was I insane not to let it be?

In the end I realized that my thirty-year longing, my prayer to the universe for fame was, in fact, answered, but not in the

way I'd wished for. I almost missed the message. It dawned
on me that it is entirely possible to get what you have wanted
your entire life and not recognize it. People may have their
prayers answered, realize their own American Dream, and not
even know it—because it comes in a different package than
they expected.

An Imposter Impersonator

Loud screaming fills my ears. Not the screams of adoring fans
who have sighted a beloved celebrity but screams of pure anger.
A Joan Rivers impersonator is pissed off. She's livid. Fake Joan
Rivers is so angry that she screeches at me, completely out of
character.

"This is not Halloween, you know!" fake Joan Rivers shrieks,
as I clutch my sweaty palms, shifting uncomfortably.

An irate Cher impersonator joins in, as do several other angry
women who now encircle me—all dead ringers for very, very famous people, all mad, all ganging up on me as if I've committed
heinous crimes against humanity. It's starting to get very, very
ugly.

"We take this very seriously and don't want people to make
fun of us!" hollers faux Carmen Miranda, who wears a headdress
of fruit, worked up with veins pulsating from her neck. She
states the blond wig I'm wearing not only discredits Austin Powers "tribute artists" but also the entire celebrity-impersonator
community at large! Furious, she elaborates: "I don't think the
real Mike Myers would appreciate what you're doing!" (I think
he would!)

"A real Austin Powers impersonator would never wear a wig like that!" imitation Roseanne Barr berates, throwing in her two cents.

Adjusting my thick glasses and dropping my half-Chinese Austin Powers accent, I futilely try to defend myself (noting there's nothing worse in the world than being screamed at by a bunch of female celebrity impersonators). Where do I begin to explain to this angry celebrity-doppelgänger mob that this was the only wig left at my local costume shop, and was not worn out of tribute-artist disrespect? How did my ploy of being under-cover at the Fourth Annual Vegas Celebrity Impersonators Con-vention and live the American Dream of being a recognizable face the public adores, go wrong, horribly wrong?

The convention's director (a miniature blond woman with no resemblance to anyone famous) points to faux Joan Rivers and adds through clenched teeth, "She spends a lot of money on her outfit, and you come here and mock it!" And finally, "As the di-rector of this convention, I'm telling you to take off that wig! I want you to go into the bathroom and take off that wig right now!"

It hurts; it really, really hurts. What choice do I have? The Arnold Schwarzenegger impersonator might squash my head like a grape! The Robert De Niro look-alike could accuse me of wanting to fuck his wife! Imitation Michael Jackson could tell me to "beat it!" Obviously the idiot for making an improper wig choice, and like a kicked, but famous-looking, puppy, I do as I'm told. My pursuit of the American Dream has been rained upon in the land of imposters. These guys are pros and can surely smell a true phony trying to imitate someone famous rather than a professional (trying to imitate someone famous). Lending no credibility, my dreadlocks stuffed beneath my wig make Austin Powers look like he has a medium-size brain tumor.

Yes, I've been unmasked midconvention, outed as an imposter impersonator!

The American Dream is in thrall to the ideal of "celebrity." People aspire to be idolized by millions, loved and admired. They desire to possess that face, one that is recognizable by all privileged to lay eyes on its renowned entity. Some achieve this by moving up the showbiz ranks. Others simply spend their entire careers imitating the famous, taking a sleigh ride on their coat tails, further feeding into cult of celebrity—except one generation down. Driven by constant exposure in the media, fame is an essential prerequisite for celebrity status, though the reason for fame is often minor; such as those who are famous for being famous. In this cult-of-celebrity obsessed world, simply looking and acting like a famous celebrity is an American Dream.

Let's Backtrack to Before My American Dream Went Horribly Wrong

In the buffet line, heaping food on to paper plates are the (visual) likes of Kenny Rogers, Ozzy Osbourne, Tina Turner, Snoop Dogg, and Prince, not to mention three Shania Twains.

"Hey Willie, don't forget to pay your taxes," riffs a Sean Connery with a fabricated Scottish accent to a pigtailed dead ringer for Willie Nelson holding two plates of food, while the dozens of attendees schmooze in the vocational regalia, as their respective renowned characters.

The Vegas Celebrity Impersonators Convention, along with the Sunburst Convention of Celebrity Impersonators in Orlando, are the two big industry events that bring together look-alikes, tribute artists, agents, and producers for several days of seminars, showcases, and schmoozing. Since 2007, the Celebrity Impersonators Convention has joined with the Reel Awards, which honors the best look-alikes and tribute artists in the business.

The Vegas ranch locale for the big opening convention barbecue—for those who resemble the famous—is more surreal than a Salvador Dali dripping clock. Put on by the man behind Imperial Palace's Legends show, if this were a party with the real, actual celebrities being portrayed, it would be the best party ever!

Still, this soiree is nothing but eye candy: several Marilyn Monroes mingle among a Paris Hilton; a paunchy, overweight Ponch from CHiPS; and Seinfeld's Kramer (though not screaming the n word). Then there's me: a third-rate, blond Austin Powers who can't get his catchphrases right and utilizes a slight Chinese accent: "Yeah, ladies!" I blurt to everyone who passes, shaking my hips to level 11.

"That's Austin Powers with a big brain tumor," a Liz Taylor impersonator interjects, pointing to the back of my head where my hair is visually stuffed under my wig. "Have you got a big brain tumor, darling?"

"Shag-a-delic, baby! It's malignant!" I slur, making my way towards the alcohol (to fuel my Austin Powers characterization), while rubbing elbows with fake Snoop Dogg (he's appeared on MTV, as, well, Snoop Dogg).

"Is that Cher?" fake Snoop's real cousin (and manager) asks, pointing to six-foot-three transvestite Cher.

"That's a man, baby!" I reply with China's number-one Austin Powers inflection, passing dozens of the Elvises (or Elvi) present, clad in various stages of the King's career (leather jacket Elvis, jumpsuit Elvis, rockabilly Elvis, etc.). Perhaps the granddaddy of all celebrities who are impersonated, it's estimated that there are roughly thirty thousand Elvis impersonators worldwide (enough for a small Elvis-impersonated town!).

"The weird part is when you meet people who actually think they're the character," shares cool Elvis. "That's why I'm wearing the shorts," he says, who's too cool to wear an Elvis outfit—he's saving it for the stage. Hailing from Arizona, he's kinda like the Elvis who hangs out with his best friend Sonny and the boys around the pool and then shoots up television sets.

As long as there have been the famous, there have been those who look like them: Mikheil Gelovani, a Georgian actor and Joseph Stalin look-alike, played the Soviet leader in propaganda films of the 1930s and 1940s, while once in the thirties, Charlie Chaplin entered a Charlie Chaplin look-alike competition and, ironically, placed third.

"I'm going to be on *The Tonight Show* next Monday," interrupts Clonan, the overly active, carrot-topped Conan O'Brien impersonator.

Asked if he's nervous, the red-haired impresario replies with the confidence of a pro, "Not at this point in the game!"

"Are you going to be doing your Clonan act?"

"I'll just do whatever hits me," Clonan replies, then breaks into a Conan O'Brien dance. Rather than "officially" being booked on *The Tonight Show*, Clonan's plan simply involves sitting in *The Tonight Show* audience and somehow getting on the show that way.

Looking around, I ask Clonan, "Who's the most famous celebrity impersonator here?"

"I am!" Clonan boasts without hesitation, shaking his red-haired head, then handing me, along with everyone else, a copy of his resume. "I got the most TV credits!"

Looking over the resume, I question Clonan (whose real-life name is Bruce and also works in restaurant and hotel management in New York City), "What was your role in the Howard Stern movie *Private Parts?*"

"You know the part where AC/DC is in concert? I was in the crowd scene!" Clonan nods, describing his contribution among hundreds of other extras just like him.

Has Clonan ever met the real Conan O'Brien?

"He knows who I am," Clonan replies with the intensity of Rupert Pupkin and tone that almost implies restraining order. Imitation is the highest form of flattery—or it can be plain, downright creepy.

There are several levels of impersonators present. First, there're tribute artists: those who perform as their idol in Vegas-style acts. Then there're look-alikes: it's pure genetics (or cosmetic surgery). They were born into the role and find work at parties or trade shows as atmosphere or as stand-ins for the actual resembled stars. The problem with some attendees: you don't know if they're impersonating celebrities you're not familiar with or if they are simply civilians. While a Hank Williams tribute band kicks out wicked rockabilly, I turn to the creepy-looking man standing hunched over the buffet line, "Let me guess, Dr. Strangelove! Right?!"

Becoming mildly offended, he flatly says, "No!" and abruptly walks away (he actually owns the ranch).

The Country Music Channel coaxes various impersonators to get in front of their cameras (such as third-rate Austin Powers), allowing attendees their clichéd fifteen minutes of impersonator fame. Following in the footsteps of, say, a Susan Sarandon or a Sean Penn look-alike, I use the podium of television to spout my celebrity-impersonator political views regarding the Iraq War.

"Who do we have here?" asks the Country Music Channel's cameraman, turning his crew's attention from fake Paris Hilton to myself. "Why, it's Austin Powers!"

"Yeeeeeah, baby!" I bellow, moving my hips, hamming it up for America's TV viewing audience. And then: "It would be really shag-a-delic if we brought our troops home from Iraq! George Bush out of the White House would be simply groooooovy!" Stunned silence. I proclaim, "Free Mumia, baby!" Further silence. The crew immediately turns their camera light off and moves on to one of the numerous Chers.

It doesn't go any better with a camera crew following a "Vogue"-era Madonna impersonator for the documentary sequel to Madonna's *Truth or Dare*. After Britney Spears and Madonna re-create their famous MTV kiss for the cameras, I jump in front of the cameras for my sixteenth minute of fame, acting like an Austin Powers impersonator who just can't get the catchphrases right.

"Let's misbehave!" I spout in the accent of the Chinese. Occasionally placing my bottom on fake Madonna, I then utter, "It's horny time! It's time for horny!"

"Austin and I once starred in a movie together," fake Madonna, who remains composed, tells the Truth or Dare sequel cameras.

"Yeah, it was my movie *The Spy Who Shanked Me!*" I announce. "Shank-a-delic!"

Then with gyrating dance moves: "I lost my moped, baby! Oooooooh, groupies!!"

More cameras are shoved in my face.

"Who do we have here tonight?"

"I'm the world's foremost Steve Guttenberg impersonator," I share. "You might remember me from *Cocoon*, *Three Men and a Baby*, and my more recent work, *Dancing with the Stars!*" As an Arnold Schwarzenegger impersonator walks by (not *Kindergarten Cop* Arnold, but *Terminator* Arnold), I suddenly shout, "It's the Govennator, baby!"

Fake Arnold Schwarzenegger completely ignores me, like I'm on the impersonator C-list. "I just got dissed by Arnold Schwarzenegger, baby!!" I cry, then conclude by singing a few drunken bars of "I Got You Babe" with man-Cher.

As the night wears on (and the alcohol pours), my thoughts turn to hitting on either the Cyndi Lauper impersonator or one of the numerous Chers (definitely not man-Cher). Remember, what happens at a celebrity impersonators' convention stays at a celebrity impersonators' convention! Chatting up circa-sixties Cher (a former medical student who drove out here from Arkansas with her dog and cat), while making some valuable Cher time, Jack Nicholson walks by and whispers important impersonating-career advice, "If you want to make some money, lose the wig!"

(**Pause.**) "I lost my moped, baby!"

No sleep for the famous looking. After the barbeque, a face-value ensemble, which at quick glance could be mistaken for an Academy Awards after-party, storms a karaoke bar on the glitzy Vegas strip. Will our visually recognizable collective be stormed by the fake paparazzi upon arrival, snapping shots of our merry band drunkenly fucking up or exiting cars without panties? (Are you listening, fake Roseanne Barr?)

"Oh, my god! Can I take a picture with you?" an adoring fan's request of the blond, fun-loving Austin Powers who appears to be afflicted with a minor brain tumor.

"Free Mumia, baby!"

The karaoke bar puts on the full VIP treatment, seating us in a special section away from the common civilians (resembling only themselves), who look on with thrilled admiration at our famous faces. Hey, if they can't have a chance to see their idols in this celebrity-obsessed culture, then we are the next best thing!

Tina Turner, Prince, and one of the Elvi look on with up-staged jealousy, as more thrilled tourists flock over, my fake star charisma pulling them in. A birthday girl asks for a kiss. A bachelorette party gets me to dance wildly with them. More pictures. More kisses. Love me! Love me! Love me! I'm as beloved as the real deal, and all I did was rent a costume. In your face, faux-Roseanne! In your face, faux-Jack Nicholson! Up yours, faux-Robert De Niro! There's a new impersonating sheriff in town, rapidly climbing the tribute artist A-list, and you better believe he's blond and has a big brain tumor!

Celebrity Impersonators Convention: Day Two

"Hi, George Washington," the men's-room attendant says to me, looking at my now-disheveled blond wig and crumpled frilly shirt, totally missing the mark on my Austin Powers persona. A

Liza Minnelli impersonator enters the men's room, taking the urinal next to me. She bursts into a Broadway show tune.

"That's a man, baby!" I blurt to the men's-room attendant.

Making my way towards Imperial Palace's conference rooms for an afternoon of celebrity-impersonator workshops, my hung over and unshaven Austin Powers (with bits of hair sticking out of my wig), faces the moment I've been dreading but that I knew would be inevitable: I've spotted another Austin Powers—a rival. The other Austin Powers—a chubbier version than my rendition—eyes me with extreme contempt. We stare each other down.

"Saucer of milk, table for two! Meow!" I say in passing.

In regard to the celebrity-impersonator game, last night Lucille Ball explained, "The ones who you look out for are the people with the one gig. They're so involved with the one character that they take on the character!"

True, there's slight derision, since you're vying for the same jobs, another similar imposter on the landscape means artificially flavored food off their table. Also affecting their meal ticket, scandal in a real celebrity's life directly impinges on the careers of those impersonating. (You don't see many Hitler impersonators.) Dancing a love/hate tango with the famous, when the public turns on a celebrity, they also turn on the celebrity impersonator.

This year, controversy has greatly decreased the number of Michael Jacksons and Seinfeld's Kramers in attendance. (Not to mention Phil Spectors and Robert Blakes.) Can you imagine your entire career being cock-blocked when a star is slapped with pedophilia or murder charges?

Other times it's the impersonator who fucks it up for the stars. A few years back, a gossip rag reported that Robert De

Niro picked up a woman at a bar in the Hamptons and had a torrid one-night romantic tryst. Around the same time, accounts surfaced that Robert De Niro had embarked on a spree of freeloading and fraud. A police investigation revealed that these crimes weren't linked to actor, Robert De Niro, but instead, Joseph Manuella—a Robert De Niro impersonator. The former New York City firefighter immersed himself so deeply in the role, he'd carried a credit card in De Niro's name, enjoyed hotel discounts and free meals at swanky Manhattan eateries, conned fans out of money, and indulged in starstruck, but not very bright, groupies. He'd handed out autographed photographs of himself, which he'd signed "Robert De Niro." He even fooled the head of Sony Pictures, who saw him on the studio lot, shook his hand, and thanked him for all his years of good work.

"I get better treatment in restaurants," Manuella once said, before he was arrested. "Owners have even thanked me for eating in their establishments."

Two counts of criminal impersonation were charged to the celebrity impersonator, whose blessing/curse was becoming too used to the cult-of-celebrity trappings of the American Dream.

Sitting down at a table with a big-nosed, gray-haired man who's situated next to a pudgy woman in a sparkly dress, I have no idea who the hell the celebrities are they're trying to impersonate. Maybe that's why they came for these workshops (Lesson one: Make sure people know who you're impersonating!) The big-nosed, gray-haired man (Jack Lemmon? Wilford Brimley!?) interrupts my contemplation.

Chuckling with those around our table, he says, "There are some people here who you just don't know who they are!" (Lesson two: Don't mock other impersonators if no one knows who you are.)

The pudgy woman (Selena? Charo?!) leans in close, acknowledging a depressed-looking man across the room wearing a blue suit and sitting alone. She asks, "Who is he?"

"That's Rodney Dangerfield," I clarify (knowing this from riding the elevator together). We glance at questionable Rodney. He truly doesn't get any respect! Questionable Rodney is being upstaged by another, more animated Rodney Dangerfield, who works the room, dishing out zingy one-liners to other fake celebrities. Nonrespected Rodney can only sadly lean over and listen with envy, fumbling with the straw of his soft drink. What an opportune time to utter his idol's classic catchphrase, "I get no respect!" The moment is lost. He remains alone at his empty table.

It's also embarrassing when you wrongly guess an impersonator's celebrity identity. Their whole career is based on the public acknowledging that simple attribute. It shouldn't be a hard stretch to connect the dots. Earlier, I said to a guy, "Hey! It's Chris Rock!" He responded, "Actually, I'm Marvin Gaye." Awkward silence followed.

So, I devised a solution to the identity problem. You say to the celebrity impersonator, "Hey! Do that famous catchphrase of yours!"

I turn to big-nosed, gray-haired man. "Hey, do that famous catchphrase of yours!"

Imagine my surprise: "I'm Bond, James Bond!"

Well, fuck me sideways!

After the Jack Nicholson impersonator conducts a ball-busting workshop on business insights ("You need to set up a website!"), a man in a suit, with a posh English accent, questions me as if I were an inferior piece of impersonating shit, "I assume you're an Austin Powers impersonator?" He then directs me to his exhibitor's table displaying acrylic veneer dental prosthetic teeth (eight hundred dollars), conveying it's a foot up in the look-alike business. "Tomorrow, there's a man named Richard Halpern. Check out his teeth. I made them!" he states, regarding still another Austin Powers impersonator. After boasting about secured prosthetic teeth sales from the likes of impersonators Roseanne, Kenny Rogers, and Tom Jones, comes next, he proclaims, "I don't fix teeth," he stresses. "I make teeth!"

When the dental interrogation concludes, a cameraman from the Discovery Channel informs me (with insights he's discovered), "It's sort of considered the lunatic fringe to get cosmetic surgery in order to look more like the chosen celebrity. It's more for the wannabes or the extremely high-level impersonators who have their own Vegas shows."

Like a prosthetic-teeth infomercial, the Englishman takes to the front of the room, fielding inquiries from celebrity impersonators who ask questions out of character. First, Sammy Davis Jr., "Is there a device you can put in that can change the facial structure?"

"Absolutely! What you're looking for is called a facial-plumping appliance."

"How about a big English nose?" pipes in the Rod Stewart of Canada.

"No, we don't do noses. We don't do eyes. Just teeth!"

The Arrival of Fox News

With nothing but a potpourri of those who enjoy too much attention, Clonan continues to tell the cameras (and anyone else who'll listen) he's going to be on *The Tonight Show* on Monday. Liz Taylor does a gangsta rap involving original lyrics she wrote.

"Shut your pie-hole!" screams Chris Farley, looking like he's about to pop a blood vessel, poised in a crouched posture. Everyone turns as he works the cameras, loving it. "Oh, my god, look at all these pretty ladies!"

Farley is dead on (quickly becoming my convention favorite). Hailing from the Midwest, he's only been in the Farley-impersonating game for a few months, caving after years of being told at his day job in the mortgage industry how much he looks like the rotund funnyman.

"I just memorized the few key lines," he says, quickly rattling off the essential Farley curriculum. In fan appreciation to his deceased hero, fake Farley adds with sentimentality, "I would just like to meet some of his family and tell them I thought he was really funny and a great guy!"

Since it's a huge boost to the career of an up-and-coming Austin Powers impersonator to get more TV screen time, I jump behind the trio of Shania Twains, who now sing for the camera, and start madly dancing my American Dream like I'm on the BBC.

"It's time for horny!" I cry, moving with fervor, like my impersonating life depends upon it, clearly upstaging Shania-Twain-in-triplicate. That is, until I'm pushed out of camera range by fruit-headed fake Carmen Miranda.

"That's too much!" fake Carmen Miranda reprimands, quickly teaching me a valuable lesson in celebrity-impersonator etiquette: never madly dance behind three Shania Twains while they're singing on the local Fox News affiliate. "That's really not cool," she adds. "That's their moment!"

Other professionals, though, notice star quality in my Fox TV spectacle.

"You got good energy!" remarks a fifteen-year veteran Joan Rivers impersonator, clearly seeing my inner-fraudulent celebrity charisma. Yes, from my local Fox News affiliate appearance, I've been "discovered." "First, we have to do something about that wig!" Joan Rivers exclaims, offering to take me under her impersonating wing.

"I was late to catch my plane and I accidentally grabbed my Eminem impersonator wig," I clarify, wondering why a blond wig is such a big deal in faux–Austin Powers circles, explaining it's my interpretation of the Powers character, who goes by the professional name Awesome Powers.

Joan Rivers's husband, who acts as her manager, also sees my potential, "I think you got it," he says with dead seriousness. Vigorous head nodding on my part. "You got great energy," he enthusiastically expounds. "All you got to do is memorize a few catchphrases and you can make from fifteen hundred to a few thousand dollars at trade shows just greeting people!"

"It's horny time, baby!" I shout, breaking into another sixties dance.

Pretty darn good. In a mere day, I've climbed closer to the American Dream, with professional peers now steering me up the ranks. Yes, I shall be beloved by those who'll never get the chance to see the real Mike Meyers in his most famous role. I shall become the next best thing!

"Just learn a few of the key catchphrases," he restates. Again: "I think you got it!"

Me: "I lost my moped, baby!"

The sun seems to be shining down from the artificial heavens. Except this is the part where the rug of my cult-of-fake-celebrity American Dream gets swiftly pulled out from under, and all the screaming starts.

After upstaging three Shania Twains on local Fox News affiliate, an absolutely livid Carmen Miranda went directly to the Fourth Annual Vegas Celebrity Impersonators Convention's director. It was leaked that I'm not actually a real Austin Powers impersonator, but the aforementioned imposter impersonator! (My guess it was from man-Cher!)

"This is not Halloween, you know!"

Who blew the whistle? Was it the Rod Stewart of Canada, Willie Nelson!? Prince, perhaps!!? Joan Rivers is hugely offended. Her husband won't even speak to me! No longer am I taken under their wings. A severe chewing out follows:

"How come none of the other writers are dressed up!"

"Yeah!"

"You're going to say we're all freaks!"

I should retort, "Oh, behave!" but I don't.

More screaming. More yelling. Me, making excuses. More hatred towards my wig, etc. . . . Need I point out to these celebrity impersonators, if we're talking freaks, there's no bigger freak than myself!?

The Big Talent Showcase

So now the remainder of the convention is spent trying to avoid lived Joan Rivers, Carmen Miranda, and anyone else who witnessed my celebrity-impersonator fall from grace, and wig giving-up. I lurk in the shadows, hiding behind the likes of Kenny Rogers and Jay Leno, avoiding further unnecessary confrontation, I've adopted a visor and Hawaiian shirt, disguising myself as Hunter S. Thompson so I can attend the big Talent Showcase, where impersonators display their goods for booking agents and producers, not to mention girthy midwestern tourists.

With extreme revulsion, I sadly look on at chubby Austin Powers (my rival!), now flocked by tourists clamoring for group photos.

"Say, 'Shag-a-delic!'" quips chubby Austin Powers. (That's my line.) Cameras click. I should be the one in the photo! I should be saying "Shag-a-delic!" Those should be my adoring tourists! Chubby Austin Powers shoots a smug "They made you give up your wig" look. Word travels fast in these circles.

Others can share in my dismay. Little kids flock to loveable Ozzy Osbourne for autographs. (Do they know it's not the real Ozzy!?) A much taller Ozzy stands nearby, glaring. Unauthorized Ozzy, The World's Greatest Ozzy Impersonator, is not like wacky Osbourne-dad Ozzy fielding autographs, but more like the biting-the-heads-off-bats, snorting-ants Ozzy.

Ten years ago, manifest destiny catapulted Unauthorized Ozzy, The World's Greatest Ozzy Impersonator, into his career. When working as a recording studio engineer he actually met the real thing. Real Ozzy told him, "You're a chip off the old mother!" So Unauthorized Ozzy (his real name's Peter) dyed his hair black and relocated to Vegas with his real estate agent wife.

With the intensity of a man who has been up for days, Unauthorized Ozzy goes off on a bitter triad. "Vegas is the worst! It's a very competitive town. If you're really good, people will turn against you," he complains. "I wish the casinos were more open to the act. They're afraid it would scare away the blue-hair crowd."

Pointing to loveable Ozzy—in the midst of bringing delight to children—I ask the burning question, "Do you feel competition with the other Ozzy impersonators?"

"No!" answers Unauthorized Ozzy, "Only with Ozzy himself, because we're searching for the same band members!" he boasts, claiming to play with former members of Ozzy's original band (as well as a guy from Night Ranger). He then arrogantly adds, "You got to support the other Ozzy impersonators. I've driven two out of town so far! One guy came to see my show and he left on the Greyhound the very next day!" Why? "It was so real he couldn't even deal with it!"

After ditching Unauthorized Ozzy (he was so real I couldn't even deal with it!), loveable Ozzy inquires about my new look, "Austin, where's your outfit?"

"I've gone civilian," I say, making a sad face, eyeing more tourist-requested photo-ops from Chubby Powers. "Are you performing today?" I ask, regarding the big talent showcase.

"I'm not," loveable Ozzy replies. "There are too many of them," he replies, referring to the thirty scheduled tribute-artist acts.

"All we get is two minutes onstage," exclaims the popular Rodney Dangerfield, working the crowd filtering in (as nonrespected Rodney grimly looks on). "That's one minute more than my wife gives me!"

"Hey, Tiger," Rodney then shouts to Snoop's cousin, mistaking him for a Tiger Woods's impersonator because he's black.

"He called me Tiger! That's the second time he's done that," he exclaims with a laugh.

The showcase kicks off with Cher singing "If I Could Turn Back Time." A parade of celebrity-impersonator new school (Beyoncé, Snoop Dogg) versus old school (Liza Minnelli, Frank Sinatra) follows. Ricky Martin does the William Hung classic "She Bangs." The three Shania Twains each perform (but not at the same time). Carmen Miranda (who hates my existence) dances with fruit on her head. An overachiever portrays the entire Rat Pack (Sammy, Dean, and Frank). Cool Elvis blows the crowd away, kissing the ladies and striking karate poses.

Acts that nail it are great. A chubby Prince comes out, metamorphoses into both Sonny and Cher, then Michael Jackson, and finally Elvis—all done by one man! Others, like a confusing older woman wearing a bird's beak and singing Jimmy Durante, seem like advanced karaoke.

Afterwards a sea of celebrity impersonators spill out into the foyer to the delight of their fat, Vegas-tourist fans. The fans, in turn, are doing a bit of impersonating of their own: pretending they are rubbing elbows with the real deal.

"It was so exciting!" a woman from Pittsburgh tells her friends. She then shyly asks cool Elvis for a photo—as if he were the real thing. "We feel like little kids," she shrieks.

"Fifty different egos and a hundred different acts," cool Elvis remarks in a postshowcase moment, with only one regret, "I wish I would have worn a different jumpsuit than the other guy!" Such comes with the turf in the world of Elvis impersonating.

"I'm about ready, man, for a martini," cries Sean Connery in the performance aftermath. Clad in a white dinner jacket, he takes me off guard by using his regular, thick East Coast accent.

Eight years ago, while working as an owner of an art gallery in Palm Beach, his American Dream was realized when an agent came in and said, "Hey, I can make you a lot of money." And that's just what happened! Now, traveling to big James Bond events around the world, John (his real name) also occasionally works as a stand-in for real Sean Connery. "The first job I ever did, I beat up some guy and threw him into Donald Trump's pool!" With a twinkle in his eye and boyish grin, he says, "I grew up and became James Bond!" slyly adding, "And then, there's the Bond girls!"

While the photos continue to snap, with confusion the Pittsburgh woman asks, "Who's that guy in the blue suit?"

I look over at a sad, old friend.

"That's Rodney Dangerfield," I explain (truly not getting further respect).

Taking a good, hard look, the Pittsburgh woman finally remarks, "Oh! . . .Okay! . . . Really!?"

The Celebrity-Impersonator Wedding of the Century

A true American Dream is about to be realized. The convention comes to a head with the wedding of the Arnold Schwarzenegger impersonator to one of the three Shania Twains. The two, who met at last year's convention, decided to tie the knot with an extravaganza that has attracted almost as many paparazzi as would the real stars' nuptials.

"Have you had any real celebrity weddings here?" I ask the woman in charge of Imperial Palace's wedding chapel.

"No," she answers. "But VH1 had a ceremony here where two dogs married each other. The two owners exchanged collars."

The celebrity impersonators begin to gather in the wedding chapel, while a George Bush look-alike primps, serving as Aaaaahnold's best man. I can safely say this George Bush is muuuuuuch cooler than the genuine article (probably with a much better policy on Iraq). He looks so uncannily like Bush, it's laughable. Always smiling, when this former Kansas City construction-company owner does presentations and accidentally bumbles words, the audience usually goes, "Ha-ha, he's really doing him!" Netting six figures yearly for playing the role, he actually met the real George W., who quipped to an aid afterwards, "Did you all get a look at that guy?!" The obvious question, is he a Bush supporter? "I tend to vote for my own best interest," he answers with a sly grin while adjusting his lapel.

More tribute artists file in. Clearly this is shaping up to be the celebrity-impersonator wedding of the century—to the magnitude of fake Lady Di marrying phony Prince Charles. For the blessed event, I contemplate putting back on my Austin Powers outfit so the convention organizers will chase me around the room like it's an episode of *The Benny Hill Show.*

"Can I give you the last kiss as you single?!" wisecracks Whoopi Goldberg to Arnold beforehand.

"Me, too!" pipes in Clonan (forgetting to mention he's going to be on *The Tonight Show* next Monday).

Organ music commences. George Bush enters, accompanied by a spitting image of Laura (who entertained us preceremony with a confusing pro-war rap called "Thank God George Is the President!"). Jack Nicholson and Tina Turner follow them. Impersonator love is truly in the air, and her manager just proposed to her onstage during the talent showcase. ("I wasn't expecting that," she shared with Whoopi Goldberg afterward. "I thought I was getting a contract at Legends.")

Then the moment we've been waiting for, fake Aaaaaaahnold enters, not in a Terminator leather jacket, but instead, a tux. The lovely Shania celebrity impersonator follows, as all heads turn. Numerous photographers dance around trying to get various shots. Cameras flash. Shutters click.

"This is truly a time you both will never forget," states the clergyman conducting the ceremony. "You'll look back and say, 'Do you remember our wedding day in Las Vegas?'"

Tears and an exchange of wedding rings. Fake Laura Bush is crying. Fake Tina Turner is crying. So is fake Whoopi Goldberg—not with an impression of tearful emotions, but real, actual emotions.

"What a special day," quips the cynical Discovery Channel cameraman taking in the whole spectacle of familiar faces in the glitzy Las Vegas chapel. This could only happen in America, where every citizen has the chance to grow up and one day portray someone famous and then marry someone who looks like a mega-selling country-music star—but isn't. Personally, I'd have to say this, by far, is the most beautiful celebrity impersonator wedding I've ever attended. Artificial dreams truly do come true!

CHAPTER FOUR

MILITARY AMERICAN DREAM

THE AMERICAN DREAM: IN THEIR OWN WORDS

John Grady, Association of the United States Army

If you go back to the fundamental documents of this country—the Declaration of Independence and the Constitution—it sums up the American Dream very well. "We hold these truths . . .," and "Inalienable rights," and "Right of the people to abolish it"—which means to abolish a radical or new government that would most likely affect American's safety and happiness. That is, I think, the fundamental part of the American Dream.

Without a strong military is it possible to live the American Dream? The answer to that question is no, we could not. How are you going to protect the people of the United States from attack from the outside? How are you going to keep people safe in their homes if you allow lawless bands to run loose in the streets? You have to have a strong military.

You have to remember that the United States Constitution was the first written Constitution of any English-speaking people. The balance that the founding fathers tried to achieve was to create in the federal government three coequal branches of government—which was imitated in the fifty states.

There certainly is a need to be wary of having a concentration of power. But this is why we have a tri-party form of government. The Executive carries out the will of the people through the legislative act, making sure that nobody oversteps their bounds, as well as basic fairness. I'm not going to say "justice," but basic "fairness" and "equity," which exist through the courts. Regarding the concentration of power, we periodically need to remind ourselves of how much we want to give away in terms of personal freedoms and liberties in the global war on terrorism. Those are major concerns, and they need to be continually reviewed.

Think about how many of the people who were at the Constitutional Convention were Revolutionary War veterans? It was a very high proportion because they did not want to see the Revolution that they had fought for flounder with the chaos.

Does the American Dream change? I'm saying the fundamental part, the pursuit of happiness, and the best of tranquility—those are broad, overarching terms. The specific parts of the dream obviously have to change. In the 1940s, if the nation were not at war, would a white person be overly concerned with the civil rights of blacks, or how Chicanos in California, New Mexico, and Texas were being treated? I don't think so. So it does change. It has to. These documents that I refer to, they are living documents. Each generation has to interpret the American Dream in its own way.

Power to the People's Army!

In the sight of my high-powered weapon is a bald businessman's head. Waiting for the word, I'm ready to fire and forget.

"So, all I have to do is lock on this bald man's head, fire, and walk away?" I once again clarify, making sure I'm clear on the operating instructions.

"That's all you have to do," replies the man with a nondescript European accent; he's wearing a well-tailored suit and square-framed designer glasses.

I engage the firing mechanism on the Remote Weapon Station, and then make loud exploding noises, with my mouth forming horrific screams. I imagine the damage that could be done to the bald businessman, knowing in mere seconds his head would explode like a ripe watermelon hit with a sledgehammer.

"The U.S. Army is our biggest customer," the man with nondescript European accent says; his company, the Kongsberg Group, recently received a $1.35 billion contract in 2007 to supply the army with sixty-five hundred of these puppies.

"Who else do you sell to?"

"England, Finland, Holland, Ireland, Australia. . . ."

"What about to the Revolutionary Armed Forces of Columbia?" I ask, hopeful. At one time Saddam Hussein was on the weapon-selling good-guy list, so why can't I be?

The man with the nondescript European accent makes a disapproving unhappy face. Why should he? Business is business. Today's demons are yesterday's friends!

Every February the Greater Fort Lauderdale/Broward County Convention Center holds the Association of the United States Army annual military hardware trade show where the latest in weaponry, surveillance, and defense technology is displayed. The AUSA Winter Expo is set up like your average tradeshow—with industry exhibits, booth babes, and slick sales presentations—but instead of companies selling the newest innovations in plumbing supplies, it's the latest in military weaponry.

Freedom and the American Dream have a price. That price means going to war and fighting for what we believe, keeping the world safe from evildoers.

To the patriotic sect, the American Dream involves maintaining a strong military force—especially since 9/11; protecting the American Dream as we spread democracy for the side of decency; preserving the United States' role as powerhouse, protector, and police to the rest of the world. It is a dream inextricably linked with our belief that we are the One World Superpower.

As Americans, it's in our best interest to fight. But when a price is paid for liberty, who profits? Weapon and defense manufacturers who reap big fat billion-dollar military contracts. With a $475 billion yearly defense budget, the Iraq War has been costing Americans $720 million per day, $500,000 per minute, equaling enough money to provide homes for 6,500 people and health care for 423,529 children. Like a happy marriage of politics and commercial interests, the AUSA Expo actually encompasses two American Fun Dreams: capitalism and military strength; a direct realization of the military-industrial complex—a term President Dwight D. Eisenhower coined to warn of the dangers of the close, symbiotic relationship between our nation's armed forces and its private defense industries. Hurrah! As Billy Bragg once sang, "War what is it good for? It's good for business."

AUSA—Supporting America's Best— It's All About the Soldier

In the shadow of the Sea Escape Fun Cruise gleams the Greater Fort Lauderdale/Broward County Convention Center. The parking garage ticket gate has a sticker that reads, No WEAPONS—irony! Held in the same city known for Spring Breaks Gone Wild and bars that constantly play Jimmy Buffet's "Margaritaville," the AUSA PR guy told me over the phone, "It's in Florida. It's a sexy show!" Let's see how sexy.

KNOWING THAT A PRECISION STRIKE CAN HIT YOU AT ANY TIME! Such warm, inviting welcome signs are still diligently being hung at the Outdoor Pavilion near a fleet of Stryker Mobile Gun Systems—the eight-wheeled light-armored fighting vehicle equipped with MK19 automatic grenade launchers.

Inside, a massive sea of blue and gray suits dotted with those in military fatigues descends the escalator towards the registration desk. ($500 for government personnel, $700 for AUSA members, and $1,000 for nonmembers.) It's a building full of Dick Cheneys. Lords of War. These are the very rich men whose corporations profit from war, defense, and national security, every second the quagmire in Iraq drags on. I can rest assured the CIA is in attendance. Thus a need for a little undercover preparation.

PSEUDONYM: Hank Leonard

DISGUISE: I stopped at Target and bought a gray suit and porkpie hat. Think of Target like a rental house but without the rental charges—they take returns on virtually everything.

GOAL: To live the American Dream by buying a missile launcher for the People's Army (while at the same time not having representatives of the Expo escort me to an area for questioning). Some might not agree with the policies of the People's Army, but remember, you're only a terrorist if you're on the

losing side; Hank Leonard's People's Army has no
intention of losing!

"Good morning, sir," salutes one suited stern-father type to another, clearly knowing each other from previous military-
weaponry conventions.

"Randy, we're in the same spot as last year," the man replies,
whose company, Lancer Systems, manufacturers a translucent
thirty-round magazine developed for the 5.56mm M16/M4/AR15
rifle.

Some pass the time in the registration line making Hillary
Clinton jokes. This is pure Bush/McCain country whose "one
hundred years in Iraq" mantra resonates hard throughout the
convention center with every new billion-dollar contract.

"Was he involved at all in the prison scandal?" I overhear an
Expo attendee say.

"Well, he didn't end up getting court-martialed," is the response, leaving me wondering if booths will have the latest in
water-boarding technology, new torture devices, or those fashionable black Abu Ghraib hoods, where booth babes beckon,
"To my left is the future of prisoner interrogation. . . ."

America, FUCK YEAH!
Coming again, to save the mother-fucking day yeah,
America, FUCK YEAH!
Freedom is the only way yeah
                                        —Team America

AUSA Winter Expo is a huge blue- and gray-suit pickle
party. Filled wall-to-wall with the war industry, with hundreds

of military defense-based corporations present, on the massive showroom floor, the large video monitor blazes a Humvee tactical vehicle ad trumpeting, WHEN HELL AND BACK IS A DAILY COMMUTE. A flood of military weaponry defense company's sales slogans sell both the American Dream and the fear of being attacked:

**WHEN THE MISSION IS DEFENDING FREEDOM,
THE WEAPON IS MADE BY FNH USA**

THE THREAT IS REAL—THE RESPONSE IS NOW!

THE ENEMY IS VULNERABILITY

Business is booming! Contracts for the top ten weapons contractors were up 75 percent in the first three years of the Bush administration alone. Before war can be fought, the military needs to align with these companies to stock up on the necessary weaponry to squash those we don't agree with in the world. (Or sell to those who'll train others to do so.) Through the years there's been so many places to choose from: Iraq, Vietnam, Korea, Russia, Panama, Nicaragua, Bosnia—the list goes on and on. Bow down and pray to the government for striking fear into the psyche of Americans as profits soar.

"You have your trajectory. Then you have its axis," explains a diligent sales professional for NAMMO AS—the leading manufacturer of ammunition systems and missile and space propulsion products.

"This is interesting," says a serious man with an American-flag tie, who looks over the warheads.

A constant uncomfortable feeling, like rusty acupuncture applied to every inch of my body, rushes through me. Sober is how I describe the atmosphere. Cocaine and bourbon would be the drug of choice. Though I'm trying to blend in with a suit, I still seem to look like a guy who just got out of prison.

"Determine if target is friendly or hostile before detonation," entices XM 7 SPIDER exhibit ($301 million was budgeted to produce 907 Spider systems); a land mine device remotely triggered wirelessly by an operator (command-detonation). "The XM Spider enhances the effects of friendly weapons!" the sales pitch states. (How friendly is any type of weapon?).

Adding an international arms dealing flavor, the French army is present, along with the Israeli, Australian, and Canadian, just to name a few, each parading around in packs in their nation's perspective military uniforms. A Russian man talks adamantly on his cell phone. Asian businessmen look at assault rifles, lengthening their arms to show the proper requested weapon size. I can only imagine the power-schmoozing done here. Steak dinners and martini lunches, deals sealed with a slap on the back and hearty laughs, safe in the knowledge the outcome will help fuel future or existing skirmishes and the usual results that follow.

"They weren't looking at me, they were looking at her," shares an anti-tank guided missile salesman with his cronies. Like a comic-book convention, let's not forget the booth babes. Disappointed they aren't clad in bikinis, holding rocket launchers, and go-go dancing on top of tanks, I notice instead that the booth babes are dressed in more conservative clothes—like body armor.

"To my left we're showcasing the future of the battlefield," announces a tiny woman wearing high heels and an army helmet. Holding an assault rifle, she gives a demo to gathered men with

folded arms. Standing under a large banner that reads, Sup-
PORTING THE SOLDIER, the tiny woman gestures with her assault
rifle as part of her trade-show demonstration. "In my hand I'm
holding an M4, which is to enhance soldiers' targets. It incor-
porates the future of combat systems."

The gathered men remain glued—sex still sells when it comes
to phallic-shaped weapons.

Weapons and surveillance. What I fear is some sort of face-
recognition software zeroing in on me, after which I'll be taken
to an undisclosed area for interrogation. An array of Patriot Act,
Big-Brother gadgets enable the government to check on our nation's citizens and ingrain fear and paranoia into our country's
psyche. Who will get the billion-dollar contract to develop new
devices for the Terror Surveillance Bill, which makes it easier to
eavesdrop on phone calls and e-mails?

"Sell me on this!" I inquire.

"It can even read license plates from covert standoff positions.
Even in high-speed conditions," explains the rep for Gyrocam
Systems—industry leader in airborne surveillance solutions,
$43 million military-contract recipient.

"Sell me on this!"

"In London the average person is filmed roughly five hundred
times a day. Chicago now has more cameras than London,"
boasts a chubby, excited man with glasses, regarding the Funnel Cloud Homeland Security video surveillance equipment.
"The mobile video sensor system only comes on when you need
it," the chubby man says with a growing smile. He then points
to my chin. "We have video equipment now where you can see
a pimple on your face from five miles away."

"Where can you find that equipment?"

"That's classified stuff!" he smiles.

"Is this classified?" I say, pointing to the Funnel Cloud.

"There're different levels of classified!"

"Do you have surveillance equipment that monitors what people think?" I ask.

Before he can respond, the chubby guy starts looking over my shoulder. A group of soldiers stand behind me.

"You got your Funnel Cloud?" interrupts army guy in officer fatigues. In these circles, this upstaging is the equivalent to Brad Pitt entering a Hollywood party.

FRIENDLY OR NOT?

WHAT'S OUT THERE?

WHERE ARE THEY?

WHO ARE THEY?

"Can you use it as a weapon?" I ask the man at Tough Book, a laptop resistant to sand and water, demonstrated as such by pouring sand and water on it.

"No!"

I then ask, "What's your favorite weapon you've seen this year?"

"There's a giant laser on a tactical vehicle from Boeing," he says with growing excitement. "It's used to explode unknown ordinances, but I'm pretty sure they're going to use it to zap people!"

"What!"

"Yeah, it's a normal Humvee that shoots a missile on one side and a laser on the other."

Like a little kid about to see Star Wars for the first time, I rush over to the Outdoor Pavilion, passing the A160s HUMMINGBIRD UAS, a sleek, bullet-shaped unmanned helicopter that fires machine guns. (A $75 million contract was awarded to design and test four A160s).

Slightly out of breath, gesturing wildly with my hands, I blurt to the pair of attractive booth babes behind Boeing's tactical vehicle showroom desk, "Which vehicle has the large laser beam on it?"

"A laser beam?" one of the women repeats, wrinkling her brow.

"Yeah, a guy told me one of your vehicles was equipped with a laser beam. (Pause.) You know, for zapping people."

The two Boeing women look at each other like I just told them humans evolved from volcanoes. "There are no vehicles with laser beams!"

"It's classified, right!?" (Was I duped?) Quickly, I then inquire, "What about the briefcases that turn into jetpacks? Where are they!?" More brow wrinkling.

Disgruntled by the interaction, I then do some shopping next door at Lockheed Martin—the largest weapons contractor in the world, situated in an elaborate tent like one would have for an extravagant wedding reception. Lockheed's former vice president chaired the Coalition for the Liberation of Iraq, a bipartisan group formed to promote Bush's plan for war in Iraq. And then in 2001 the company was awarded $200 billion—the biggest weapons contract ever!

Two large, Dick Cheney types joke with the salesman. Phrases like Integrated Survivability are used as key selling points for armored tactical wheeled vehicles.

"How many can I get?" cracks one of the gray-haired men.

"We take Visa and Mastercard," the salesman retorts, laughing.

"Give me a quote, and I'll talk to Robby and get an okay."

The salesman gestures to one of his colleagues. "Tony, take care of these guys."

A deal is done; further building of the American Dream with growing military might.

Rapping my palm on the side of one of these puppies, I ask, ""How many can I get?" (No laughs.) "What would one of these puppies run me?"

"Twelve million," replies the Lockheed salesman like a snotty boutique clerk. Regardless, he suggests, "Jump on in and watch your head." I enter the six-person cab, which gets a whopping eight to twelve miles per tank, imagining the hell of a grenade being drop inside this confined, claustrophobic space.

"Stand up on the seat," the salesman suggests, like it were a used car, allowing me to peer out the gunner's crow's nest.

I exit the vehicle with an expression like someone just did a bad smell. "I'm going to do a little more shopping around, thank you. Who's your main competition?"

"BEA is around. They're unveiling a new one today."

Yes, the unveiling of the new BEA/Navistar's armored tactical vehicle is one of the big events at the AUSA Expo.

"It's going to replace the Humvee, so it's huge," explains a superfriendly, stocky guy, who, along with Oshkosh and ATK, sells a competing armored tactical vehicle. Excited, he gestures to the BEA Systems/Navistar Defense tradeshow exhibit. "It's a $3 billion project. We're bidding on it," smiley guy explains, regarding the competitive market. "It's a head-to-head competition. The best proposal wins! We want to show our competitors here today that we're the best out there."

"Do you move a lot of these babies?" I ask, referring to his company's armored tactical vehicles as "babies."

"We sold 110 already," friendly guy says proudly—mere hours into the expo.

I kick the self-inflating tires. "Do you sell just to the U.S. Army?" "No, anyone who wants to buy it," he confirms. "We sold to the Australian army, the British army, the French army. Anyone who wants to buy it."

"How about the People's army?" I inquire, handing him a business card with a P.O. box in the Cayman Islands. "I can pay in cash?"

Sadly, it takes a little more paperwork to get these babies fully loaded with all the cool toys. But friendly sales guy steered me right; a large crowd of corporate suits gathers for the 2:45 BEA/Navistar joint light tactical vehicle unveiling, currently concealed under dark cloth. You'd think the Pope was coming to town in his shiny new Pope-mobile. Expo attendees jockey for prime visual positioning. A bustle of anticipation. Cameras poised. While I'm standing behind a guy whose T-shirt reads INTRODUCING TERRORISTS TO 72 VIRGINS SINCE 9/12/01, the ceremony kicks off.

"On behalf of Navistar, we're bringing a very unique and broad spectrum to the battlefield!" expresses the blotchy-skinned president of BEA Systems. "We have the opportunity to build the vehicle of the future to bring into battle, into nation building."

Suddenly, speed metal blares. A light show commences. Cameras flash. Anticipation builds. Excitement follows. The vehicle of the future is unveiled just as someone's loud cell phone goes off.

> Terrorist your game is through cause now
>   you have to answer too,
> America, FUCK YEAH!
> So lick my butt, and suck on my balls,
> America, FUCK YEAH!

Holy shit. Team America has come to life! Sprayed with stars and stripes with a big, kick-ass American Eagle plastered on the hood, the red, white, and blue armor tactical vehicle of the future is unveiled—ready for battle. Wait till the Iraqis see this coming. We'll kick their asses while strains of "The Star Spangled Banner" blast from loudspeakers, sung by Tom Cruise! Let the $3 billion bidding war begin! America, fuck yeah!

"We were a bit afraid to show the vehicle to our competitors, but then again we want to show it off!" the blotchy-skinned man says with pure ass-kicking American pride. "We want to show the army and military that we're ready and that we have the best vehicle designed!"

"U.S.A.! U.S.A.! U.S.A.!" I chant, hoping others join in (they don't).

The floor is opened for questions

"Is this based on your MST design?" inquires a serious man who has done his homework, asking the question I was going to ask.

The answer is muffled however, because none of the microphones seem to work properly—BEA can design the future of light tactical vehicles, but they can't seem to get an operational sound system.

Afterwards, men in suits take turns getting into the vehicle departing with big smiles and firm handshakes. Networking is done. Business cards exchanged. The $3 billion dollar bidding war is well on its way. Joint light tactical vehicle humor follows:

"This is going to replace the Humvee?" a man in a suit remarks.

"Let's kick the tires and see if it falls apart," replies his colleague. (Laughs.)

"We feel fantastic," exclaims the blotchy-skinned company president to a camera crew. "This is a landmark day!"

ADVANCE

PRECISION

KILL

WEAPON

SYSTEM

"Let me get your information," a booth babe says, scanning my badge, as my name and address pop up. Worried that facial recognition software has keyed in and men with earpieces are trailing me, I need a break. Venturing to the parking garage, I'm off to the public sector. Strange. My rental car's door is mysteriously open. I'm positive I locked it. Has a tracking device been planted inside? Am I being followed!?? Is it because I know too much!? Have I become a code-red national security threat!!?

Back at my place of lodging, paranoia—almost conspiracy theory–esque—has me practically unscrewing the light bulbs looking for hidden microphones. Is a black van pulled up outside?

The Enemy Is Chaos

Late for the second day of the Expo, accidentally, I leave missile company brochures scattered all over my hotel room. Has Homeland Security already been alerted?

AVENUE OF CHANGE reads the projected slide as I arrive for the morning opening remarks from the AUSA president—a four-star general who stands uniformed at a podium in front of an American eagle emblem. He addresses his blue- and gray-suited troops in the large conference ballroom, packed with various Dick Cheneys and career military.

"That $660 million is just tip of the iceberg," the general states, regarding corporate profit margins and military budget increases. Like a CEO addressing shareholders of the business, a series of charts appear behind him. "We produce thirty-two vehicles a day. Humvees. We'll increase the number to forty-two total units," the general informs. (Happy payday to those companies.)

SOLDIER AS A SYSTEM now reads the projected slide. This refers to the corporations' most valuable—yet expendable—(a $12 million tactical vehicle isn't cheap) weaponry commodity, as mounting death tolls can attest.

"If you think about where we were at the start of this war, and where we are now—that's progress!" the general declares to the somber crowd, confident we're achieving the American Dream, both winning in Iraq and expanding the American empire. "We're growing the army at the same time we're fighting a war," the general adds, defending the army's overextended state. A story: "The other day, my wife came in with hair on fire. She said, 'I just heard on CNN that 19 percent of the soldiers going in are felons!' I said, you might have heard it on CNN, but it's bullshit!"

Huge Dick Cheney laughs. I shift uncomfortably in my chair.

"All felons are not created equal," stresses the general. Realistic examples: "A young kid sets fire to a beehive in his parents backyard. It accidentally catches the tree on fire, and then burns down the neighbor's house. Should we let him in with a felony waiver?" he poses. Pausing for dramatic effect, "I ask why the hell wouldn't we do that!"

(Applause.)

Full military amnesty is given to felons who've burnt down beehives! "They lay claim their past foibles for the United States Army. God bless them!" Same holds true for potheads and the physically impaired. "A high school quarterback who throws his shoulder out in the big game. Why wouldn't we let him in with a medical waiver!"

(Nods of agreement.)

Good news for shareholders: "The next few decades are going to be just as turbulent as the previous. Rest assured if you're concerned about the state of the soldier in Iraq. Our business is to provide soldier precision."

(Big applause.)

"Thank you for doing what you do," the chairman concludes to the corporations. "The partnership with the private sector is the reason why we can do what we do!"

(Huge applause.)

"We don't fight fair fights. We don't fight home games. Victory starts here!"

"U.S.A.! U.S.A.! U.S.A.!" I chant.

Good place to wrap things up, except the general starts talking about joint force command and JFCOM, rapidly walking through the crowd.

For the Full Spectrum of Warfare

So many missile companies, so little time. Today is dedicated to missiles and missile launchers for the People's Army. Loudly I talk on my cell phone about missile purchasing: "The rebel forces are counting on me to make the purchase!" I shout. "Viva la Revolution!"

The competition present makes it hard to choose. Sales videos look like minor Michael Bay productions. Filmed from a helicopter and set to speed metal, missiles destroy vehicles, buildings, and everything in their path—you can run, but you can't hide—explained how a second shot is laser deployed. Soldiers go, "Woo!" Other sales videos take the opposite approach. Like the end sequence of *Apocalypse Now*, strains of classical music coincide with missiles operated by a satellite tracking system that blows up Iraqi houses.

One missile company has a jar of M&Ms on their counter. (M&Ms and missile purchasing—is there a connection?) Hardened, scary men who look like they've seen it all run other booths; the weight of destruction caused by their product doesn't fall heavy on the shoulders of these merchants of death—it only makes them harder.

"I did it thirty-seven years ago. I was Airborne at the tail end of the Vietnam War," remarks a mustached round guy with glasses from the Lauders-Rocket Family.

"Sell me on it!" I say, pointing to his largest missile.

"We just came out with a new case adapter section. Safe body. We just cut out the joint. It's just one joint. You may not notice a thing."

"You're right, I didn't notice."

Soon, I become the lingering creepy guy. "These are some darn good missiles," I express to the salesman at General Dynamics, who looks like a well-groomed dad in an eighties John Hughes movie. "Sell me on it!"

Pointing to the 120-mm tank ammunition, he gives a rundown of each displayed missile, mentioning such selling points as "propellant."

"This is very good against certain obstacles such as vehicles at close range. It explodes like shotgun pellets."

"That's incredible!" I say, nodding my head. There's no hard sell when it comes to missiles—these babies sell themselves.

"This might get the guy standing on the corner, but it's also going to take out the building."

I make an unhappy face.

"The anti-armor tungsten penetration is suitable for export."

Happy face once again!

And then: "This is the Silver Bullet!" We stand in awe of the Cadillac of missiles. "Because of the Uranium it's only for the United States," he says, stressing pesky international restrictions.

"Whom do you usually sell to?" I ask, stroking the side of the Silver Bullet and going "Mmmmm!"

"Whomever the United States sold the Abrams tank we've sold to," he replies. "We want to expand to Israel."

"There's lots of money to be made there."

We laugh.

Looking off at the sea of blue-suit Dick Cheneys, he says proudly, "To be out here in person gives me a chance to meet with our customers. (Pause.) I have a lot of customers here." He adds, "Esterline Defense Group is our main competition with missiles."

The word competition is unsettling. It means a competitive marketplace, where global peace would put competitors out of business. I look over at ESTERLINE—WORLD LEADER IN COMBUSTIBLE ORDNANCE. Business is bustling. The company holds court. Big laughs. Slaps on the back. Deals sealed.

"Can I buy just one Silver Bullet?" I ask, becoming intense like a twitchy, over-acting Nicholas Cage.

"The tank round is five hundred dollars per missile. They're sold in thousands a round. If you buy a thousand it's very expensive. If you buy two thousand, it's very inexpensive."

"What if I buy five thousand? Can you swing that!?"

"You have to go through the State Department, and you have to go through the U.S. government, then we'd be able to sell to you. We're not going to risk General Dynamic's reputation," he says, raining on my Silver Bullet parade. "We got to make sure you're not a foreign power."

In 2006 alone, the U.S. military sold a $20 billion weaponry package to Saudi Arabia and another $10 billion to various other Arab countries, which include warships, advanced missiles, and precision-guided bombs. "A good omen, a divine gift offered to the Muslim fundamentalists by their enemies," an intelligence officer for the Islamic Republic of Iran commented regarding the transaction. Since, he predicts, some weapons will eventually fall into capable hands and be used against the United

States, imagine egg on America's face when our troops are fired upon with these Silver Bullets.

I get indignant: "I hardly think the People's Army is a foreign power." I laugh. Then stop. Then add, "No, really, we're not."

When the Shot Counts

The French army circulates in a pack, wearing fashionable uniforms that make them look like an eighties new wave band, browsing remote operating machine guns and unmanned robots. It looks like in the future we'll have armies of fighting Robocops operated thousands of miles from the battlefields in boardrooms. I follow at the French army's heel. Aren't we supposed to be hating the French? I guess our hatred of the French only extends to gladly selling them weapons—everything has a price!

It's missile-launcher time! One of the French officers simulates blowing up a house, utilizing Javelin's Precision Terminal Guidance. This causes adamant French discussion.

Like two fully grown kids, the gung-ho salesmen love their Javelin missile launcher. With a big excited smile, one asks, "Do you want to play?" using the word "play" to mean annihilating enemy targets and blowing shit up. I smile. He smiles. We both smile.

"Let's do it!" I cry.

The happier of the two points out features that blow away their competitors.

"It's a two-piece command launch. It weighs forty-nine-and-a-half pounds. Both pieces fit on your back.

It's direct attack. Low profile. Top attack default. Just fire and forget."

"That's incredible!" I cry, delighted, situating myself on the stool. Looking through the scope of the long, green cylinder, I switch to infrared night vision.

"It's based on army video games. You don't have to see your target. At any point you can readjust your missile frame and change the course of the missile. Initially, you don't even have to see the target; just fire and forget!"

I'm instructed to lock on to a moving truck off in the horizon, utilizing the weaponry that has a degree of precision no one ever dreamed of.

"How many seconds will it take from firing to hitting the target?"

"Eighteen seconds," he gleefully replies. "Once you lock on, you can just fire and walk away."

"So I could lock on an any enemy target and just fire and forget?" I clarify. "Like this truck." (Pause.) "Or an abortion clinic?" (Pause.) "Just fire and forget, right?"

"Yes!" he exclaims, watching the locked missile veer towards the enemy target then making direct contact. "All it takes is a two-week course to become an expert."

My response: "That's incredible."

SHWAG OFFERED AT WEAPONRY-EXPO
BOOTHS:
- Golf tees
- Tote bags
- Pens
- Pencil sharpeners
- Jars full of candy
- Lapel pins

RAFAEL ADVANCED DEFENSE SYSTEMS LTD.: SHARING OVER 60 YEARS OF EXPERIENCE IN THE WAR ON TERROR has the best free shwag. It's a pen with the company logo. It gets better. On the side of the pen, hidden in a secret compartment, I shit you not, is a scrolled prayer! Again, I shit you not. This almost beats my fantasy of seeing a missile company open their booth by having everyone get down on one knee and pray to Jesus.

Like loveable Ronald McDonald, Rafael's logo is Rafman, a funny animated superhero who looks like a blond, goofy version of Superman. Rafael Advanced Defense Systems has made weaponry kid-friendly! What Joe Camel is to cigarettes, Rafman is to missile launchers and door-breaching rifle grenades, making weaponry much more appealing for all those boy soldiers in Africa.

A video. Rafman flies through the air. Bubbly animated words pop onscreen:

To Destroy!

To Defend!

To Protect!

Tanks fire at loveable Rafman, boom! boom! boom! Missiles bounce off Rafman's chest. Animated Rafman flies away unscathed. In reality, though, if an actual real tank missile hit a person in the chest, their body would explode like a human piñata, spraying internal organs and body parts rather than candy (much to the undelight of children).

Rafael Advanced Defense Systems' product line includes:

- Door Breaching Rifle Grenade
- Matador WB
- Shoulder-launched wall breaching munitions.
- Maulent shoulder-launched anti-STRICKER munitions

A cute Israeli woman is situated behind the Rafael Advance Defense Systems' weaponry display. I point to funny Rafman.

"Did you create Rafman?" I ask, catching her attention in a flirty manner.

She smiles. Rafman brings joy to people. "Yes, that is us."

"No, did you create the Rafman character?"

"I don't know, but there he is," she says curtly.

"Sell me on it!" I say, pointing to their lightweight missile launcher, handing her my Cayman Islands business card, trying to feel if there's any chemistry between us. (There isn't.)

She situates me behind their missile launcher in the popular fire and forget genre—a direct competitor to Javelin's Precision Terminal Guidance.

"It's a missile. It has a range up to 8k," she clearly explains with her sexy weapon-explaining voice. She points to the features. "You can see the image from high up and adjust. You lock on to the target."

Looking up, I lock my eyes on her—my target—then fire and forget a coy glance.

"Why not try for the house," the cute Israeli woman casually suggests.

I effortlessly explode the house. War gets easier and easier. Damn, a child could operate this missile launcher. Pooh-pooh on the clunky Javelin missile-launching system and their pesky two-week course. I could become a Rafael Advance Defense System expert in minutes and start exploding the People's Army's enemies tomorrow.

"That's crazy!" I lock on one more fire-and-forget target and scream, "Let's nuke Iraq back to dust!" The screaming stops; I sooooo don't want to be swooped up off the expo floor in broad daylight, taken to a secret interrogation area and waterboarded.

More huddled suits. More sales made. Why build all these new toys if they're not going to be used? It's all very funny on a smug, ironic level; very sad on a real level.

Happy Hour!

What do people who profit from war have in common with those who oppose it? Happy hour! (Remember, if we forget happy hour, then the terrorists have won!) At the end of the long day, after the billion-dollar deals have been made, there's an open-bar happy hour on the showroom floor among the most powerful weapons in the world.

"I feel like a little kid," the bartender says, in awe of all the military weaponry, as he hands me yet another drink. (I just hope I don't get trashed and piss off a four-star general.)

"Let's fire it up!" I exclaim, gin and tonic in hand, to the team at HyperSpike—the world's most powerful electro Acoustic Speaker, whose IP-controlled audio deterrent shoots a signal up to two miles.

"We did a little bit ago!" the sales rep replies with a laugh as drinks flow.

Are drunken guys already using the surveillance equipment to scout out the booth babes (like the one in short-shorts promoting gear winches)? Will a weaponry company drunkenly rev up a tank? Is a fire-and-forget strike zone being put on my head?

"You shot the hostage multiple times," a large man with military haircut says to his buddy, knocking back beers, taking turns with the Lasershot assault-weapon video-training simulator, both thoroughly enjoying the simulation of killing people in an Iraqi home-siege scenario—just like a giant video game, but with more realistic kills.

"He was a collaborator," he replies with a laugh, adding, "I got to get one of these in my basement for my kid's birthday party. I can see kids telling their parents, 'Mommy, Daddy, we got to shoot people!'"

My turn. With assault rifle in hand and alcohol surging through my veins, I simulate killing Iraqis. "Take that, stupid towelheads!" I scream. Shared laughs. Middle Eastern guys pop out of corners. "Die, in the name of Jesus! Die! Die! Die!"

I shoot the terrorist. I shoot the hostage. I shoot random people. I keep shooting long after people are on the ground dead. I shoot women. I shoot children. I shoot anyone who'd get in my way. I shoot because it becomes fun to shoot.

"I think he's dead," the burly Lasershot rep notes. I keep firing. He adds, "You sure like shooting people in the face."

Through the marvels of alcohol I've befriended two brothers from Arkansas who design metal casings for missiles. We join forces, with vigor downing drinks like they were enemy aircrafts. For the finale of the AUSA expo, dinner is served upstairs in the main ballroom.

A large slide depicts the silhouette of four soldiers with assault rifles on a large screen while attendees eat surf-and-turf meals.

"Let's find a table with some four-star generals," the Arkansas brothers say, like two teenage girls wanting to get closer to their favorite boy band.

The remaining seating options leave us at a table with three serious men in suits (four-star-general tables are taken). They linger, huddled in deep conversation throughout the meal, perhaps plotting military coups, leaving the Arkansas brothers and myself getting increasingly drunk on war (as well as boisterous and lippy). The sound of silverware starts clanking against glasses.

The quieting of conversation. After-dinner words. The Honorable Wilson Ford takes the stage.

"The task of bringing the army back to balance will take years of commitment.

We can bring the army back into balance by 2011."

Very serious looks on the attendees' faces. Some listen with heads lowered, like in church. "We need to increase the basic budget of the army—that's our mission!"

Standing ovation follows. I rise to my feet. (I don't want to be put on "the list.") Fat-fingered men raise their glasses. I want to strip off all my clothes in the name of peace, now sadly knowing more than I care to about the ways of the world, wishing for my old naïvetée. War is the American Dream at a rate of $720 million per day. War means corporate profits, and we're the top dog—you'll work with us, cuz you sure as hell don't want to work against us. And judging by the expo, we're going to be at war a long, long time—perhaps forever. Yes, hello, Iran!

Staggering back to my hotel, I stop at the Food Mart to buy beer. Loud gangsta rap plays throughout the store. A girthy guy with dreads stands behind the counter.

"How's the convention?" he asks, looking down at the pass still stupidly hanging around my neck.

"Do you like big weapons and stuff that blow things up?" I reply, setting the beer on the counter.

"Who doesn't!" he exclaims.

"Then it's great, just great!"

Momentarily, only the sound of gangsta rap fills the Food Mart.

CHAPTER FIVE

BIBLE-THUMPING
AMERICAN DREAM

THE AMERICAN DREAM:
IN THEIR OWN WORDS
Shirley L. Phelps-Roper,
spokesperson for God Hates Fags

It doesn't matter how many children of Doomed America are shipped into the Iraq sausage grinder to "fight" (NOT) for our freedoms—if there are not people standing on the soil of this nation of rebels against their God with NO cause, where the real threat to this constitutional democracy is being waged, and fighting that fight, there will be no First Amendment!

The servants of God at Westboro Baptist Church talk to you daily about eternity and your never-dying souls, most of which are headed straight to hell. We talk to you daily about the destruction of this nation because of her filthy, unrepentant manner of life that God has never let ANY nation engage in without serious consequences. IN short, if you forget God and establish policies of filth and disobedience and murder (not to mention your filthy sex practices) in your nation, WORSE than Sodom and the cities about her, you will suffer her fate!

Every person in this nation should have a Ph.D. degree in ancient Sodom and her destruction and in the antediluvian world, and her destruction—but this generation will not even mention those two events that the prophets and the apostles warned were examples of what will happen to any nation that forgets God. And God says this to such a people:

Psalm 50:16

But unto the wicked God saith, What hast thou to do to declare my statutes, or that thou shouldest take my covenant in thy mouth? KEEP YOUR MOUTH SHUT ABOUT THE WORD OF GOD.

17 Seeing thou hatest instruction, and castest my words behind thee.

18 When thou sawest a thief, then thou consentedst with him, and hast been partaker with adulterers.

19 Thou givest thy mouth to evil, and thy tongue frameth deceit.

20 Thou sittest and speakest against thy brother; thou slanderest thine own mother's son.

21 These things hast thou done, and I kept silence; thou thoughtest that I was altogether such an one as thyself: but I will reprove thee, and set them in order before thine eyes. This nation of rebels think that God is blowhard like they are and his promises to deal with them are not true—but you do greatly err, not knowing the scriptures nor the power of God!

22 Now consider this, ye that forget God, lest I tear you in pieces, and there be none to deliver.

We do all this work free of charge to you—we ask for nothing and take nothing from you! And you deal with us in such a way that we must also fight for your freedoms— WHERE IT COUNTS!! This nation of rebels is a danger to themselves and to others!

In short—today, the American Dream is a fraud, you had blessings from your God—you forgot God and went awhor-

ing after other gods that are not gods and you worship everything BUT your God so now, it is a Doomed American nightmare! Stay tuned for the final act!

God Hates the World!

"Sweetie, you don't want the POPE IN HELL sign. It's not a Catholic
Church."

"I want it!" whines her little curly haired son who looks like
he could be cast in a Fruit Roll-Up commercial. "Please, Mom!"

Motherly, she explains, "Sweetie, you want the GOD HATES
FAGS sign."

With spastic little-kid energy, the curly haired little boy, strug-
gling to raise his sign, clarifies, "GOD HATES FAGS works at any
church or protest."

"Okay," I say to the little tyke, while standing next to him holding TOO LATE TO PRAY.

It's an all-American moment here at Topeka Bible Church.
Families, dressed in their Sunday best, begin arriving, passing a
multitude of day-glo signs blazing such things as 2 GAY RIGHTS:
AIDS & HELL and YOUR PASTOR IS A WHORE. Irritated but unfazed,
they've seen this spectacle for the past seventeen years. It's old
news here in Jerry Springer America.

"Shouldn't you be happy that at least people are going to
church?" I ask the woman in charge.

"No, hon, these people tell lies that God loves everyone. We
picket here because they should be joining us, but they did the
opposite." Looking towards her sign-toting minion, she adds,
"Christ told us the response."

Yes, America has gone to hell because of all the gays and for-nicators, and leading the charge to defend us from eternal damnation is the Westboro Baptist Church (WBC) in Topeka, Kansas, and their subtly named picket group God Hates Fags. Founded in 1991, these religious zealots have called for gays to be killed, praised terrorist attacks, and mocked the funerals of AIDS patients. They have picketed the funerals of tornado vic-tims, the Amish schoolgirl shootings, and the dead coal miners in West Virginia. Even worse, they're anti-Swedish.

No matter how heinous it might be, their vicious actions are protected by the First Amendment: the right to free speech—one of the pillars of the American Dream, along with religious free-dom. Strictly following their interpretation of my favorite work of fiction—the Bible, the WBC is led by Fred Phelps. Affection-ately known to his congregation as "Gramps," Phelps is one of the most hated men in America. A mere three days after 9/11, he stated in his sermon the reason behind the attacks:

> This evil nation has smeared fag feces blended with fag
> semen and dyke feces on the Bible!

Needless to say, Fred is a little antigay. It gets better. Since June 2005, the WBC has been picketing soldiers' funerals, out of the twisted logic slain soldiers are going to hell for defending a country full of the fornicators and adulterers. They've protested over 330 funerals in forty-seven states, garnishing a massive amount of media attention—all from a group comprised almost entirely of the Phelps' clan. With thirteen children (four es-tranged) and roughly fifty-two grandchildren, comprising the majority of the seventy-member congregation, Gramps wields absolute control over his followers in his delusion that he is the only righteous man on Earth.

Beginning in 1952 as a street preacher who warned of the dangers of dirty jokes and sexual petting, Gramp's ideas remain simple: every tragedy in the world is linked to homosexuality—specifically society's increasing tolerance and acceptance of what he calls the Homosexual Agenda. The group maintains that God hates homosexuals above all other kinds of "sinners." Sounds like someone has got some issues.

Fred's daughter Shirley Phelps-Roper is the acting spokesperson for the group that the majority of society deems crazier than a box of frogs. After buttering Shirley up via e-mail about her screaming match on Fox TV's *Hannity & Colmes* ("I don't like those guys either!"), I receive an open invitation to the inner circle of God Hates Fags.

Going as a journalist, rather than infiltrating, allows me full access to the group, especially for those quiet family moments (though I'll make sure to cover up my San Francisco dreads, surely deemed long fag hair). Yes, for three days, I shall walk in the shoes of the Westboro Baptist Church, deep in the heartland of America, seeing the world through their fire-and-brimstone eyes as I live their American Dream!

Oh, Jesus!

Topeka's zip code is **666**04 (Fred Phelps has vowed to have that changed). A cold Friday night on Churchill Street. A large house in a comfortable middle-class neighborhood. Nothing unusual except for the large, fenced-in backyard. On closer inspection, an upside down American and Canadian flag wave shamefully from a flagpole. On the pristine fence someone has spray-painted GOD HATES THE PHELPS. This is where I'm supposed to meet up for the 6:30 picket.

I approach the house, with its mirrored outer door that prevents me from seeing inside, and ring the bell. Shirley, who's in her early fifties, answers directly, wearing a turquoise running jacket.

"You're famous!" I exclaim, immediately recognizing her sunken eyes and long, gray-dashed hair from her *Hannity & Colmes* appearance.

"No, she's infamous," corrects a small child by her side (saying this twice).

"It's an easy, simple life," surprisingly upbeat Shirley says, as she leads me to her large backyard that resembles an elaborate playground. "The Holy Spirit directs us," she adds, then reprimands a cluster of small boys with biblical names like Jonah, Zion, Luke, and Joriah, who are gleefully jumping on the family trampoline.

Quite a handful when you've got eleven kids ranging in age from preteen to thirty (her eldest son was born sinfully out of wedlock).

"The neighbors like us because we don't cause any trouble," Shirley smiles.

Considered a notorious stain on the local Topeka landscape, maybe that's because roughly fifty-seven of the seventy Westboro Baptist Church members live in the same neighborhood, most in the cluster of houses joined together by the large fence that separates them from the outside world. On the surface, their lifestyle resembles a Brady Bunch existence—a suburban American Dream. School drawings hang by the refrigerator. Little kids play everywhere. I imagine the backyard filled with potato sack races and water-balloon fights. Within these fenced confines, the

Westboro Baptist Church has created its own utopia, one inflamed by hatred and backed by frequently recited Bible verses. Topeka is the ideal home base: "It's dead center of the country so it's easy access to picket anywhere in the United States. We don't want to be in the belly of the whale!" Shirley laughs.

In the sixties, Gramps worked for the law firm opposing Jim Crow laws (although he was later disbarred for harassing a court reporter). Many of the Phelps also practice civil rights law. Need I mention irony?

"This involves our nation falling apart," Shirley states, clear to distinguish between the discrimination of minorities over gays. Why? "God didn't say abolishment for blacks or women!" Clarification: "It's a sex act. There's no Rapist Pride Parade!"

(Pause.) "I see."

Friendly neighbors/relatives wave from across the street.

"We're growing tomatoes!" exclaims Shirley's husband, Brent, a pencil-thin man with a wisp of curly hair, getting his hands dirty digging in the garden.

"Where are you from?" asks Shirley's white-haired brother, Fred Jr., walking his dog on a leash.

"I'm outside the fag capital, San Francisco!" I say, warming to him.

Big laughs.

Shirley knows San Francisco. That's where she picketed the 1994 funeral of gay journalist Randy Shilts ("Some fag who died of AIDS.") "He pressured this nation to call it AIDS. It's a gay disease, a plague from the Lord our God!"

(Pause.) "I see."

Shirley made a deal with the San Francisco police. If allowed to hold up their GOD HATES FAGS signs for five minutes, the group would pack up and leave. "Hon, those fags were twenty rows deep. They were beating on our van. It was awesome. It was invigorating," she fondly remembers. "We were jumping, we were so happy. We were like jack-in-the-boxes!"

The sign-holding actually only lasted a minute and a half: "They threw eggs! They threw bricks! They threw bags of urine!"

"Weren't you afraid of being pummeled silly?"

"No. The Lord our God, I know, was watching over us." (Pause.) "We were the top story on the news! Hon, that event exploded our group on the radar!"

At other events, unsurprisingly, God Hates Fags members have had the living shit kicked out of them for their antagonistic tactics. "Most recently, they drove their cars at us," Shirley says, as we trudge through the neighborhood toward this evening's picket along with her sister Abigail, pondering whether the Lord keeps them safe, or causes people to drive their cars at them? "We know our God is the one that gave us this ministry—to make it crystal clear to them what they've done, so the wrath can rain down on them." (On a roll.) "God Hates Fags gets them." (With mockery.) "Oh, yeah, God loves everyone." (Rational.) "This nation's gone the way of Sodom and Gomorrah. September 11 should have been the time to repent." (Reasoning.) That was a juggernaut sent by the hand of God to repent." (Result.) "God is sending the nation's soldiers home in body bags from Iraq."

(Pause.) "I see."

Worse than tossed urine is the $10.6 million judgment slapped across the face of Westboro Baptist Church. In 2007, a grieving father won the settlement after WBC picketed his son's funeral with signs like THANK GOD FOR DEAD SOLDIERS. Some might also see this judgment as an act by the hand of God. Shirley doesn't.

"Here's what happened: I don't think there was a media outlet that wasn't at the picket. Not one person testified that they saw us at the funeral. We stood out of sight, out of sound. You couldn't be closer than a thousand feet; we were twelve hundred feet away. The father happened to see us on the news." Visibly angry, Shirley claims trouble began when the father came across her blog, which she dismisses as a cut-and-paste rehash of Deuteronomy Psalms—so what's the big deal!? "At the trial he was so over the top, it was pitiful. He said he cried for three hours after he read it. He said he vomited."

Lance Corporal Matthew Snyder was twenty years old.

Shirley has remorse. "We're driving into this town for the funeral, and Becky's reading the obituary, and I'm crying. It said, 'He's the love of our life.' Well, why didn't they teach him what the Lord our God intended?" Her reason for Matthew Snyder's death: "Because his father was such a pervert!" stretching the term to mean "not teaching him the Lord's words."

(Pause.) "I see."

"It's painfully hard for them to hear the truth," Shirley says. "These people engage in conduct not fitting to God!" Worked up: "These are church times!"

Go to Hell, Funnyman

Tonight there are bigger fish to fry. "We're going to picket a performer who's in town," Shirley beams.

"Really! Who?"

"Ron White," she replies, referring to the star—along with Larry the Cable Guy—of the Blue Collar Comedy Tour.

"You mean Tator Salad?!?" I exclaim, mentioning him by nick-name. I'm confused, and more than a little delighted. "We're go-ing to picket standup comedy!?" (Pause.) "Is Ron White gay?"

"He's a filthy adulterer," Shirley's sister Abigail contributes as we plod past a schoolyard. "He's the one who always has the bourbon."

"Do you find Ron White unfunny?"

Shirley thinks for a moment. She smiles. "He's got some funny stuff."

"Then why picket his comedy show?"

"He's got a pulpit," she stresses. "We like him, but they all could be teaching God and the way of life. They have responsibility!"

"Tator Salad!?" I once again inquire out of disbelief. "Isn't a co-median's only responsibility to get laughs?"

"They can do that and be faithful and sermon about the Lord."

Shirley and I aren't on the same page with numerous things—this being one of them.

"Do you picket other performers?"

"Yeah!" Shirley turns to her sister. "Who's that one singer?"

"Burt Bacharach?" I randomly blurt and sing a few bars of "Do You Know the Way to San Jose."

Joke's on me: "Yeah, we've had him, yeah." She then beams like a schoolgirl, "Jerry Seinfeld talked about us onstage."

"What did he say?"

"Something like, 'Did you see those picketers outside?'" (Pause.) "Okay."

"And who's that dyke?" Shirley asks Abigail.

"Paula Poundstone."

"Do you think she's funny?"

Shirley chuckles. "That zucchini bit she has is pretty funny." Boasting: "We've had several people cancel because they heard we were coming!"

Is it out of fear or just another reason to avoid this redneck hellhole?

Becky, also kin of Shirley, picks us up along the way in a mini-van; a stringy-haired woman with glasses wearing a THE SIGN OF THE TIMES sweatshirt.

"Larry the Cable Guy used to be so funny, then he got nasty," Becky says. "Apparently if you're not in the dregs of the sewer, you're not funny!"

"What are you doing watching Larry the Cable guy?" I inquire.

"Flipping channels." (She mimes.) "Sometimes you got to watch something for a couple of minutes to see what kind of trainwreck it is."

Pulling up early to the Topeka Performing Arts Center, a large, gray building in the heart of a dismal downtown in a culturally re-pressed part of the planet, fans of standup comedy slowly trickle in for the show. Already a few members of Westboro Baptist Church—mostly women and teenaged boys—are perched on the sidewalk with such visually colorful, warm, and inviting signs as:

FAG TROOPS, GOD HATES AMERICA

FAGS DOOM NATIONS

It looks like something straight out of *The Onion*—but with-out the irony. From the sign pile in the back of a pickup, I grab, THANK GOD FOR $10.9 MILLION, being that it seems more bitter than offensive. As comedy fans do bewildered double-takes, I procure a position next to another kin of Shirley, whose placard reads, THANK GOD FOR 9/11. She stands with an older glossy-eyed teen. Quiet. Bespectacled. Somber.

"What's the video camera for?" I ask the woman.

"For our protection," she replies. "If anyone attacks us, I'll video them."

"Fuck you, dumbasses!" a man screams driving by in a pickup.

With the pep of a callous cheerleader, Shirley rouses the group, suggesting a musical number from their picket-song repertoire. "What's a good harmony song?" she poses to the group. "How about 'This Land Is Fag Land'? If little Daniel comes, that's his favorite."

Instead they settle on a military song parody with a "funny" twist:

> First we fight for the fags
> Now they're coming home in body bags
> And your army goes marching to hell!

The comedy crowd, mostly clad in baseball caps and denim, watches in bemused disbelief at the musical sideshow spectacle.

"That's not even funny," a guy yells.

"What's the message!?"

> With the IED God's blown them up
> No toes left for toe tags
> Thank God for IEDs!

The women really ham it up in campy style, singing and having corny fun. It's enjoyable for them. They crack their voices in a zany fashion at the end for funny emphasis.

"You're retarded!" screams a man with a mullet.

He's right. I do feel retarded—very retarded! As I stand in a sea of idiotic sign wavers, I'm worthy of a bag of thrown urine (though I hope it doesn't happen).

Then, the reinforcements arrive! Cars pull up. Dozens of little children jump out and come running out of breath; huge smiles and the joys of childhood plastered on their faces.

Like a candy-filled piñata just burst, the cute little tykes jockey for signs. An excited, chubby, red-haired girl grabs FAGS ARE WORTHY OF DEATH.

With the addition of small children, a rousing rendition of "God Hates America," breaks out.

> God hates America,
> Land of the fags . . . .

Reactions are mixed:

"I think God hates the Phelps!"

"That would be good if you believed in him."

"Then why are you here in America!?" a chubby cowboy with a goatee snaps. "Go back to Canada!"

Fending off the onslaught of heckles, Shirley retorts, "Obey your Bible!"

Boom! You've been served! We're taking down Ron White comedy fans left and right. Sure, no immediate impact (if any), but we're planting seeds in the subconscious of standup-comedy-going heathens.

Closer to showtime, the jovial crowd now arrives in droves. Laughing. Smiling. Until they hear the melodic sounds of "This Land Is Fagland," being sung by small children. With the most vigor, even the tiniest join in, big smiles, swaying their heads like it were the Barney the Dinosaur song. The chubby, red-haired girl actually jumps while singing—she's that happy.

A biker stands on top of the stairs and mockingly pretends to conduct the picketers.

Two redneck guys act like they're a couple, planting a kiss on each other's cheek, achieving the opposite of the WBC intended actions—encouraging small-city gay tolerance, while not a single damn passerby agrees with their statements.

Focusing his attention on the children, a kindly man wearing a leather vest comes over. "There's a whole world that's not full of hate," he sermons. The kids seem confused. The man gets down on one knee to address them. "You see, young man, hating people is wrong. . . ."

Shirley is outraged. "PROTECT THOSE CHILDREN!" she screams.

"You see, you don't have to hate. . . ."

Code Red! The picketers close in around the children to whisk them away from the bad man.

"He can't talk to these kids like that!" she barks. "Sir, have you been drinking?" (To the group.) "He has drinking breath!"

Another Code Red! A girthy guy jumps on the top of the stairs and slowly undoes the belt on his jeans. "Everyone turn your heads!" screams Shirley. There's much fanfare. The Westboro Baptist Church covers their eyes like it was *Raiders of the Lost Ark* right before all the Nazis melt.

The guy drops trou, moons, and starts slapping his chubby butt cheeks at the God Hates Fags picketers as Ron White fans squeal with approval.

"Is it okay to look?" asks Shirley's perky college-aged niece, Libby, who hides her eyes.

"Yes," I say (butt cheeks are still being slapped).

"Let me put this on here," requests a large woman emerging from the crowd, wielding a bumper sticker that says, You Can't Fix Stupid. Direct face-to-face conflict! Outstretching her arm, she steers her attention towards Libby's Fags Doom Nations sign. Once again, Code Red!

The large woman focuses on me. "Can I stick this on your sign?"

"Oh, you better not," I reply sarcastically.

Directly across Thank God for $10.9 Million the bumper sticker is slapped.

Libby immediately tears it off. With concern for the team, she asks, "Are you all right?"

"I think so," I reply with faux shock.

"You can't tell what a person is going to do when the freaks deface signs."

Yes, freaks: the one's who don't picket standup comedy shows.

Now it gets personal: "Keep your whore hands off of people's property." Shirley barks. "Do you know what you do with your whore hands!?"

"Are you calling me a whore!?" the large woman screams from the stairs, gesturing her head Jerry Springer–style. "Do you want to come here and call me a whore!?"

Where did the love go?

Shirley eyes the local rednecks with disgust: "This is the best our country has to offer!" (Really a reflection on fans of the Blue Collar Comedy Tour.)

Back in the minivan Shirley seems giddy, almost euphoric, all wide-eyed and smiles. This was fun for her.

"How did this compare to other pickets?" I ask trying to gauge against, say, a soldier's funeral.

"It was a little rowdier," Shirley professes with a grin. "Hon, they're all middle-aged drinking freaks."

"What do you feel you've accomplished?"

Without hesitation: "The nation is leading towards destruction so fast."

More talk of the Bible, verses quoted, Jonah and the whale mentioned, Shirley talking more at me than to me, seeming happy to have someone to put on the full show for.

My Dinner at the Phelps

"Are you hungry?" Shirley asks. "Do you like salmon?" Shirley has opened her home to me, and I'm invited to dine with the Phelpses.

"Do you ever have problems with going out to restaurants?" I inquire, since we're ordering in.

"No," Shirley replies as we drive towards the Phelpses' house. "Most of us they don't know too well. I mostly get recognized in airports." (Pause.) "I'm not very anonymous anymore."

True. Shirley is the media's go-to man to fulfill the obligatory role of crazy-extreme-opposing-viewpoint-for-engaging-in-screaming-match. She's been on the likes of *Howard Stern*, the *Adam Carolla Show*, *Tyra Banks*, and of course an outraged *Hannity & Colmes* (for the antisoldier stance, rather than antigay).

"Hannity, he's nothing," Shirley laughs. "We don't serve him. They have us on to try and beat us up and bully us." Without laughs: "We're not going to be bullied!"

"Bad publicity is still good publicity," I throw out.

"Exactly!"

Like the ugly girl at the dance, thrilled everyone is now talking about her, Shirley gets thousands of press requests and answers all of them. "I don't draw the line." The FBI contacted her to speak at a course called Understanding the Mindset of a Terrorist. Shirley felt both offended and flattered. "Whenever there's a new editor at the local paper, I send them a basket with a crying towel," she adds.

Next to the kitchen is the brain-center of God Hates Fags, an office with several desks and computers. Shirley's husband is busy assembling a wheelbarrow with tools laid out on the floor, while her chaste eldest daughters, Meagan and Rebekah—both adorned in exercise clothes—sit at desks doing homework.

"Why didn't you go to the picket?"

"I had a finance exam," Meagan replies in a flirty manner. "Then I went jogging."

Always a family affair, Shirley took nine of her children to picket a military base in Texas.

"How did that go?" I ask Rebekah about being put in the crosshairs of the enraged.

"Awesome!" she glows. "One guy got arrested. He made a beeline for my mom."

"Is it ever scary?"

"Yes!" she exclaims. "Especially the Wisconsin protest."

God Hates Fags showed up at UW-Stout after three students died tragically in a fire, with signs depicting a burning house and reading GOD'S FURY. Outraged students came out in mass to run the Topeka group off campus.

"There were a thousand against four to protest our little group," Rebekah proudly recalls, like, somehow, they were the anger-evoking David to an infuriated and disgusted Goliath. "The cops aren't the ones keeping you safe. It's the Lord!"

(Pause.) "Okay."

"It was awesome!"

Despite thirty-seven states enacting laws banning picketing at funerals, Shirley assures, "He knew the Last Days were coming, and

He knew he had to get us on a path to get that First Amendment so we can say these words." Further arguing for the protection of hate speech, which fans the flames of her American Dream, Shirley adds, "Boy Scouts can say, 'God bless this family,' at funerals, but we can't say our message? It's either both or none!"

Shirley receives hundreds of negative e-mails a day, with every threat imaginable against her and her family. Websites like KillFredPhelps.com have been launched. Certainly not helping matters are the group's own press releases, sent to every possible media outlet:

> Judgment in West Virginia! Thank God for His Out-
> poured Wrath and for 12 Dead Miners. WBC to picket
> their Memorial Service. "God is not mocked!" God
> Hates Fags! & Fag-Enablers! Ergo, God hates the Sago
> Miners and is tormenting them in Hell!

With their us-against-the-world fashion, it's almost as though the Westboro Baptist Church is addicted to infuriating people, and the repercussions fuel their plight—like a personal vendetta. On August 20, 1995, an IED was set off in front of their house. "It put a hole in the side of the van and a hole in the fence."

Shirley recollects, "It was some fag student. The judge didn't do anything. He called it arson. The guy ended up spending six days in jail. And he served it on the weekends."

Then there was Heath Ledger's funeral.

"All hell broke loose! All day the phone rang from every radio show in Australia. It was cool!" Her Rashomon version of the story: "We got to preach to a new country!"

"Is it a failure if it doesn't get any press?"

"No, then that's God's plan."

"Health Ledger wasn't gay," I inform her.

"He was committing adultery on the screen and to his wife!"

A few of the boys are now on their knees helping dad assemble his wheelbarrow.

"Do you ever get e-mails that say, 'You're saying what I'm thinking'?"

Shirley thinks for a moment. "Not very much," she admits.

There was one guy from England. From an affluent family, he came to Topeka because God told him to. Other voices were also in his head. "He was off his meds," Shirley explains. "He started off very friendly and cordial. He really knew his Bible." Trouble soon brewed. "He began yelling at cars, 'You're going to Hell!' I had to explain we really don't do that."

"The reason you don't do it is cuz you're a coward!" he snapped. Then a kid started swinging his skateboard at the WBC picketers. "Ignore, don't respond—you walk away. Don't engage," Shirley describes the protocol. "He wanted to fight him."

Neighbors later called and complained that he was laying in their yard. "I had to resist every impulse to mother him." Things came to a head when he started parading around Shirley's neighborhood with a hand-scrawled GOD HATES YOU sign till late, late at night. His four-day WBC stint ended in the county jail. "A police officer picked him up after neighbors called. He was almost noncommunicative at that point." They determined that he was bipolar, and that the one rare, new WBC member was also off his meds!

Dinner's here. Hurrah! As handfuls of little kids play video games, we're steered toward the large dining room table. Shirley has chicken and a salad. My salmon is simply delicious.

"So which standup comedians are we going to picket tomorrow?" I throw out for dinner conversation.

"You got to keep the sense of humor fresh on the picket line, you got to have a sense of humor!" snickers Margie—yet another sister, who works for the Kansas Department of Corrections, where she prepares inmates to reenter society. Margie will be making the trek tomorrow to Cincinnati with a group of six to picket the funeral of a marine who was kidnapped four years ago. His dead body was just returned.

"They got a SWAT team to stand by them," Shirley says, nibbling on her salad.

"We're going to get our asses kicked by three thousand bikers," Margie, rounder than her sister, laughs, referring to the Patriot Guard, or the "Bitter Bikers," whose mission is to shield grieving families at funerals.

"They formed in reaction to us!"

"Who wants to get up in their grill," Shirley adds, using the language of today. They're violent, and there're usually children present!"

Noting twenty protest signs packed for air travel, I ask, "What's it like getting through security?"

"We had incidents in airports," Margie states. "The Canadian officials were tossing our signs across the room. They asked each of us about a hundred questions. Finally they ended up having a hearing to see if they should let us in."

Since Canada has laws on hate speech, WBC was only allowed to keep four of their most generic signs. Once in Canada, they went to an art store, mocked up new signs, and accented their picket by burning the Canadian flag. But Canada had the last laugh—they passed the Fred Phelps Law in 2001 banning them from the country.

"Some fag in Congress passed it," Shirley clarifies. Claiming the congressman is now in prison, she reasons, "There are no coincidences!"

In her pursuit of the American Dream, Shirley has also been arrested. "Only once when my little Jonah stood on the flag. It happened at a soldier's funeral in Bellevue, Nebraska. I was arrested for mutilating the flag and contributing to the delinquency of a minor."

Finishing my salmon, I inquire, "Is there a country in the world that God doesn't hate?"

"God hates the whole world!" Margie confirms with a warm smile.

(Pause.) "Okay."

To emphasize this point, for dessert we gather around the laptop for the WBC music video "God Hates the World." The song, a clever rearrangement of "We Are the World" (they love song parodies), has the whole lively WBC crew sharing singing duties.

> God hates the world and all her people,
> You, everyone, face a fiery day for your proud sinning

Shirley explains her muse: "One day Gramps was preaching about the world and those words just flew into my head."

"*20/20* played it!" Meagan adds with pride.

"Congratulations."

"This is my favorite part!" Shirley says, as just the woman shtick up the chorus. "It may be a little over the top."

"I don't think it's over the top," critiques Margie. "I think it's understated."

DVD special feature: a darling three-year-old blonde girl sings a solo rendition of "God Hates the World" (ain't kids cute?). It's adorable. She clearly doesn't understand the meaning of the words; she sings just like a chimp made to wear people clothes by its trainer.

"Here's an important part about America," Margie says with fiery eyes at the video's conclusion. "It calls itself a Christian nation except it asserts itself around the world like a big bully." Worked up: "This nation was given light and understanding and spit in God's face! We're the only church that's preaching the truth! If there's another church preaching, you can't find it—teaching what the Bible actually says!"

(Pause.) "I believe you."

Dad gets up from the table. "Do you want to come to the track meet?" he asks, inviting me to see his daughter compete. Besides soldier-funeral picketing the Phelps family are really big track fanatics. Run, Phelps, run!

Onward Christian-Soldier Picketers

Today I'll be driving an hour and a half in one of two minivans to the Kansas City airport with the Westboro Baptist Church group flying to Cincinnati to picket a soldier's funeral. The group consists of five women and Shirley's oldest son, Ben, who designs the God Hates Fags website. Almost all wear matching THE SIGN OF THE TIMES sweatshirts. No one seems worried—it's like they were leaving for a Grand Canyon vacation. Waving. Smiles. Hugs in the driveway.

"You guys are plain giddy," I note, as the three young girls in back—an ultrasound nurse, a law-office worker, and a high school student—are giggly like hyperactive sorority girls going to Cabo.

"Yeah!" they reply almost in unison with huge smiles.

"How many people get to be the mouthpiece for their God?" squeals the wild-eyed one next to me. "We are the luckiest people in the world—whatever happens, happens—this minuscule group gets to be the mouthpiece for God!"

What should I expect from girls who started picketing when they were ten years old, knowing this as being completely normal.

"As soon as they're old enough to hold a sign," interjects stringy-haired Becky steering the course. "Before that they came out in strollers."

"Taylor came from Florida. She got to picket a soldier's funeral in West Palm Beach. Lucky duck," one of the giggly girls says of the spring break gone wild.

"Do you get angry when people counterprotest you?"

" I don't get angry—they're retarded. You're going to change God's standard?" the wild-eyed one exclaims.

"They had on *CNN Headline News* that they're having a twenty-four-hour precession," Ben, who resembles a tech-support guy, finally perks up from the front seat. "Four soldiers were kidnapped in Iraq. The kidnappers sent back the thumbs and fingers. Now they just sent back the body. That's kind of brutal," Ben adds. (Maybe he's not as extreme as the others?)

"He's just another dead soldier," the wild-eyed giddy girl casually says. With growing excitement: "If you get 100,000 people coming out for the funeral, that's just more people to preach to!" A squeal of delight.

Momentarily, Bible quotes take the place of conversation. Like a big Mr. Smartypants, I state, "Topeka seems like kind of a homophobic place to begin with. Judging by the reaction at last night's picket it actually seemed to draw out more gay tolerance."

Ben retorts with more Bible quotes—something to do with the Lord polarizing people. His whole demeanor changes. "We're focusing on the main sin of our generation, what we're seeing before us!" Anger emerging. "A generation that's promoting that sin day by day." Mocking anger. "'God loves everyone' is a fabled doctrine. All you got to do is say you love Jesus, and he'll be your personal servant." Ben snaps, "Come on!"

"But why picket soldiers' funerals? A lot of poor people join the military because they don't have many alternatives."

"Yeah! Who made it that way? It was God's doing!" Ben says, utilizing easy mythology to explain the world around him.

"You can also prostitute your body," reasons the stringy-haired Becky with her eye on the road.

"Yeah, but they join out of there own free will. How is that a punishment from God?"

"People don't have free will," Ben confirms.

"Of course not!" say the formerly giddy girls in cultish unison.

Turning into the most awkward van ride ever, our conversation now segues to Ben defending Adolph Hitler: "Some might think I'm anti-Semitic by saying this, but Hitler, that's a judgment straight from the hand of God for the Jews!"

To clarify, I repeat, "So what you're saying is, Hitler was sent by God as a punishment to the Jews?"

"Yes."

Check, please!

Ben steers the topic change: "Do you know how many babies in this country are killed each year because of abortion? More than killed by Saddam Hussein!"

"Saddam Hussein committed genocide against his own people," I clarify, then throw out the obvious: "Isn't what you're doing a bit, um, insensitive?"

"Insensitive? Insensitive!" Ben fumes about mocking funerals. "What's insensitive is to tell that mother and father that that person is in heaven!" he erupts. "That's a lie!"

"Dying time is truth time," Becky adds. "When you're dead, it's time to tell the truth!"

(Pause.) "I see."

"This whole First Amendment is in place so people can preach the word of God!"

"But isn't the military put into place to protect the First Amendment?"

"If it weren't them, God would find another way for us to preach," he retorts with another convenient argument. "The First Amendment is being whittled away in such a fashion by what this little group is saying, because they don't want the word of God heard! This whole nation should be outraged!" Ben viciously adds, referring to the $10.6 million judgment.

(Confusion. Isn't the $10.6 million judgment because the nation was outraged?)

"The goal was to get us to stop," Becky contributes, exiting off the freeway. "You can see how well that's going."

Like a narcissistic Rosa Parks of hate speech, Ben confirms: "We decry China's human rights violations, and in this country it's also horrible." With conviction: We're the only true patriots in this country!"

Pulling into the Kansas City Airport we park the minivan in utter silence. The fearless six get on their plane. Nobody says goodbye to me, or even acknowledges my presence.

High Five!

Other outsiders have also gotten Westboro Baptist Church's
cold response. Recently, Sasha Baron Cohen (aka Borat) at-
tempted to pull one over on God Hates Fags as part of his new
movie, Bruno—featuring his gay German character. Unfortunately, everyone recognized him right away.

"Do you have the *Ali G Show* in Germany?" one of Shirley's
kids immediately asked.

When no one reacted to Bruno's antics, he started getting
pissed off. WBC decided that if Bruno didn't get what he wanted,
he wasn't going to put it in the movie (or DVD special feature).
So they arranged to have Bruno come to their next picket. Ben
laid ground rules, "You can make fun of us as much as you
want, just get our message across (fags should die)."

Bruno arrived in a minivan, hopped out with a raccoon tail
sticking out of his ass, and hooked together with another man
to make it appear they were engaged in a sex act. Still, he
couldn't get a rise out of anyone, and started grabbing for
people's signs. Shirley warned Bruno, "If you don't take your
hands off people's property, we'll call the police!"

Back in the Van

The only thing more uncomfortable than the ride to the airport
is the trip back to Topeka. Just two large Westboro Baptist
Church men and myself—both with schoolyard-bully demeanors.

"Those kids don't have boring lives," Steve Draino laughs, unfazed that his high school–age daughter will soon be facing

hordes of angry bikers at the soldier's funeral. "They don't need summer camp!" Shirley's brother Tim, who works for the Kansas Department of Corrections, drives in silence.

"I came out of curiosity. It turned into something more significant," Steve explains about his first visit to Topeka in 2001 to film a documentary that focused on people's ignorance of their own religion. Steve had a spiritual awakening. So impacted was he by meeting Fred Phelps, not only did Steve change the focus of his film, but also moved his entire family from Florida to live across the street from the Phelps compound. Steve then made his family join the Westboro Baptist Church—one of the rare few members not related to the Phelps. "Fred Phelps told me if I made Westboro Baptist Church look like buffoons, my film career would be over." Unlike other documentaries that mock Phelps, Steve had a different vision: "You can't make him look like a fool! You can't make God's servant look like a fool!" Originally, Steve had eighteen people helping with his documentary. As the film's focus became clear, his crew ran for the hills. "When it came time to edit, I was on my own," Steve recalls.

Once completed, the documentary didn't get the warm reception he expected. It was banned in Canada. It was banned in Sweden. It violated both countries' hate crime laws.

"I sent a copy to a childhood friend, and I never heard from him ever again."

Same cold reaction from the Telluride Film Festival. Prior to his "awakening," he worked on the festival crew, where he was known by his nickname, Draino. "Telluride takes care of their own. It's a no-brainer for the crew to get projects into the festival.

I submitted the film. Bam! Radio silence." Other festivals had similar reactions. So did PBS. Easy explanation: "Gramps said, the whole entertainment industry and media are slaves to the fag agenda." (Funny, I thought it was the evil Jews.) "If you question that lifestyle, you're done!"

Draino's film projects now center on Fred Phelps's love crusades, primarily the Sign of the Times website. "It made jurors cry at the trial they were so angry," he boasts.

The site contains feel-good video testimonials that ridicule the hate-crime murder of Matthew Shepard, dead soldiers, victims of hurricane Katrina, and much, much more!

Clearly, Draino has lost the fucking plot in his newly adopted American Dream.

As we pass Famous Dave's rib house he solemnly confesses, "The Lord has been kind and merciful in the long history of my folly. I'm ashamed of the sins I committed in the past. I'm not proud of it." Draino's American Dream defined: "To live in the reverent fear of God is a gift from God."

Tim mocks with a laugh. "My American Dream is a nice house, white picket fence, golf pants. . . ."

"I'm living one of the most fortunate lives in the history of man—completely by lottery. I didn't even earn it," Draino continues, looking damaged by deep, hidden secrets. "Any hobo can preach, 'Do not steal!' We're preaching the unvarnished word of God, cover to cover!"

My stomach begins to ache. I miss the giggling girls. I hope they don't bury me in a shallow grave out by the shed because that's how they interpret God's word.

"Look at how small our group is. They're mad at the word of God! They're mad at the Bible!"

Like a biblical comedy team, Tim and Draino set each other up for Bible verses, occasionally finishing the other's quote.

Tim's floodgates have opened: "We're at that time. How much further will we go before that switch is triggered?" With disgust: "I got some global warming for ya! You can say it's a fairy tale or holy shit. It's just a chair shift on the deck of the Titanic." Clearly worked up: "The economy is collapsing, but the bars are filled—with forceful people full of lust chasing each other!"

Am I soon going to receive Gwyneth Paltrow's head in a box? Cuz Tim is starting to sound a lot like Kevin Spacey in Seven. As farmland careens by, Draino rants like a white-knuckled alcoholic telling of the evils of drink: "There's a moral decay! It's like a body so rotten, you push into and guts fall out—that's our nation." From the front seat he mimes pushing his finger into a rotted body.

Man! Are we there yet? Are they pissed off at fornicators cuz they're not getting any!? Is this part of the indoctrination? I need air . . . or heroin. Why is it that those who scream, "Sinner!" are, almost always, the people concealing the deepest, darkest sins?

The topic then changes to "fat chicks."

"Some fat chick came into the jail, and she had a whole bag of drugs and five hundred dollars."

"Did she have a Michelin flap?" Draino crudely snorts.

"That's not where she was carrying it!"

Laughs.

Afternoon Delight

Dad is heating up pizza slices and fish sticks for the kids who are running hyperactively around the house as we gear up for the Saturday afternoon picket.

"Do you want a pizza slice?" he asks with smile, wearing a matching red hat and shirt. Still nauseous from the minivan ride, I decline.

Shirley is on the phone in the middle of a brainstorming session: "Cops die and God laughs. That's good." (Pause.) "As opposed to 'Cops die in Hell'?" (Pause.) "These cops in Baltimore are going to hide our signs again, and we're not going to stand for it!"

Shirley is a regular Burt Bacharach. When the call concludes, she proudly proclaims, "I added another verse." She describes her composition as a "perfect song," a musical parody focused on slain cops burning in hell.

"There's a dead cop in Baltimore, and he was killed by another cop," she excitedly explains about another scheduled upcoming picket. "Three of us are going. In the Scriptures a three-fold chord is always strong." I'm handed a copy of the police oath regarding upholding the First Amendment. "They take this oath swearing to Him. I think it's in their best interest to obey the law of this land!"

Looking at her sign that says THANK GOD FOR DEAD COPS, I ask, "How do you think this will go over?"

"They're not going to like it," she confesses. "We've had cops in our faces on many occasions. One time the police chief's son was the dead guy who they were burying. They keep pushing us, and we're going to push back." Due to the Phelps family's antics, the federal jury in Maryland determined that WBC is liable for invasion of privacy and intent to inflict emotional distress. But that doesn't worry Shirley. "Know what I'm going to pack?" she says. "A step stool!" Her confidence grows: "If some guy is there with a gun it will backfire, cuz the Lord is on our side!

God's not going to put it into people's minds to do something like that."

"So, what if the gun doesn't backfire?"

"Then he'll deliver us!"

Jubilant little kids pile into the minivan. Once again, it's picket time. Everyone is happy. Everyone is excited. Children with curly, tussled hair, ready for their regular Saturday-afternoon family outing.

"What if someone picketed your family's funeral?" I ask as we drive off.

Shirley blurts without indecision, "If I had a dead child, the last thing I'd be concerned about is a bunch of picketers." (Awkward thing to say in front of your own kids.) "My job is to make peace with God."

"Have you ever been swayed in an argument?"

Shirley momentarily thinks. "Interesting enough, it was on a fag radio show."

"What did he say?"

"He said, 'So, should we picket you? You failed him as a mother.'" The radio host was referring to Shirley's estranged son Josh, who under the cover of darkness packed up four years ago, moved to Kansas City, and disassociated himself from the Westboro Baptist Church, recently becoming a father out of wedlock. On his Facebook profile it says, "To make a long story short, there's too many good things, and life is too short to spend it hating someone." Shirley's mask lets down for a moment: "I didn't fail him, because I taught him the Scriptures."

"Do you still talk to him?"

"No," she says abruptly. "He hates God. He cut himself off." (Pause.) "I know he's drinking."

"Will you ever see him again?"

The mother flashes through. Hesitant with her words, she legitimizes: "No!" (Pause.) "We taught our son all the doctrine, and he turned his back on it."

"You going to carry that big sign, babe," dad says to his curly-haired son wearing a green tie-dyed T-shirt, as assorted children joyously sprint for the pickup truck. I snatch FAG LAW SCHOOL (surely a bitter WBC personal vendetta).

"This was the very first message we ever had, GOD HATES FAGS," the little curly-haired kid (is it Jonah or Joriah or Luke?) tells me with hyperenergy about his sign, though mentioning his favorite. "I like GOD HATES IEDs."

The little kid starts going on about snow cones and the flavors he likes and doesn't like, while the Phelps clan—all shapes and sizes—careen down the block and break into song.

"I love the song 'God Hates America.'" The curly-haired kid's eyes light up as music fills the busy intersection.

"What's your favorite thing about picketing?" I ask the little guy.

He racks his little kid brain. "I like when they drive by and yell things, cuz I like yelling back at them—the Truth!" (Pause.) "Have you heard of the Million Fag March? They march by our house and yell things." Without benefit of a segue: "Have you heard about *Brokeback Mountain?* It's a sick, disgusting movie." (Pause.) "My mom told me about it."

"Hey, Jonah," interrupts Dad with a concerned tone. "Can I talk to you?"

My little amigo is whisked away, perhaps in fear he might say something that would embarrass the group.

The younger WBC members seem happy to have a fresh face to chat with, since the rest of the world must find them repulsive. ("Marvel not if the world hates you.") Libby invites me to play in tomorrow afternoon's family soccer game, asking permission first from an elder.

"I went to San Francisco when I was little for the fag parade," she shares with more flirty excitement. "The police put us in the paddy wagon to protect us, cuz fags are violent!"

"How was the track meet?" I ask Shirley's youngest daughter, now joining us.

"Awesome!" she gleams, now holding her message to the world, FAGS ARE WORTHY OF DEATH.

"She cut thirty seconds off her time."

I try stirring things up by waving my sign vigorously. Still no honks. No flip-offs. Rarely do people yell, "Fuck off!" Westboro Baptist Church seems to have blended into the Topeka backdrop like a kitschy local absurdist theater. I imagine they'd be a local attraction you'd show gawking out-of-town visitors. I keep taunting the message. Little kids keep talking about video games. Am I the only one taking this seriously?

"After you've been here for over a decade, people are kinda over themselves," Shirley reasons.

The thrill is gone baby. The thrill is gone! Finally, finally, someone honks and gives the finger. "Fuckers, die!" they scream.

Ecstatic, I wave back and brightly smile.

"Mom! Can we go buy gumballs?" asks little Jonah, as we slowly walk back to the minivan.

"You need to practice for thirty minutes," Shirley says, disciplining Jonah about his piano lessons.

A duplex by the minivan is now adorned with an American flag. A large woman stands in the driveway holding a flag, alongside a long-haired man wearing an American-flag bandana, an American-flag T-shirt, and American-flag baggy pants. Normally, I'd deem this bunch "scary," except in this context, it's refreshing.

Shirley mocks their display of free speech. "They sometimes put notes on the windshield of our cars," she sneers. "They used to infiltrate our pickets and mingle among us. When they'd throw stuff at us, they'd hit them," she laughs.

As we drive off, the patriotic couple gives the car in front of us the bird. Dad finds this funny. "He just flipped him off, and he's not even with us!" (He says this twice.) Shirley keeps making references to the Roman chapter of the Bible.

Ford in Hell!

The rest of the afternoon is spent with Shirley's lanky fifteen-year-old son Zach, who wears a Bob Marley T-shirt and gives me a tour of the Westboro Baptist Church's elaborate sign-making shop built onto the garage. Fully outfitted with a printer, laminator, and cutting board, without these astute signs how would free speech prevail?

"These are all about the fag agenda over there," Zach casually says in a soft-spoken manner—gesturing to the archive of some three hundred signs. God sure hates a lot of people over the years:

FAG ELTON (Elton John), FAG TUTU (Desmond Tutu), FAG MTV (MTV), FAG FLAG (All countries).

Some have human stick figures to illustrate the international symbol for "man sex."

"What's your funniest sign?" I ask, momentarily forgetting I'm the only one here who sees these with ironic detachment.

Zach is stumped. "I'm not sure what you mean?" He ponders. A few silent moments. Then: "I think I know what you mean." Zach begins describing a sign that has a symbol of some fag pulling down his pants. To emphasize, Zach mimes pulling his pants down. I mime the same for clarification.

"We'll put a sign out, and they'll get really mad," says Draino (He's back!), whose back and has come to supervise sign making for the police officer's funeral in Baltimore. "They'll say we're hate mongers, because that's what God says about the matter," he reasons about the threatened use of violence (you'll burn in hell!) for the purpose of creating fear in order to achieve a religious goal.

"Will you please explain this sign?" I ask, pointing to FORD IN HELL plastered with President Gerald Ford's face.

"He's an adulterer," Draino reasons. "He sinned more than Saddam Hussein."

"Gerald Ford!? Really? How?"

"He gave himself over to the fag cause!"

(Pause.) "Ooooooh!"

As we stare at Gerald Ford's face, Draino reminisces. "There was a time when Gramps did all the signs by hand. He'd cut each of the letters out."

That's clearly a man with a mission: cutting individual letters, forming every word on each hate-mongering, I mean, word-of-God-spreading sign.

"Those look terrific," I remark to lanky Zach, who laminates a beauty that reads GOD KILLED YOUR COPS, still using the same Boulder font Gramps originated. "Really terrific," I add.

Zach beams.

"How does this rate as far as signs go?" I ask, pointing to PRAY FOR MORE DEAD COPS.

"The contrast is fine. It needs to be readable from a long way away," he says, like a fine-art critic. "The thing is not to get cute."

"Cute?"

"Cute from a design aspect."

"Is this too cute?" I ask pointing to MATT SHEPARD 7 YEARS IN HELL.

A moment of pride: "Every time a high school does a production of the Laramie Project, they re-create our signs—that's wonderful stuff! All these beautiful signs!" Draino looks around the room, taking it all in. Draino looks crazed again. "People offer to buy them. They try to make a mockery of it—mocking our message. As long as Christ gets preached, we don't care."

Who's Jesus' Daddy?

A big day for the Phelpses. Besides their weekly Sunday service, there're four whopping pickets beginning at 8:30 AM. Quality family time today is focused on churches. Like a cleaning chart, there's a rotating list on the kitchen bulletin board so each child knows the correct picket to attend.

"You can come to my picket," Libby swoons. (Is she making a dreamy look?)

While we look at the list Shirley is plain excited. "We'll start with Holy Name, then Topeka Bible, then the park!" They explain that the Catholic Church picket is a lot of fun because there's a lot of interaction.

The next morning, the girls drive me to meet up with the others, because I overslept (God's will!) and turned up at their house late. More talk of the family soccer game. Meagan amusingly refers to her mom as "the old lady." If the topic of banishing homosexuals to Hell never came up you'd momentarily think they were quite normal. At times I almost expect them to wink and say, "Gotcha!" (But they never do. And the topic does come up.)

Outside of Holy Name Catholic Church, Shirley now has the addition of an American flag in her belt loop. "Several of our teachers go here," she says, boldly waving her message.

"Do they take it out on the kids?" I ask, looking at the multitude of smiling children holding signs like FAG PRIEST.

"There are teachers that do," she admits regarding her children, who are top students. "There was one biology teacher. It impacted Libby's grades."

In retaliation, WBC created a picket sign dedicated to the biology teacher. Her likeness was transformed into a witch's face. Pickets aren't all about the gays; they're also about the bad grades.

"Someone must've called the police," Shirley cries with concern. Two cop cars pull up, parking mere feet away. For the first time Shirley looks worried. "I don't want to say people lie, but they don't like the words."

"Do these police officers know who you are?"

"They know Tim and some others, cuz they work in law enforcement."

Quickly, everyone's instructed to pack up and head to the minivan.

"I don't know why I felt nervous when those police showed up," she tells me. "Old habits."

The Park Where It Started

The morning pickets conclude on the edge of Gage Park where in 1989, Gramps, on his angry-man Don Quixote quest, began screaming, "Fag!" into the midday sun. To show hometown spirit, a mega–TOPEKA, CITY OF WHORES sign is displayed to trumpet that the whole city—other than the seventy Westboro Baptist Church members—are sinners.

Gramps's first picket was against "All the fags having sex in the park." Gays, as you know, can only have sex in parks. What put Gramps over the edge was the afternoon he cycled with one of his dozens of grandsons: "They tried to lure that child into the woods," Shirley claims. Gays, as you know, are so deviant they can't even draw the line at pedophilia in public parks in the middle of broad daylight.

With the same commitment he instilled in his children in the seventies, when they reportedly were the family's main source of income, selling candy door to door, Gramps felt it was time to stand up against the scum and the filth. The first signs Gramps constructed (one letter at a time) simply read GAY PARK and GOD HATES GAYS.

Immediately, students from the University of Kansas held counterprotests, only enraging Gramps, who upped the ante. As a vendetta, he came back with even larger, more elaborate signs, evolving to the present day with such gems as the just-plain-indignant, IT'S THE FAGS, STUPID!

"Why isn't Gramps here?" I inquire, looking at all the kaleidoscope of happy little tykes, spanning almost an entire block; spreading his message without him.

"Gramps doesn't come out often," Shirley says. "He's got a sermon to prepare on Sunday and a radio show."

If antigay crusader Ted Haggard was caught doing meth with male prostitutes, what's Fred Phelps's dark sin? What shameful incident does he harvest, causing him to be so angry and hateful and to legitimize it with an interpretation of Bible quotes? Was he queen of the glory-hole circuit? Was it a jilted male lover that sent him spiraling on personal vengeance against the world to the point where the freedom of his American Dream infringes on the pursuit of happiness of others?

"Where do you think the group will be ten years from now?" I ask Shirley on the stomping grounds of the God Hates Fags conception.

"Ten years from now? That's optimistic," she scoffs, looking into the distance. "This won't be going on ten years for now!"

"The bikers are getting madder and madder, openly threatening us, telling cops they're going to kick our ass." A multimillion-dollar judgment hangs over their heads. Funeral-picketing laws are being passed. Locals are less fazed by their presence. Increasingly their cruel message is being silenced by an outraged and disgusted America.

Besides, the world—according to Shirley—is coming to an end.

"We'll have the Red Sea in front of us and the Romans at our back," Shirley recites with a glint in her eye. "When 9/11 came, that said the words."

And if Shirley happens to be taken out before then, certainly a higher power would have a reason for it.

"God's will, right?"

"Exactly!"

Heeeeeere's Gramps!

It's all been fun and games till this point—cute little hyperactive kids holding signs, giggly girls, salmon dinners. Westboro Baptist Church's weekly service is held Sunday at noon, led by the patriarch of the family, Gramps, who decried Jerry Falwell for not being antigay enough.

Meagan leads me to the chapel built next to the sign-making shop in the backyard of the Phelps compound. As we make small talk about the family soccer game, nervousness shoots through me, like I'm about to get a tooth pulled with rusty pliers.

Lines of pews. Cheap wooden panel walls. Women's heads covered with scarves. Fred Jr. playing piano. Family members dressed in a mix of church clothes and God Hates Fags T-shirts. The seventy-member Westboro Baptist Church has gathered. Intimate. Tense. Somber. Uncharacteristically jittery, Shirley curtly instructs me to sit in back near a large, round, corn-fed midwestern guy, also named Zach—the only recent addition to the Westboro Baptist Church. (Is he off his meds?)

"I've been seeing their signs for years," Zach says leaning forward in his pew. "I grew up here and used to belong to the other Baptist Church."

Five weeks ago Zach made the leap and become a WBC member. "This is the only church that truly follows the Bible," he adds with a big grin, finally blessed by both God's grace and a lack of mental evolution since biblical times.

"What do you parents think?"

"I'm sure they're not happy."

"Why?"

"They hate these people—but I don't care."

(Is this Kansas-style youthful rebellion?)

Like most churches the pulpit is adorned with signs that read DYKE HILLARY, FAG MEDIA SHAME, and the obligatory, GOD HATES FAGS—messages straight from their Lord.

Zach leans forward again. "The women cover their heads like in the Bible and the men should keep their hair cut short."

"Didn't Jesus have long hair?"

"I'd take that hat off!" snaps a scarved woman. Fat chance. I'm not going to expose my long San Francisco fag hair for the most hated man in America to point out and ridicule during his service.

A sharp hush comes over the congregation. Kids sit up straight. Zach stops smiling. Enter Gramps. Did they just unfreeze him? Gramps isn't a kindly old man like Wilford Brimley or the guy on the Quaker Oats box. Gramps looks more like an old man that would strangle kittens with his bare hands while quoting Bible verses.

"This exceedingly adulterous generation!" he berates the room, red-faced, voice bouncing off the cheap, wooden paneling. With an icy-cold stare, he is one no-nonsense mofo. Some real fire and brimstone is about to go down.

"Word came from Cincinnati," he addresses from his pulpit, with raising and lowering vocal inflections. "Four of our women and one boy were set upon by the marines in full-dressed uniform, who seized our property, for free speech—our signs," he erupts like a sci-fi villain about to blow up the earth.

"Which ones? GOD HATES FAGS? QUEERS DIE, GOD LAUGHS? FAGS ARE WORTHY OF DEATH? World-famous signs! Beautiful signs! Never put in our thoughts that the marines would be attacking us for preaching—five of them—they should put them in jail!" he spits bitterly. "Five people, four women and one boy."

For good measure, Bible quotes are thrown in with the unfiltered anger beneath the surface of everyone here. Ironic detached element is hard to muster as Gramps starts rattling off names of signs: "NO TEARS FOR QUEERS—the Bible teaches that! GOD IS AMERICA'S TERRORIST!"

No sugar coating here; it's the true face unmasked that hides under the Brady Bunch surface, directly from the man who imbedded it into several generations, right down to little Jonah who begs for snow cones and robotically utters the same discourse.

"Why would it take four members of the SWAT team—four of them—in full riot gear to protect our loved ones?" He froths, glaring at the congregation with snake eyes. "For a dead marine, laying down his life for a bunch of fags and faggy neighbors! We got our armed forces to keep you in your sin!"

This guy's got some serious issues. Substitute the name of any minority group, and suddenly we have ourselves a Klan meeting. I really hope I turned the ringer off on my cell phone. Crazy Draino sits with his family looking like Judgment Day has a cometh. The message continues to be battered into these children, like it was to their parents, and will to those not yet born.

"You're right; fags are worthy of death. GOD SENT THE AIDS!"

I try to go inside my personal cave. His voice hits right to the stomach. You can hear a pin drop between red-faced screams.

"We're looking down the face of a barrel," Gramps sneers, scoffing at all the presidential candidates for being promoters of fag rights. "This nation deserves such a president—like as a PUNISHMENT to give pure FILTH as a leader."

How time stands utterly still. I'm paranoid a pipe bomb might go off at any moment.

Gramps's ranting segues into his sermon that has to do with why God hates us—Jesus as the schoolyard bully ready to kick your ass for eternal damnation.

"You don't know His WRATH, cuz you've been listening to the kissy-poo preachers about LOVE! What are you going to do with all these verses—you and your kissy-poo preachers! They say you don't preach the Jesus of the Bible—THIS IS THE JESUS OF THE BIBLE TALKING!"

For some reason, I won't be playing in the Phelps family soccer game, running on lush green grass, passing the ball with huge smiles. What's going through all these little children's minds as

Gramps turns them against the world? How will this be processed? Bitterness about the lawsuit. Bitterness about the world that doesn't share his views. Biblical wrath a-comin'. Delusional about their mission, when in reality it's simply the waterskiing squirrel at the end of the newscast. Heaven's Gate about to catch the mothership. A Jerry Springer episode.

"Safe in the Arms of Jesus" is what we sing to close the service. Tim scratches his head and hands me a hymnbook. We rise to our feet as I stare dumbfounded at the lyrics, which don't even have one mention of fags. As it turns out, large Tim has the voice of a sparrow—just like a little bird. What caused their Jesus to be such an asshole?

After the service, Shirley holds her tiny, gurgling grandchild, the great-grandchild of Fred Phelps. "He looks just like my kid," she glows. The baby looks to the world with innocent, impressionable eyes.

Is it the Lord making me bolt for my car and the airport, the Red Sea in front of me and Roman soldiers at my back? Blessed be the scoffers and mockers—my likeness on a picket sign. The devil is going to come posing as the holy, smiling and serving you salmon. Let Babylon be builteth here. And remember, Jesus hates you!

CHAPTER SIX

SWINGER
AMERICAN DREAM

THE AMERICAN DREAM:
IN THEIR OWN WORDS
Greg Freeman, organizer
for the First Annual SwingFest—
the largest swinger convention
in the country

I think the phrase American Dream has been pretty bastardized over the years, but if you break it down to the words of Thomas Jefferson, "created equal . . . certain inalienable rights . . . life, liberty, and the pursuit of happiness," you see that those in the swinger lifestyle are living the American Dream. Most Americans don't actually know that the word liberty means "the freedom of choice"; swingers choose this lifestyle in their pursuit of happiness.

It's about doing what people want to do and not following traditional ideals on how couples should behave. It's interesting, because there's people who you'd think wouldn't be skeptics of the swinger lifestyle—like celebrities—who'd say that the lifestyle will destroy your marriage or relationship, despite the fact that there are several thousands, and probably millions, that have proved that to be incorrect. It's like a lot of things; you don't know about it until you've done it—you don't know what you don't know!

I tell everyone starting out to try the lifestyle three times. The first time you get over the culture shock, such as, "I was taught this," or "I was told that this was supposed to be wrong." The second time you realize that it's not wrong—you observe more and get past the shyness of it, and realize there's nothing odd about it; you feel that its people living their lives, doing what they want to do, and realize that there is nothing wrong about it. By the third time, you can make the decision whether the lifestyle is right for you or not—and it's not right for everybody, but it is for many people who have found comfort in the lifestyle.

My first experience with the lifestyle was about fifteen years ago with a couple who were trying to meet people online. Over the past few years, there definitely has been an upward swing—pardon the pun—of swinger parties, events, clubs, and websites, due the Internet. It has brought people together and made them realize, "Hey, I think this way too." The online world has given people better ways to put themselves in touch with one another, and made them realize they're not so strange after all.

Because of the upward trend for the lifestyle, there's been a demand for SwingFest—the World's Largest Swingers Lifestyle Convention and Party. It's our American Dream. It's been a nonstop roller-coaster ride. We keep bringing on staff just to keep up with the demand—it's going to be extremely popular. Basically, anything any sexually liberated couple could want, or people they would want to meet, will be there. Overall we're really going to push the message to come and have a good time with a lot of like-minded people. However, I hope that people will walk away with a sense of camaraderie and a message of sexual freedom. People might take notice that the lifestyle isn't a bad thing—it's their own common experience.

Behind Suburban Doors

A fully clothed, overweight, bespectacled couple sits solemnly in a corner with blank expressions, watching the porno movie playing on the TV mounted to the wall. Strange, since the exact same action they're watching on TV is playing out all around them (but without those who resemble porno stars).

Are they happy? Are they sad? Is this a good night for them!? Others who've already "finished" lie silently caught up in the intricate porn movie plot.

Witnessing a roughly eighty-year old guy grunting, "Uh-huh! Yum!" and then goosing a random woman (the Viagra must be kicking in), I wonder, "Do you ever see couples get into fights at these parties?"

"Oh, yeah, it definitely happens," our tour guide replies. "Some newbies think they're both up for play. Then they see someone having sex with their partner, and they're not cool with it."

"Especially when one of them is getting way more into it than the other," his wife adds.

"I've seen people screaming at each other in the doorway before."

Is this what Thomas Jefferson had in mind when he scribed, "life, liberty, and the pursuit of happiness," groups of people in the suburbs engaging in sex with others outside their own relationships? Did our founding father envision a land of couples swapping partners for noncommittal sex? The swinger lifestyle embodies the American Dream: doing what you want to do—as long as it feels good and doesn't give you AIDS! Yes, sexual freedom in the U.S.A. is as American as baseball, apple pie, and ribbed condoms. That's why I shall become a swinger and live the American Dream!

Under the guise of swinging couple Ken and Debbie Stamos, I steer towards the California Swingers Club website, e-mailing every damn swinger organization in the area. With minimal effort, Blue Moon Socials–Swingers United answers the call. Hurrah! They're swinging this weekend at a big Sacramento swinger soiree! As the male representative of the fictional Stamos swinger couple, an application is first required for attendance.

Swinger Application Highlights:
Q: Are you HIV/AIDS free?
A: Yes!
Q: We require everyone who attends a social to shower before playing and frequently during the evening. Is this understood and agreed upon?
A: Absolutely!
Q: Have you ever been told "no" when asking someone for sex?
A: All the time!

Next hurdle: a woman named Wendy requests a phone interview. This will determine whether Ken Stamos is a fine, upstanding citizen worthy enough to have sex with multiple strangers in a suburban Sacramento home—politely asking permission first! The American Dream is just a phone call away!

Let's Talk!

Using swinger lingo, where a lot of terms are put into "quotes," I relay to Blue Moon's Wendy: "We're kinda new to the 'lifestyle,' but we're really 'open-minded,' and like to 'play' with others!"

Wendy explains, "Well, we have two parties a month. The party tomorrow is for women who want multi-male experiences!"

What the!? I glance over at the Blue Moon website:

> For those ladies who just can't get enough—The BLUE MOON RENDEZVOUS is a high-quality multiple-male experience that will leave you breathless!
>
> Also known as a GB or gangbang, this gathering of sexy, hungry ladies & men are ready for a freaky-good time! NOTE: This is a true gangbang party—a function in which women gather and have multiple-male sexual experiences—lots of women participate in this modern-day stress reliever each month.
>
> Let's Get Freaky!

"That sounds great!" I somehow hear myself saying. (Pause.) "Let's get freaky!"

"For tomorrow, I think there's going to be four single women and twelve single men," Wendy says, regarding her gangbang lineup taking place in a three-bedroom suburban townhouse. "We also have six couples lined up."

"Terrific," I hear my voice resonate. Then, "Let's get freaky!"

I click on the party pics from the last get-together. *Eeeew!* They sort of look like those Abu Ghraib photos: flabby, pale, naked bodies twisted together, emitting expressions of great pain. A multitude of men cover each woman like bees swarming a beekeeper. Details: "Our single men go through a more stringent application process. So we require them to come to these parties first before they ever get invited to our couples' parties." Creepier: "This Saturday, all the lights will be on!"

That's a hell of a lot of dudes' *junk* to endure for an entire evening—under bright florescent lights mind you. I once again hear myself express, "That's great!"

Specifics: "We ask people to shower between 'play.' Especially if you and your girlfriend are not using safe-sex practices and then you play with someone else. We enforce safe sex. Oral sex is at your own risk!"

"At your own risk," I repeat. "Got it!" (Pause.) "Let's get freaky!"

The cost for Wendy's gangbang party: fifty dollars per couple, which will feature swingers hailing from diverse occupational backgrounds. "There's everything from blue-collar people to people who don't need to really work. We have law enforcement. There're even a couple of judges!"

"Courtroom judges!?"

"Yes!"

Swinger age also varies: "I have this woman who's in her mid-forties, but her husband is seventy. He doesn't want to play, but he likes watching her," Wendy shares. "He was really funny. He's like, 'I'm not expecting to play, but trust me, I'm not going to turn it down. I'm realistic; I'm seventy years old!"

(Pause.) "Let's get freaky!"

The Stamoses are in! A swinger gangbang awaits!

Meet the Swingers

For the role of Debbie Stamos, I've recruited a stripper friend of mine, who is on a stripper leave of absence due to a rash outbreak (don't ask), a nice insane monkey wrench to throw into the swinger soup. My only direction: "Dress real slutty!" Adding to the evening's fun, she's completely shitfaced when I pick her up.

STAMOS CATCHPHRASE: "We're 'open-minded.'"

Before the big suburban Sacramento swinger gangbang, Wendy has scheduled a seven to nine PM happy-hour meet-and-greet at a bar called Liquid.

> You can come chill out with us beforehand, before everything gets OUT OF HAND ;-)

Yes, "chilling out"—before everything gets "OUT OF HAND"—will provide a chance to meet the complete strangers who you'll soon be either

1. having sex with;
2. watching them have sex with your partner;
3. standing next to naked in line while waiting "your turn."

My palms are clammy. Butterflies race through my stomach. Why? This is the most primordial, primitive activity in the world. Chimpanzees do it, for god's sake—on a regular basis! This is what people would do all day long if inflicted with medium-size head injuries. One problem: I don't even like getting naked in front of strangers in the gym locker room. Will this experience not only turn me permanently off of sex, but also human beings in general?

DISGUISE: Sleazy; leather pants, too much jewelry, bad Walgreens cologne.

Liquid is a working-class sports bar far from other establishments. Enter "open-minded" Ken and Debbie Stamos: insurance

salesman and preschool teacher by day, swingers on the weekend. Looking around the sparsely filled bar, I wonder what
swingers look like? Is there a secret swinger handshake? Do
swingers walk among us and we don't even know it? A young
couple sits at the bar. Swingers or civilians?

Eye contact initiated: "We're 'open-minded,'" I throw out for reaction (no reaction). "Let's get freaky!" (Eye contact now avoided.)

The only collective bunch is a long table of ten leering men off
in the corner by the pool tables. These must be the multi-males,
who've bonded due to their shared love of multi-male/female
gangbang (or GB) experiences. With drunk, sluttishly dressed
Debbie Stamos at my hip, I apprehensively approach.

"Let's get freaky!" I announce to the group with award-winning
swinger smile. "We're here for happy hour."

"Great! Come and grab a seat!" exclaims an excited cross-eyed
guy (the leader?), who's happy to have us, especially with the introduction of a sole female (do they really think I'd share?).

"We want to chill out before things get OUT OF HAND!" I
trumpet, shifting in my seat as we awkwardly settle in with
these multi-male gangbang degenerates: cross-eyed guy, man
next to me sporting big scar on face, another with bug eyes
jumping out of skull. No wonder they need to get laid in multi-
male–female fashion; who else would have sex with them!

"Where's Wendy?" I ask. (Pause.) "We're open-minded!"

"Wendy?" repeats the cross-eyed guy, racking his brain for the
whereabouts of the gangbang coordinator. "Wendy? Wasn't she
the one at the Valentines' Day party who was dancing all
wildly?" He begins imitating a wild dance by madly waving his
arms. Others at the table start madly waving their arms.

"We're new to this!" I stress uncomfortably, happy when the
arm waving has stopped. (Pause.) "But 'open-minded.'"

Swaying in her bar stool, drunken Debbie Stamos, suddenly blurts, "We want to have sex with multi-people as a couple!"

The table becomes very silent.

The cross-eyed guy clears his throat. Then, "How did you hear about the Sacramento Cacophony Society? Did you go to Santa-Con?"

I look around the table. These aren't swingers; they're just nerds. *The Sacramento Cacophony Society* pulls such stunts as bowling while dressed in Santa suits. My bad.

"I think we're at the wrong group?" I clarify, now noticing individuals at the bar gravitating towards the foosball-table area—ho, matey, these are the swingers!

"We were looking for the group-sex party?" drunk, sluttishly dressed Debbie Stamos proclaims—attention firmly on her. Quickly we descend upon the true swingers, comprised of roughly thirty people: mostly men who look like cops and ex-military, mixed with a small smattering of women who are either overweight, old, or Asian—firmly gripped by a male companion. Though not "Elephant Man" hideous, it's not exactly the glamorous-Hollywood-swinger crowd either, really just average and almost forgettable—less creepy than the table of nerds.

"Do you want a beer?" inquires one multi-male to another—a bald, short pudgy fellow resembling Uncle Fester.

"I'm drinking water," Uncle Fester replies, adding with a grin, "I got to keep my energy up. It's going to be a *loooooong* night!"

A knowing laugh by both. The pair breaks into talking about football. ("The Green Bay team had an impressive season!") Clearly a multi-male–female experience perk: while waiting in the gangbang line plenty of guys around to talk sports. (Not to mention all the high-fiving!)

How does one cross the threshold and become a lone man who attends multiple male–single female swinger parties? Like an army troop ready to move out for an operation ("We're all in this together!"), they seem to bond together.

"This is one of the things you just got to experience in life," remarks a man in a long black jacket, who was previously talking about software development. "I can cross it off the list."

Confirming that she's Wendy, a very round, short woman holding a clipboard provides an introductory rundown: "We have a very strict policy: anything past 'no, thank you' is considered aggressive behavior."

"Let's get freaky!"

"If someone gets pushy or anything, we ask you to come to us right away. So it should only be a 'no, thank you,' and that should be the end of the conversation."

"We're 'open-minded,'" I confirm, then inquire, "What about roofies?"

"Absolutely not!"

"I mean in our *own* drinks."

"Can you see pictures of the people before going to the party?" Debbie Stamos loudly interrupts.

Blank stare from Wendy.

"What do you do to stop being so nervous?" I quickly question a man with pointy ears, while the butterflies continue to race in my stomach.

"This is how!" he interjects, gesturing to his beer bottle.

"I left the wife at home," remarks a large guy with the buzz cut, while an older man with a comb-over, who wears a sweater vest sits cross-legged on the edge of the group, eyeing everyone while playing with the straw of his drink.

"How does she feel about you going to a swinger party?"

He smirks. "Just as long as I tell her about everything that happens, it's okay."

"But maybe she's going to another swinger party?" I question.

"No!" he abruptly answers, with an angry tinge. "She wouldn't do that!"

Multi-male–female etiquette inquiry: "Do you have to stand in line long for your turn?"

"Usually it goes pretty quick," he says, and recommends with a laugh, "Just make sure you have a position already in mind!"

Latecomer males walk into Liquid, with arms firmly around female counterparts, claiming territory (before other men claim their territory), gripping their companions tightly, as though they were the ones to talk them into doing this, but need to show confirmation of love before swapping begins. It's a friendly bunch (otherwise no one will swap with them). The friendliness, though, has a creepy undercurrent, with initial awkward interaction, as if to say, "Sure, I am just meeting you, but I'll soon see you naked and having an orgasm!"

"Can we do designer shaves on each other?" the male half of a clingy couple, who wears dark shades (though it's night), sleazily propositions Debbie Stamos.

"On you, or me, or both?" she replies.

"On each other!" he makes clear.

Hey! Why am I left out of this equation? I can easily see these evenings ending with long, silent car rides home. Boundaries are being crossed. New doors are being opened. Anxiety mounts for what's to come.

"Are they going to be filming the party?" questions a chubby woman, part of two couples sitting at a table—previously talking about their kids. "I got a very distinct tattoo on my back of a turtle. Everyone at my work knows I have it," she says regarding her receptionist job for a civil engineer. "If I go in there, I'll just have to hide it!"

Just underneath the surface of normalcy, these are yuppies that think they're being wild—mundane lives made exciting on weekends, breaking out of the rut of the monotony of the everyday grind with their scandalously saucy little secret.

"We're the Stamoses!" I announce to the table, sharing our newbie status while holding up my drunken companion.

"This is our first time, too," exclaims the chubby woman. "We didn't know what to expect. We thought there would be people here with no teeth."

"Hey! In certain situations that's not a bad thing!" I throw out with a wink, executing swinger humor.

Gesturing to her boyfriend, who looks like a marine, she adds, "We've done 'things' with friends of ours, but that list is really short." Her fingers are used to imply list shortness.

"I guess it's time to expand that list," I reply, licking my dry lips, noting you can say things as sleazy as you want and no one minds!

"I just want to make my man happy!" Debbie Stamos shrieks, having difficulty standing.

The chubby woman looks at her boyfriend. "We said, we're going to go and check it out, and if we decide to join in, we'll join in," she says, with a tone suggesting this was well discussed. Her boyfriend immediately plants a possessive kiss, but also checks out other people, because that's part of the bargain.

"Everyone always says that and they always end up joining in," blurts a stocky middle-aged guy (law enforcement member?)—veteran in the swinger ways, whose wife was the first to suggest they give it a try.

Gripping her drink, Debbie Stamos questions the group, "Do you ever think this will spice up the romance, cuz the sex at home is getting really boring and routine?"

The table falls silent, shifting uncomfortably, neglecting to answer the question. Then Debbie Stamos accidentally drops her wine glass, doing a great job freaking out the swingers.

Looking for the signs, I can now tell swingers when they enter the bar. An older woman (the only females who come on their own) with fuzzy poodle hair, looking like her trailer home just caught fire, sizes up the group of men in their fifties surrounding her, who could prospectively occupy every one of her orifices. The guy with the comb-over grabs her rump—old, familiar swinging buddies. Not only do I not want to see these people with their clothes off, but I don't particularly enjoy seeing them with their clothes on.

"He's my partner in crime," says a newly arrived rotund woman with large breasts and slightly thinning hair, motioning to a guy in a stripy button-down shirt.

"Like Batman to your partner-swapping Robin," I state.

The thinning-haired woman confesses on preferring parties over swinger clubs: "The *Power Exchange* is weird. Like we were having sex there, and I looked up and there was a large group of men jacking off all around us. (A lifestyle hazard!) "Some were getting a little too close. I had to keep stopping and tell them to back off!"

With curiosity: "What's it like to have sex in front of a group of strangers?"

Her chubby face lights up. "You just go for it and don't really think about it!"

"Are those double Ds?" interrupts Debbie Stamos, grabbing for the woman's mammoth breasts, highlighted by a frilly red bra peaking out from her low-cut black dress.

Men leer at drunken Debbie Stamos, thinking perhaps she's going to be one crazy participant with a long line veering down the suburban townhouse hallway, as she starts falling all over me—literally! (Mostly to hold herself up.)

"Some people chicken out," exclaims a man with pointy ears, who hails from a small farming town.

"Not us!" I proclaim.

Swingers start filtering out of the bar, like a pumped-up squadron shipping off to sexual war, making their way to the party blazoned with huge Christmas-morning grins, ready to unwrap their presents and play.

But a monkey wrench is thrown into the Stamoses' multi-male–female gangbang swinger experience. Debbie Stamos has disappeared. Going outside, I find her passed out in the passenger seat of my car. The creepy nerds stare at her through the window. Our swinger multi-male–female experience will have to wait for another day, my friend—the American Dream is put on hold.

A Swinger Tradition

Serious recasting is done in terms of the Debbie Stamos role. Surprisingly, not an arduous task. The more friends I told about swinger gatherings, the more became interested. Strange what lies just beneath the surface of unassuming people. Thus the recruitment of a more reliable Debbie Stamos (Debbie Stamos II)—a nonprofit worker who'll help make the leap into the next stage of the American Dream. Creepified by the whole multi-male–single female debacle, my virgin swinger foray needs a more nurturing scenario. Enter Barry and Shell:

> Barry and Shell have been hosting swing parties for couples and single women for thirty-five years. We offer a safe and pressure-free place to explore sensual fantasies and meet like-minded people.
>
> A delicious buffet is available throughout the evening.

Held the second Saturday of each month, Barry and Shell's is a swinging institution—the mom and pop store of swinger parties. With over three decades of swinger-party hosting under their belt, these must be really *old* swingers—a throwback to the early seventies heyday (most likely featuring many of the original cast members). Unlike kids today with their multi-male–single-female experiences, this is the swinger equivalent of a 2008 KC and the Sunshine Band reunion tour.

Adding to the swinging fanfare, it's Shell's birthday tonight. Over forty swinger couples are expected to attend. Condoms and plenty of towels are provided. I wonder if cake will be served? Like firearms, swinging and hard alcohol don't mix; guests are only allowed to bring wine.

"There's no pressure whatsoever," Shell told Debbie Stamos II over the phone like a *kindly den-mother-of-having-sex-with-multiple-partners.* "You don't have to do anything. You can play. You can watch. If you bring toys, we got outlets in all the rooms."

(What kind of archaic or industrial toys does she have in mind that aren't battery operated?)

Thoughts race through my head as we drive towards Barry and Shell's three-level home in a lovely East Bay neighborhood: Will I end up having sex with someone's wife? Will someone's grandmother hit on me!? Will images from this evening cause me to wake up screaming like a traumatized Vietnam vet?!? Did I again leave the iron on in my house!?

"Don't you dare leave me alone," stresses a nervous and concerned Debbie Stamos II, as I park my car in the designated area blocks away from the party.

A quiet, nondescript neighborhood. With my silk shirt unbuttoned down to my navel, I've added a few gold chains to my sleazy look, accompanied by my swinger partner, who is dressed like a frumpy schoolteacher. Reluctantly we make our way toward the door decorated with cheesy Christmas lights. Faint music emits from beyond. To the untrained eye there's not a clue of what goes on inside this closed entry of normal suburbia. A moment of uneasy anticipation. A ring of the bell. A knock on the door. The sound of a lock being opened.

"We're the Stamoses!" I declare with arms open to a thin woman wearing a red corset top, giving my best "I'm-ready-to-swing" look.

"Come on in!" she says, neither friendly nor unfriendly in manner.

With the hesitancy of someone who's afraid of large birds and covered in breadcrumbs, we enter the swinger abode, letting out periodical staccato nervous laughs. Immediately I can tell this isn't your ordinary Saturday-night middle-class suburban house party. A dank smell. Seedy lighting. Walls painted pink. Occasionally, a man clad only in a towel walks by. Is this house haunted, cuz various grunts and groans bellow from upstairs . . . and beyond!

Names checked off the reservation list. "That will be eighty dollars," the woman in the red corset says in a manner neither friendly nor unfriendly, while perched under a sign that reads, "You have to wear a condom. If you don't, you won't be invited back."

"We're new to the *lifestyle*," I stress to her boyfriend Mike, who is dressed entirely in black. Unlike the corset woman, Mike is very friendly and talkative. Years ago Mike lived down the street from Barry and Shell, and that's how he started attending their parties. His girlfriend, though, is a relative swinger newbie in many ways.

"I'm fifty-four, and she's twenty-one," Mike shares, gesturing towards his red-corseted girlfriend (who is neither friendly or unfriendly).

"Did you guys meet at a swinger party?" I ask surveying the situation as another man walks by wearing only a towel.

"No, we met at work," Mike replies. "I work for a program that brings arts into schools.

"She's an administrator. Are you a musician?" he asks, adding, "Cuz I'm really into rock and roll. I saw Jim Morrison play!"

"No, I'm a girl's basketball coach."

More men walk by in towels.

Bringing the focus back, I blurt, "Since we're new, can you give us the tour?"

"Sure," Mike enthusiastically says, while continuing to talk about "rock and roll." His quiet twenty-one-year-old girlfriend remains quiet (did they meet when she was still a student?). Commencement of swinger house tour. "The living room is the main social area. No *play!*" Mike stresses.

"Let's get freaky!"

Then the wide variety of "playrooms." Steam rising in the air. Various naked couples frolic in the hot-tub room. With twenty-one-year-old girlfriend in tow, Mike matter-of-factly explains the rules. "Don't finish in the Jacuzzi!" (*Eeeew!*) "When you're ready to finish, go to another room, but don't do it in the Jacuzzi!"

(Pause.) "Let's get freaky!"

"There's a downstairs area where you can watch," Mike says, leading us towards the red-lit bowels of the house. A more pungent smell hits me first, before the visual. Wall-to-wall mattresses. Crumpled stained sheets. The sounds of grunts and groans mixed with body parts slapping together. If you ever wondered what it would be like if your parents had sex, this would be it. A room full of naked unattractive couples, some to the point of plain obese, with rolls of flesh one could get lost in, twisted into a variety of random sexual positions. Lotion is accessible. Garbage cans scattered for used condoms, with signs posting their purpose. How could a germ-phobic person possibly get aroused and partake on these crumpled sheets used and reused by a rotation of numerous strange couples? Like a horse corral, a long railing separates the area and provides something for spectators to lean on, watching the action unfold with wide eyes and melancholy expressions. Far from arousing, it's more comical; the looks on people's faces, the ridiculous noises they make, the crowd of zombies watching on. I wish the *Benny Hill* theme would suddenly start playing.

"You can rent a lock for five dollars," Mike suggests, as we pass a room upstairs equipped entirely with health-club lockers in case we want to exchange our clothes for towels. "And this room is just for couples," he says, gesturing to weird hanging blue sheets separating small individual mattresses—for privacy—though various tops of heads and gyrating feet dangle out from each end of the compartment with a noise that sounds like someone getting a tooth pulled.

"Put your name on your wine bottle," Mike says, handing me a Sharpie, as the tour concludes in the kitchen—though people share partners, they don't share wine! Then: "You should come join us in the Jacuzzi," friendly Mike beckons with big friendly smile and silent twenty-one-year-old girlfriend by his side, staring at us a little longer than comfort permits.

"Yeah. Maybe later," I say (but not too convincingly), leaving Debbie Stamos II and myself in the pink-walled kitchen.

A seventies-era framed copy of *Cheri* magazine is the room's artistic centerpiece. Naked Shell (of Barry and Shell fame) graces the cover, along with a photo spread of naked, contorted bodies and hot-tub action, capturing the quintessential pre-AIDS California swingers' experience, during a time of innocent sexual experimentation and massive amounts of cocaine.

"You look like first-timers," remarks an affable Hispanic guy named Carlos sitting in the corner adorned with a crew cut and crisp button-down shirt.

"Is it obvious?" I ask with fear in my eyes.

"No worries, just ease into it," assures Carlos, breaking into a big, affable smile, with his full-figured wife Yvonne perched on his lap.

"It took us about a year of coming to parties to start participating," Yvonne adds, wearing a low-cut print dress accentuating her mammoth breasts.

Carlos explains their indoctrination: "We used to go to swinger clubs in San Francisco, but they'd only have girl's participate." Gesturing to his wife: "She would participate, but only with other women so I felt left out. Here, I can have some fun too!"

"They can be cliquish," Yvonne pipes in about the San Francisco sex clubs. "You go there and you have to be really slender and look like a Barbie doll. Here you can just be yourself."

"This must be your American Dream?" I throw out to Carlos.

Carlos ponders. Carlos enlightens: "Yeah, the *sexual* American Dream!"

We high-five.

"So how do you let people know you're interested in play?" Debbie Stamos II asks, shifting uncomfortably, as towel-adorned people linger around her.

Affable Carlos demonstrates. "You kind of come up to them and massage them." Carlos rubs his hand over my fictional wife's back. "Then you see where it goes." Carlos lowers his hand and boldly grabs her ass. A complete shocked look crosses Debbie Stamos II's face, completely mortified by his groping. Carlos plays it off with a huge laugh.

"So that's how it's done," I say witnessing the display in front of his own wife.

"Girl, you're the one in charge here," Yvonne interjects to Debbie Stamos II, stating that the woman usually is the one who instigates things; most often with another female. "You got the power. If you're not ready, you're not ready." (Pause.) "It's the woman's choice!"

Suddenly a woman appears with the word *juicy* across her shirt and bottom. She immediately starts fondling Yvonne. Carlos lets out a big, pleased smile. Lone men continue to circulate the kitchen in towels, trolling the party for fresh newbie meat. Some couples arrive and head directly to the various sex rooms—that's all the socializing they need. Barry and Shell's has the atmosphere of some weird, sleazy family reunion with the average age around fifty-five.

"There're a lot of cops and judges who come to these parties," Carlos says. (What's up with cops and judges?!) "Some people really don't talk about their jobs, especially if they have a high profile position."

"Are you a cop?" I ask with concern.

"No. I work as a Spanish teacher," Carlos replies.

"I do interpretation for the deaf," Yvonne adds. "We came all the way from Sacramento for the party, because there's no chance of running into someone you know."

A funny story: "We were at one party and were engaging in sex with a couple. A few weeks later we were having parent/teacher conferences and one of the kid's parents showed up."

"I happened to be there," Yvonne exclaims. "I said, 'Sweetie, I recognize them!' They were the couple from the party!"

"Did you give each other some sort of secret handshake?"

"They acted like they didn't recognize us." Carlos then adds the cliché, "What happens here stays here, is the motto!"

More high-fiving.

Once again Carlos demonstrates what is needed to initiate play. This time, he tries rubbing my fictional wife's chest. Another shocked look. Zero success to follow.

"What about guys hooking up with other guys?" I instigate, massaging Carlos's shoulder.

"That doesn't happen here!" he says abruptly.

"Is there cake?" I loudly blurt due to awkwardness. "We heard it's Shell's birthday today. We're going to find cake!"

"Do you guys want to join us later in the Jacuzzi?" Carlos asks, still eyeing Debbie Stamos II with a broad, friendly smile.

"I think we got to warm up a bit. Sort of dip our toes into the pool first," I say (hoping that sentence isn't a double entendre). I then mention the golden rule to Carlos: "Remember, don't *finish* in the Jacuzzi!"

The Spread

What a confectionary letdown. Yes, there is cake. No, it's not even shaped like something sexual or a body part—just plain old, stupid cake.

The living room, dotted with Barry's erotic paintings, is where the swingers reenergize between strenuous "sessions" on the spread. This consists mostly of cheese, peel-and-eat shrimp, and bowls full of potato chips. Hard to stomach a plateful of pickled mushrooms as an old guy with a flabby ass parades around wearing a G-string with a chicken on the front. I don't want to touch anything (peel-and-eat shrimp, potato chips, Oreo cookies). Especially the potato chips. All it takes is one swinger who didn't wash their hands after group coitus, and it's hello, hepatitis!

"I've been coming to Barry and Shell's parties for the past thirty years," says a creepy older man with gray, puffy hair like a Vegas lounge singer, who's wearing only a towel and munching a second plate of peel-and-eat shrimp. He licks his fingers. Less friendly than the others—Puffy-hair is strictly business.

With a dead look in his eye, he's one of the rare males allowed to attend parties on his own. "I worked for them," he explains. "Then I worked at several other swinger events."

"What do you do when you're not at parties?"

"I give private tennis lessons," he says, becoming a sleazy seventies cliché. ("Here, Mrs. Van Buren, let me help you with your backhand!") "It's the Bush administration," he rattles on about the decline of swinger parties. "If McCain wins, I'm sure more will start popping up," he shares his political ideology.

Sensing someone staring at the Stamoses, I look over. It's Mike! He's down the hall with a big, creepy smile plastered across his face and his twenty-one-year-old girlfriend glued to his side—both now wearing towels. They're sort of following us around the house.

"We're going to the couples room. Do you guys want to come with?"

Mental note to self: must avoid Mike!

In this era of Demi Moore, there's a broad difference in ages, but it's mostly the women older than their male companions.

"It's our first time, and we just took the plunge," states a Scandinavian man with glasses, who is clad in a towel and scarfs down food along with someone who looks maybe like his mother.

A skeleton-skinny old woman in her sixties, drunk out of her head, tries to tantalize me into dancing by lifting up her turquoise dress revealing a matching pair of turquoise old-lady panties.

"How's your night going?" I ask, noting she smells like a cross between mothballs and Grandma's house.

"If you're asking, I haven't fucked anyone," she slurs like a drunken sailor, with swinger jealousy waving its ugly head.

(Pause.) "Okay."

More jealousy: "If he's fucking someone, then I'm going to go fuck someone!" she blurts; anger is in her voice, and alcohol on her breath.

This is the opportune time to test the validity of Carlos's instigating tactic. I begin massaging her bony shoulder. (Will she end up giving me five dollars in a birthday card?) Confrontation. The man who's the other half of Skeletor jealously emerges from the smoking room. Wearing only red underwear, he looks like a funny sitcom next-door neighbor. Is this another *Jerry Springer* moment?

"That's Gary," says Skeletor.

"*Barry*?" I exclaim. "Is this your party?"

"No," he clarifies, "I'm *Gary*."

Gary fills me in on trouble in swinger paradise. Though they still throw their monthly swinger parties together, Barry and Shell have split up.

"That's like Hall and Oates breaking up!" I exclaim.

"Barry's here with his girlfriend," informs Gary, regarding the road bump in the American Dream, leaving me wondering since Barry and Shell are broken up do they still have sex together, since everyone here has noncommittal sex with other people's partners?

"Do you want to join us in the hot tub?" Gary suddenly exclaims, utilizing strong eye contact.

(Pause.) "Absolutely not!"

After momentary refuge in the bathroom—equipped with industrial-sized bottles of mouthwash and antibacterial soap—I'm actually starting to get bored with the swinger scene. "I guess we could go look at people having sex again," I shrug my shoulders and unenthusiastically suggest to Debbie Stamos II.

Another potential *Jerry Springer* moment: A superskinny black woman, wearing a mesh, see-through dress, clearly ready to leave the party, fumes, watching her man give oral pleasure to a large woman on the side of the Jacuzzi. Needless to say, that's going to be one long silent car ride home.

Carlos and Yvonne are also in the hot tub. They've both hooked up with other people. Yvonne's caressing and kissing another woman. Fully aroused Carlos stands in a circle with a group of guys, who, in turn, get oral pleasure from a submerged woman, reminding me of a trained circus seal who can play several horns with its mouth. Both seem pleased.

Here comes the image that will permanently burn into my retinas! Slowly emerging from the Jacuzzi, dripping water, skeleton woman is now completely naked as the little flesh she has hangs downward toward the ground. Yes, there comes that point when you know it's time to leave.

Last Call for Play

Closing in on two AM the party clears out pretty quickly. Two gray-haired men in suit jackets stand by the door talking about city council issues and zoning laws. Are they the aforementioned politicians conversing in shoptalk? Or bankers? Or lawyers? Or accountants? Or schoolteachers?

In the locker room a man with a comb-over and an older Asian woman put on their civilian clothes, both with blank expressions—neither happy nor sad—more stricken with the malice of life.

"Did you guys have fun?" I ask, being they look like they've just lost a loved one.

Comb-over mumbles something to the effect of both, "Yes," and, "It's none of your business," like one involved in the lifestyle for a jaded long time (maybe cautious of newbies, cuz he's a high-profile judge?).

The empty group-sex room aftermath is not pretty. Crumbled, stained sheets. Peculiar, lingering smells. The porn movie turned off. Remnants of strange bodies that laid here through the course of the evening, some not even knowing one another's names—instigated by a rub of the shoulder. Those whose ho-hum bland lives were, for an evening, made to seem edgy and spicy by their sexual drive and participation; a glimmer of excitement to think about during the working week when teaching Spanish, doing data entry, or interpreting for the deaf. An American Dream fulfilled through their ability to live sex fantasies in the swinger scene, where they can feel attractive, sexy, and wanted by others, and make acquaintances with shared, deviant camaraderie.

Imagining the industrial cleaning that will be needed tomorrow, Debbie Stamos II looks at the room. She blurts, "I don't think I ever want to have sex ever again."

As more tired swingers suit up and head towards the door, I finally encounter the legendary Shell. Looking like a kindly mom, she's cleaning up empty cups and plates in the kitchen. Shell turned sixty-three years old today.

"Do the neighbors know about your parties?" I ask.

"There are much louder parties than this on the block," Shell replies, gathering more party leftovers for the trash. "That's why I have people park down the street."

I look over at the framed copy of *Cheri* magazine with her photo from decade's past, and ask about the golden age of swinging.

"We used to throw parties three times a week," she says with a twinkle in her eye. "Then it was once a week. Now it's only once a month." Shell puts some cans in the recycling. "My parents were nightclub owners, so I grew up around this."

Swinging has not only been Shell's *lifestyle,* but Shell's *life.* Throwing these parties has for her been a long-fulfilled thirty-five-year American Dream. With Barry still nowhere to be found, Shell is left on her own to empty the bowls of potato chips and discard the peel-and-eat shrimp remains.

CHAPTER SEVEN

HOLLYWOOD AMERICAN DREAM

THE AMERICAN DREAM: IN THEIR OWN WORDS
Ali MacLean, writer, performer, and TV host who lives in Los Angeles; she is also a VIP

So you want to be a movie star. Not any star, but an actor that does important films. Oscar-worthy fare. But how does one achieve the Holy Grail of the golden statuette?

First, you have to realize that you are more talented and beautiful than anyone else you know. You know this because your parents have told you, your boyfriend has told you, and your high school/college/community theater play director has given you a lot of encouragement (plus some questionable back rubs). Now, this is not enough alone. You also must have determination, drive, a bit of disconnect with that ugly word reality, plus a nice nest egg to fall back on for your big trip to Hollywood!

When you arrive, you must not look like you are fresh off the bus from Omaha. But no matter what you do, your in-experience among the well-groomed jackals and shape-shifters will scream out "Naif Waif Waiting to Be Swindled!"

199

Still, keep up the false mask of superiority over the other film extras living in the Oakwood Apartments temp-housing condos.

Get a job to pay the bills and get in an acting class pronto! You can find a class at the Samuel French Bookstore, Back-stage West classified ads, or written in magic marker on the back of an envelope and posted on your Oakwood temp-housing condo bulletin board.

Once you begin taking these classes (while waiting tables at Cheesecake Factory) you will definitely realize that you are way more talented than anyone. BUT. You need to get an agent or none of it matters. You'll also need a whole new wardrobe of low-cut, strappy tank tops and mile-high pumps. Oh, and some veneers, extensions, and plastic surgery wouldn't hurt either.

After suffering through hundreds of cattle calls and worse, commercial auditions, you do a stint on a sketch show and a few parts in a few big films. One film launches the career of everyone who is cast under the age of thirty . . . except yours. You get an agent who sends you out for the role of a pregnant teen. You're closer in age to Luke Perry than Hilary Duff, but you make the hour-long drive in your car, with the broken air-conditioner, arriving sweat drenched and unprepared. The casting director tells you the part is for an African American girl. You tell her you're great at doing accents. She still sends you home. This incident repeats many times. You fire your agent.

You begin writing, because it's easier. It doesn't hurt quite as much auditioning for the part of the town whore. Plus you don't have to cut all the carbs from your diet. You write a suc-cessful play and work on some kitschy TV shows. A power-ful agent expresses interest in your work, and asks you to accompany him to watch another one of his clients do standup. Somehow you end up at his place with him chasing you around his pool. You won't sleep with him. Ipso facto, he tells you he won't sign you as a client. You fire yourself from writing for TV. Coincidentally, reality TV hits and takes over prime time, rendering both TV writers and literary agents useless.

No one in this town wants your smarty-pants ideas. No one wants to put Shakespeare on film. How silly to think that a town that gives away acting roles to athletes and heiresses would care anything about iambic pentameter.

You retreat to doing radio and music journalism, which are faceless jobs, but come with the perks of the plus one: you plus one guest for shows, parties, and events. These often have free food and open bar. This softens the blow of having to interview people who you knew way back when, who are now famous stars.

It is several years later. The stars on the Walk of Fame used to glisten with the residue of angel dust and pulverized meth vials. Now the litter is of the Starbucks variety, and there is a Gap and a Hooters on the corner.

They've built a mall around the famous handprints, which has a massive stone "casting couch" that fat tourists take turns posing on. They think this is fun. You wonder if they'd laugh if they had ever been on a real casting couch.

You scowl at the stupid tourists and stride quickly to avoid the guys selling maps to the stars' homes. You're not on that map yet and this makes your stomach churn.

You pass a young handsome guy wearing a Batman costume. He's on break, maskless, talking on his cell phone while enjoying a hot dog.

"What a waste of a gorgeous face and body," you think.

He probably lives in the Oakwood temp-housing condos and moonlights as a waiter at California Pizza Kitchen. He takes acting classes, goes to cattle calls, and when he has a day off, he ferociously works out at the gym and then drinks beer with friends on the patio at one of their temp-housing condos.

You realize that you are far from being Kate Winslet. But you've just spent five dollars on a latte and later on that night, you are on the list at that big music show. You have VIP tickets, which means you'll have free food and booze and most likely some local publication will take your picture. It's not the cover of *Vanity Fair*, but people in the scene know who you are. You don't live at Oakwood. You have a cute apartment in the Hills with eclectic furniture and a vast music and clothing collection. You aren't famous, but you're good at what you do. And you like what you do. And suddenly that's more than okay. It's better.

Generating Hollywood Heat— German-Style!

In Hollywood, it's all about HEAT! Generating an industry buzz in turn creates HEAT, and most important, HYPE. On the whole, Hollywood lives the old adage of the emperor's new clothes. It's a town full of people who can't really think for themselves and need reassurance from others in fear of losing their jobs; people who must berate underlings over delivering the wrong soy latte just to make themselves feel good; people who need to be told who is talented and who will be the next big star rather than come to these conclusions on their own.

The worst of these naked emperors without original thought are the bloodsucking Hollywood agents, who have all the soul and integrity of, well, bloodsucking Hollywood agents. To help me live my American Dream of being fawned over as the next big comedy sensation, I contacted some Hollywood insiders— organizers for the Montreal Comedy Festival—who will not only get me in the door with some of Hollywood's top agencies, but most importantly, pass me off as a megastar from a foreign country visiting L.A. for a limited time—so they better act fast and sell themselves to me! The clock is ticking.

> **PERSONA:** German comedian Dieter Lietershvantz, who hails from Struddelsburg, Germany. By posing as a German comedian, it purely exemplifies the American Dream quest where any foreign funnyman has the opportunity to move to this great land of ours and make it on a shitty sitcom. (A German comedian is, of course, an oxymoron.)
> **DISGUISE:** All-black clothing; a stupid, oversize cowboy hat; permanent scowl.
> **HEAT-CREATING BACKSTORY:** When discovered at a comedy club in Struddelsburg, Dieter's German sense of humor blew the crowd away. He was asked to be a last-minute addition to the "New Faces" showcase at the Montreal Comedy Festival—the show Hollywood sharks attend to find the next big *Everybody Loves Raymond.*
> **HEAT-CREATING PREMISE:** Only in L.A. for one day, the agents are told that Dieter is meeting with every large agency in Hollywood. No tape on him exists. (Like the Amish, Dieter feels videotaping "steals his soul.")

With meetings set, I'm about to get cajoled over by sharks, while walking in the shoes of the next big Brad Pitt or Yakov Smirnoff, as I get to smell the rotting fruits of the enticement of fame and wealth, in order to prove my point about the inanity of Hollywood buzz and hype by becoming a ridiculous, fake person with fabricated . . . HEAT!

> GROUND RULES FOR AGENT MEETINGS:
> 1. I must be indignant.
> 2. I must speak in the worst conceivable foreign accent.
> 3. I must be devoid of any sense of humor.
> 4. I must often refer to myself in the third person.
> 5. I must get an agent to sign me on the spot!

Yes, this sojourn into the belly of the beast will not only take me to the epicenter of Hollywood—where deals are made—but it shall also allow me to take vengeance for every comedian whose had their pursuit of the American Dream squashed by sleazy agents who disregard their talent like yesterday's stale bread or the plague. Besides, it's just plain fun to speak in a bad foreign accent. To protect the not-so-innocent, all names have been cleverly changed.

Stop Number One—Very Large Hollywood Agency

I enter lobby of Very Large Agency.

"Dieter is here!"

"Are you picking up a package?" asks the security guard.

How dare he! Doesn't he know I'm the biggest fictional comedy star in all of Deutschland?! I give him my icy-cold German stare.

"No! Why would Dieter be here to pick up a package?!"

"I'm very sorry," he profusely apologizes. "I just have to ask; it's my job."

People have been fired and replaced for less. The woman in the reception area on the fourth floor is more attentive.

"Dieter's appointment is now!" I announce.

The obligatory bottled water is brought to me as I sit in a large plush chair, posed like a rigid statue, glaring into the distance.

"Dieter?" I hear a disembodied voice state from across the lobby.

I meet Large-Agency woman, clad in sensible business attire, and enter her office. A bandaged, injured puppy limps around the couch area. Large-Agency woman explains how she rescued the bandaged, injured puppy from the streets, and about her volunteer service at a homeless animal shelter. The bandaged, injured puppy is taken to another room by her assistant.

"We're a big agency with a small client list," explains Large-Agency woman.

As I sit among a pile of dog toys while she speaks, my look conveys the possibility that I'm a man who can't figure out $1+1=2$.

"I don't know if you understand," says Large-Agency woman. "I mean, your English seems fine."

"Maybe if you speak much slower," I insist, looking like I'm still trying to figure out the math problem.

I now have Large-Agency woman speaking not only much slower, but also much louder. She's very animated, trying to break through our language barrier—almost using mime—rattling off their agency's client list.

"Jim Carrey, do you know him?"

"Ja! He is the man who makes the funny faces," I confirm, quickly asking if the agency represents other German actors. Large-Agency woman thinks for a minute. I prompt her.

"How about famous German actress Helga Wasserstein?"

Large-Agency woman answers, "No, you would be the only one." Then she adds, "Oh, we represent Claudia Schiffer. You can ask her about our agency."

"Dieter shall do that!"

"So you're from Germany," Large-Agency woman interjects very slowly and loudly, wanting to find out more about me.

"I vork on German television, on a show with much fighting." For emphasis, I punch the air with my fists.

"Oh, like wrestling?" Large-Agency woman says perkily.

"Noooo! Like . . . Van Damme!" I make rapid kung fu motions.

Large-Agency woman asks if I have any ideas for American TV shows.

"Maybe like Chuck Norris. On a show with fighting; much fighting." Again, my fists move in the air.

A nondescript man in shirt and tie enters the office. Large-Agency woman asks if he knows the name of the kung fu show that was on CBS with Arsenio Hall. He racks his brains. While racking his brain, she then makes introductions.

"This is Dieter; he is going to be in Montreal. He's a comedian from Germany," she says. "I'm getting the scoop, which is pretty fascinating, actually!"

"I'm married to a German," the nondescript man states, asking what part of Deutschland I'm from.

"Struddelsburg!" I confirm.

"Why am I blanking out on the name of the show?" ponders Large-Agency woman, still wanting the name of the program that had both Arsenio and much fighting.

"I can find out, though, and get back to you," the man in shirt and tie says, leaving, clearly on the case.

"I can tell you the general process," Large-Agency woman continues, getting into the nuts and bolts.

"Slower, please!"

"Let's assume that your act is very different, which I assume that it is. Probably not what you usually see," she says. "Sometimes people love that, and sometimes people are scared of that."

"Is Dieter frightening?!" I scowl.

Suddenly, the bandaged, injured puppy comes bounding back into the room.

"How did you get back here?" exclaims Large-Agency woman.

"Do you put little hats and human clothes on the dogs?" I ask in thick German accent.

After answering no, Large-Agency woman concludes with the hard sell.

"I think you're very interesting, and I can't wait to see your act!"

"Ja! It will be enjoyed!"

"Look, if you meet another agent and you love them, and they want to sign you now—then, that's what you have to do. I recommend waiting; I certainly would like the opportunity to see you. I risk losing you by saying that, but they should definitely see your work."

We make plans to meet in Montreal, along with my fake German manager, "Heinred."

"Hymen?" she attempts.

"No, Heinred," I correct.

"Heinwren?" she attempts again.

"No, Heinred!"

As my parking is validated, Large-Agency woman shows curiosity and competitiveness, asking how many other agency meetings I have set. Stroking the heat, I tell her five. She lists agencies. I randomly tell her yes or no.

"Let me guess. CAA?"

"Ja!"

"William Morris?"

"Ja!"

"UTA?"

"No!"

"Girsh?"

"Perhaps!"

As I break for the elevator, she restates, "Now don't sign with anybody yet!"

"Ja! Our meeting is done!"

In the elevator, as if I were rushing a sorority, someone's assistant advises, "You should really sign with [Large Agency]."

Stop Number Two—Medium-Size Hollywood Agency with Great View of Century City

A well-groomed man in white shirt with tie comes into the reception area.

"Dieter?" he inquires to the five of us waiting. Enjoying how that sounds, I wait for him to say the name two more times.

"Dieter?"

"Ja!" I exclaim. All eyes turn to my stony, cold stare. I demand more obligatory bottled water.

I soon find myself sitting in a large conference room with a nice view of Century City. Two similarly well-dressed men come in. Then another. Then one more. It was hard enough fooling one person; now I have to fool four—and for forty-five minutes! The key, I decide, is to speak as monosyllabically as possible. Monosyllabic and very morose.

"Dieter! I heard you're very, very funny," says the one who I assume is the leader.

"Ja! That information is correct!"

He continues, "We know nothing about you except what we were told."

"Vhat were you told!?"

"That you're very, very funny. That they made an extraspecial opening for you at the Montreal Festival, and that you made them laugh . . . a lot!"

I don't respond.

"What did you do to make them laugh?" asks the one who might be considered second in command. I explain slowly.

"I talk about the things in my life." (Pause.) "The problems with the police!" (Pause.) "The problems with the parents!" (Pause.) "The problems with the drugs!"

"Okay," he says after an awkward silence.

"And the stories about them," I clarify. Then I abruptly stop, giving no further information. Four identically dressed men give four identical blank stares. I rest my hand on my chin and scowl.

The leader goes into his song and dance.

"What makes our agency different, we help create something different, comedy-wise," he states. "We treat you as an actor, and the comedy is separate. The comics we have are all known and respected."

I move my eyes back and forth as if I only partially understand and comprehend the words coming out of his mouth. The one-who-I-assume-is-the-leader then explains that my career will be handled as they handle their other clients' careers. He mentions a few names; I act like I don't know them.

"Howard Stern?"

"Dieter is not familiar!"

The one-I-assume-is-the-leader explains as if he were talking to a child: "Howard Stern is a disc jockey in this country who went on to do other things."

"Ja!"

"All these different things, we helped create that!"

"Do you have tape of your act at all?" requests the one farthest from me.

"It is best to see Dieter live!" I confirm.

"Yeah, good answer!" quips one of the four.

It's time to turn up the heat.

"What if one who is agent signs me before the festival?" I ask.

"If you sign, what we'd offer before—we let people know who you are and what makes you special," the leader explains.

"We'll sit down with your manager," the second in command adds, saying that I shouldn't sign with anybody until he's seen me perform.

"Then if they really love you, you still have to sign with us, because we gave you the best advice!" one-I-assume-is-the-leader states with a laugh.

I restate his premise as if confused. "Sign with you, but not sign before."

"Navigate those waters very carefully," advises the leader.

"Ja! Good."

Four identical cards are put in my German hands by the four identically dressed men.

"You're going to blow up, man," proclaims one of the four. "It's going to be great!"

"We'll grab a drink up there; we'll meet your manager and have a good time," says another.

"We'll see you up there," says the one-I-assume-is-the-leader.

"Are you all right?" asks the second in command, noting confusion crossing my face.

"Many cards," I say like a perplexed German.

Stop Number Three—Big but Slightly Cheesy Hollywood Agency

There's an addition to my wardrobe. I'm now wearing a black pirate eye patch! I thought this would make a nice final touch and add to my star appeal. Catching my reflection in the lobby glass door, I look creepy—very creepy.

For the last agency meeting, I make sure I'm twenty minutes late to show how pompously busy I am.

"Ja, Dieter is here!"

The receptionist looks mildly frightened, giving me an "I can get security up here in ten seconds" look. Unlike at the other Hollywood agencies, I'm not offered the obligatory bottle of cold water. (Are they discriminating against eye-patch wearers?!)

Though late, I'm left waiting another fifteen minutes. Dieter will defiantly not be signing with this agency! I pass the time by having a fake, heated German argument on my cell phone.

"Shvanta shvieter shvieser!!!"

Finally, a well-groomed man comes around the corner with hand extended for shaking.

"Dieter?" he asks.

I raise my finger, implying I'm not done with my heated German phone argument. I wait a few seconds, conclude my call, turning my head and exposing that I am one who wears an eye patch. Though I have an elaborate backstory worked out involving an escaped circus tiger in Frankfurt, it is not needed.

We walk toward an office.

"Many people vant Dieter to sign. Dieter has had many meet-ings!" I proclaim, almost bumping into a wall because of my ob-structed vision. Another well-dressed agent joins us. He looks at me like I'd just stolen silverware. They sit in separate parts of the room, so I can only focus on one well-dressed agent at a time. I think they're about to play a "good cop–bad cop" thing.

I'm then made to tell them about my comedy act—the prob-lems with the police, the problems with the drugs, the problems with the parents, etc.—and the show I have on German televi-sion with much fighting. My eye patch blocks the view of the good cop–bad cop reactions.

The good cop explains that there's a major buzz around town about me at the moment. Heat, if you will! This is very flatter-ing to Dieter! Then he goes on to give the typical agency song and dance.

"Our agency can offer, something-something, blah-blah-blah, etc., etc."

As I see words come out his mouth, my mind wanders to thoughts of running through grassy German meadows in my lederhosen. I'm snapped back to present reality by:

"Do I want to sign you right now? Sure! But I'll have to wait and see you perform. Then I can sign you at the festival. Don't sign with anyone until they see you perform; otherwise they won't know how to sell you."

I abruptly stand.

"The meeting must now end!"

I leave.

Epilogue: Almost immediately, the Hollywood insiders who had helped me set up the ruse receive phone calls anxiously inquir-ing about when Dieter will be performing his German comedy act. The heat-hype spread faster than a Hollywood Hills brush fire.

A casting director at a major film studio called, saying the studio had heard secondhand about the heat on Dieter being added to the Montreal Comedy Festival "New Faces" roster, and wants to get a hold of him before anyone else has a chance.

One agent dug deeper:

"I just had a very interesting meeting with Dieter Lietershvantz," he said. "He's cool; he's interesting. He's got a good look. I told him not to sign with anyone before the festival, because they would only be signing on hype."

"Yeah, that and a multimillion-dollar acting career back in Germany," my insider embellished.

"Really!! Why didn't you tell me that before the meeting?!" the agent retorts, kicking himself for not singing Dieter on the spot.

And this is the moral of the story: A Hollywood agent should never sign a client on hype—unless the client has a fabricated, multimillion-dollar career in Deutschland. But for the day, it allowed me to live my American Dream of being hot, German Hollywood property.

The Pitchmaster

Time to burn more bridges in Hollywood in my quest for the American Dream. This time I'm going straight to the top by posing as a relative of a legendary Hollywood player to get my foot in the door with network TV execs, in order to pitch the worst conceivable TV-show ideas, which I thought up earlier while drinking heavily. That's right! I'm going to pose as a Spelling. Taylor Spelling, actually, and I'll live the American Dream of wheeling and dealing with those whose job it is to put our nation's shows on television.

Yes, it's been leaked that I'm the favorite nephew of deceased TV mogul Aaron *Beverly Hills 90210* Spelling (as well as cousin to plastic-surgery nightmare Tori Spelling).

In order to set up the pitch meetings, I had a very businessy-sounding associate call, claiming she was Chandelle Martin, Taylor Spelling's representation from Provoke Management. When told to forward some past credits, my prestigious list boasted all shows involving Aaron Spelling. As a topper, all my reality TV show ideas will involve the aspect of a loveable talking robot. I shouldn't worry about how stupid and inane my ideas are; they can't compare to other shows that have actually made it on air.

Any similarity to actual people, places, and events is entirely intended. Names have been withheld to protect these idiots from getting fired. Watch the magic unfold as I pitch away and our nation's viewing tastes are evaluated.

Pitch Number One—Large Children's Cable Network

MY SHOW IDEA: LITTLE SISTER

PREMISE: Think of Big Brother, only with teenage girls. Fifteen of them live in a house for ten weeks, completely shut off from the outside world. Hidden cameras capture their every move. Each week, viewers get to vote one of the girls out of the house and off the show. But here's the twist: The only guy in the house is me, who gets to hang around with them and stuff. And there's also a lovable robot named Seth that does the dishes.

MEETING: Arrangements are made through my phony manager, Chandelle, to have me meet with development executives at three major TV networks. Posing as Taylor Spelling, I'm rumored to have a hot new sports show in development at the FX network, called *Monday Night Foosball*.

A few keys to the Hollywood network pitch meeting:

- Always accept the obligatory offer of bottled water. It puts you in a position of power.
- Compliment any piece of crap that particular network has currently put on the air. React like each project is the new Citizen Kane.
- Compare your show idea to other existing hit shows. For example, say it's a cross between *Celebrity Fit Club* and *Three and a Half Men*, or *CSI: Miami* meets *Saved by the Bell*.
- Be really enthusiastic. Recite your presentation like you've just been elected homecoming queen.

I'm in the sixteenth-floor waiting room of a large office building in the belly of L.A. Wearing a pathetically cheap suit, I look like a guy trying to get a reduced prison sentence. The associate development executive emerges in well-tailored Armani and wire-rimmed glasses. "Taylor?" he inquires.

"That's me."

We walk into his spacious office, making small talk.

"Is Amy coming too, or is it just you?" asks the short exec.

Amy?! I'm almost 110 percent positive my fake manager's name is Chandelle.

The head of development is sitting at a desk, awaiting our arrival. More small talk. More bottles of water are offered. Keeping hydrated is important in Hollywood.

"I don't know if my manager Chandelle filled you in on my background," I begin, then elaborate on my faux FX project. *"Monday Night Foosball* is a real macho, real competitive, and character-driven TV show," I state, demonstrating "the Claw," "the Spinner," and a few other of the main foosball villains.

"That's very cool!" states the short exec.

"So, are you a Spelling?" the head woman blurts.

"I'm a nephew," I shyly confess.

"You're a nephew of Aaron Spelling?"

I nod. "Yeah, but I don't really like to brag about it."

She thaws. We talk about my uncle's classic show, *Beverly Hills 90210*—especially the college years.

"Have you ever been on the show?" asks perky woman exec.

I tell her about the character named Chad, who I played on a few episodes, but mostly worked as the show's consultant.

"How do you consult on *90210*?" perky-woman exec inquires.

I restate her question, in order to stall for a quick response. "Giving my two cents. Like saying 'hey, bro' instead of 'what's up, dude'?"

We're laughing. We're hydrating. It's like we're long lost friends. Enough of this Sunday-cotillion crap, it's time to play television-pitching hardball. I get down to business. The whole mood of the room shifts.

"Reality television seldom focuses on a younger audience," I say. *"Big Brother* and *Survivor* are really adult shows. I want to try to get a younger demographic by featuring younger people on the show."

Both execs nod in agreement.

"My show is called *Little Sister*. We get the same sort of *Big Brother* compound, but with a bunch of teenage girls—and we film their every move." I pause for effect. "Their only contact to the outside world would be me," I conclude.

There's an awkward silence. The perky woman finally speaks: "How long do you keep them there?" I tell her most of the summer break. Then, pulling out a piece of crumpled notebook paper, I show them a scrawled diagram of the *Little Sister* compound, showcasing the areas where the girls will have the pillow fights, comb one another's hair, and exercise. I pass it around the room. Believe it or not, the network already has an actual show in development that's very similar to mine.

"Our show has parental chaperones and a bunch of physical challenges," the head of development explains.

"Yes, but does it involve a robot?" I interrupt. *"Little Sister* features a lovable robot! That would be a huge point of difference."

"No, but it has a rat," she says.

"A rat?"

"There are two teams. They stand in a circle. At the end of the day, they meet a rat. Whichever way the rat walks, that team has to decide on one person to leave."

I'm baffled. They already have a reality show, and it's way stupider than anything I could dream up. I leave.

Pitch Number Two—Cable Network with Great Office View

MY SHOW IDEA: ROBOTIC FRIENDS

PREMISE: Seven trendy friends live together in a New York City apartment. One of the friends is a lovable robot named Marty, who's really good at card tricks.

MEETING: It takes place in the conference room of a major cable network in Burbank. I'm sitting with a

lone well-dressed development executive, who has
mannerisms like an insect. There's more bottled
water. After my pitch, he pauses reflectively. "And
this robot lives with the other friends?"

I explain with grave seriousness. "Life is tough in the city, especially if you're a robot, but you have to stick to your friends
. . ." (Pause.) ". . . for guidance."

"Is this robot anything like the one from *Lost in Space?*" he
asks.

"Yes."

"Does this robot have a job?"

"He's just a robot. I don't think robots really need to get
money," I explain. "Robots are pretty self-sufficient."

The development exec takes off his glasses, gets up, and
walks to the window. "We're going for bigger, broader concepts
than that right now," he says, purposely avoiding eye contact.
"And we're targeting an older crowd. Your idea seems more
suited for the Cartoon Network or Nickelodeon than us."

I don't even shake his hand when I leave.

Pitch Number Three—A Network on a Large Studio Lot

MY SHOW IDEA: PLANET OF SURVIVAL
PREMISE: A cross between *Survivor* and *Planet of
the Apes.* Contestants are placed on a deserted island
and hunted down for sport by people in ape masks.
The last to remain on the island wins a million dollars
and the services of a lovable talking robot named Bret.
MEETING: I meet a woman in the lobby from a
production company. I tell her about my "property,"

Little Sister. "Let me give you my card," she says,
fumbling for her bag, "because that kind of show is
all we think about."

I'm networking.

The associate and senior development executives interrupt.
"Mr. Spelling?" they ask. I am escorted to a conference room. We
all sit around a table and drink water.

"Taylor is doing a show at FX," says one of the execs. I assume
he's the leader. "Yes, it's called *Monday Night Foosball.*"

"I think I heard about that," says the second in command.
"That sounds cool." (Wow! The buzz has already gotten out.)

"We're getting about a thousand foosball tables donated to
us," I boast.

"You're kidding," says the leader.

I give my pitch.

"My show is a cross between *Survivor* and *Planet of the
Apes.* These castaways are on a desert island. And each week
people in ape masks hunt them for sport."

When I finish, everyone looks at the big guy.

"What do the apes do after they capture you?" he asks.

"You're kicked off the island."

"Do you have anything written on that?"

"Yes, I'll have my manager, Chandelle, send it over."

"That would definitely be something I would like to see."

"That is hysterical," states the second in command, looking to
his leader for approval. "What do you call this?"

"Planet of Survival!"

"It's like Paintball with apes!" says the second in command. "I
like that."

"Very cool," agrees the leader. "I like that idea a lot."

"And you'd never know when the apes are going to come!" I say.

"That's interesting," he says.

"And the apes would steal things from the people," I add, making things up as I go along.

"That's very cool," says the second banana.

I move my chair in closer. "You'd not only be competing against one another, but you would also have to band together to ward off the apes."

"So we'd get a behind-the-scenes of the two teams," the leader says. "And we'd also see the behind-the-scenes of the people who put on the ape masks?"

"No!" I interrupt. "They wouldn't be putting on the ape masks—they would be characters. Like *Planet of the Apes*." "Oh, so we see them plotting and planning a little bit?" the leader says.

"Yeah, like in *Planet of the Apes*—we'd see the council."

"Like, who they're going to capture!" he says enthusiastically.

"Or which one they're going after," the second in command puts in his two cents.

"Or we're going to get the castaways' supply tent, or take away their raft which they been building," I continue off the top of my head.

"That's very fun," the second in command says enthusiastically. "You should certainly send something over."

"Do the contestants attack back?" the leader asks with a spark of delight in his eye.

"They can, but not maliciously," I reassure him. "They would plan things to counterattack them. They would have traps to build."

"Aaah!"

The bastards are hooked. On the homestretch, I up the ante. "I'd also like to add a lovable robot," I say.

"Maybe they can go to the robot to find out answers," suggests number two.

"Yeah, the robot is like the wise mentor," I explain, "providing them with answers on how to ward off the apes."

"That's neat. That's interesting," he says. "I'd like to see more of it."

"I'll have my manager Chandelle send over more material!"

Epilogue: When the pitch meetings were over, I had "Chandelle" do a follow-up call on my hot property, *Planet of Survival.* The executives claimed that they liked the show's concept. They said they were very interested in either buying the show or bringing me (Taylor Spelling) on as a consultant for another show. Panicked that I would actually have to produce this crap, I never called them back.

CHAPTER EIGHT

REALITY
TELEVISION SHOW
AMERICAN DREAM

**THE AMERICAN DREAM,
IN THEIR OWN WORDS**
Chip Pope, writer, producer, and star
of TV pilots for HBO, ABC, FOX,
Comedy Central, and NBC (who recently
killed their script. Yay!)

To be so ludicrously rich, I wipe my ass with an endless supply of filet mignon and caviar.

To hire domestic help who are white, with good backgrounds and capped teeth, blinding in their whitenicity. (That may not be a word.)

To have "fuck you" money that tells my "fuck you" money: "Fuck you!"

To have an Olympic-size swimming pool and never swim in it.

To send my kids to private school in Gstaad and never speak to them again.

To sleep with Hal Fishman. (Google him.)

To open a chain of low-fat, low-sugar, carb-free bakeries. That's right. Finally, no-carb carbohydrates.

To drink twenty-seven bottles of Smartwater per hour. I will soon be unstoppable in my intelligence. Perhaps even after the first day.

To own Runyon Canyon and allow people to take walks in it, if I'm feeling generous.

To be a celebrity disc jockey, periodically stopping hip-hop music to scream into a mic: "What's up, L.AAAAAAAAAAAA-AAAAAAAAAAA.?" at people on the dance floor.

To have a rare breed of dog no one else has, and when someone else discovers that breed, I will kill my dog. Passé dogs are straight useless, yo.

To own a soccer team to kick Robbie Williams's and Rod Stewart's teams' asses. Take that, England! You're on Santa Monica time now!

To have a weekly basketball game at Soleil Moon Frye's house.

To eat organic chocolate out of my KCRW pledge-drive tote bag as I waltz down Montana Avenue, looking to purchase a "cute top."

To own a sidewalk café that only seats three people. The three people dine while fifty people surround them, waiting for the table.

To lose my way, totally forgetting what I'm "all about."

To know that money solves all problems, and without it, you're merely just a big pile of shit. What are you doing? Why bother?

To keep drinking that Smartwater. I need to be disciplined about it.

To be Marg Helgenberger.

Stairway to Game Show Heaven!

Yes, what TV game shows love is a big over-the-top idiot jumping around, hugging complete strangers, all because they answered a stupid question correctly in an attempt to win brand new prizes! It's the quintessential American Dream (winning big cash prizes on TV), embracing all our country stands for: appearing on national TV, competitiveness, striving to be number one, going over-the-top while sacrificing all dignity, immediate financial gratification without the benefit of hard work, etc.

This seems to be the formulaic criteria by which game shows measure their contestants. So how hard can it be to get on one and let my American-Dream living begin? Fortunately, The Game Show Network (GSN) is a whole cable network dedicated to which of the following:

    a) Game shows

    b) Women's issues

    c) Hot rods

    d) Nineteenth-century radiation-theorist Madame Curie

If you picked A, then your answer is correct. (If you picked B, C, or D, you are incorrect).

When I call the contestant hotline (310–244–4000), there's an option to pick one of the six game shows that are currently being produced. Lightning quick, I push option number four for . . . *Whammy!* Why? Because I like the sound of it: . . . *Whammy!*

Hit Me with Your Whammy Stick!

On Friday night, at a studio on Sunset Boulevard, I'm in a room full of sixty people, who also quest the *Game Show American*

Dream, waiting to audition for *Whammy!* The space has the feel of a Hollywood casting session, crossed with a Greyhound bus-station waiting room. *Whammy!* is actually a reincarnated version of an eighties game show called *Press Your Luck*. Now it's back and hosted by a man by the name of Todd Newton. The deal is, you spin the *Whammy!* board, yell the catchphrase, "Big bucks! No Whammy!" and pray the little Whammy demon doesn't pop up and snatch all your prizes (Damn you, Whammy!), crushing your American Dream in a single, fleeting moment of televised humiliation.

On my Whammy questionnaire, I make sure not to fill in a single bit of true information. Jotting down my name as *Hank*, which of the following do I put as my occupation?

a) Part-time bounty hunter
b) Babysitter
c) Hand model
d) Quantitative physicist

The answer is A: Part-time bounty hunter. More lies follow:

Q: Tell the most interesting thing about yourself.

A: I'm related to CNN newscaster Wolf Blitzer.

Q: Briefly summarize an "incident" that happened at a family gathering.

A: You haven't lived until you've seen Wolf Blitzer in the family potato sack race!

"A main thing we look for in contestants is big personalities," explains Harv, the jolly contestant coordinator. "We want each of you to stand up, state your name and why you want to win big money on *Whammy!*"

We go through the entire group of sixty. I'm number fifty-four. The *name stating* and *big-bucks desiring* gets old roughly around number fourteen, though it does give insight into the demographics of the average game-show contestant and why this is their American Dream:

- "I want to win big bucks so I can pay my bills!"
- "I want to win big bucks so I can get out of debt!"
- "I want to win big bucks so I can pay my parking tickets."

After the tedious duration of these insights, we finally work our way around the room, reaching number fifty-four. Like Homo erectus rising from his cave with a newly evolved opposable thumb, I slowly stand and give the game-show machine what they want: big personality! Yes, I exude a *big personality*, while utilizing which of the following?

a) Screaming
b) Thrusting my arms repetitively in the air
c) Facial mugging
d) Screaming
e) All of the above

The answer is E, *all of the above*. Compare to other potential *Whammy!* contestants, who seem to want to avoid bankruptcy, my big-bucks plight might come across as mildly shallow:

"I want to win big bucks on *Whammy!* so I can buy a tuxedo and . . . *party!!!!*"

I then keep enthusiastically screaming the name of the game show ("*WHAMMY! WHAMMY! WHAMMY!*"), and throw in a few *woooo*'s for good measure, then high-fiving everyone within high-fiving distance. As can be expected, the game-show people eat it up. How could they not? Not only was I a *big personality*, but I was such at level 11! Part-time bounty hunter Hank makes it to the next audition round of . . . *Whammy!*

Those who didn't make it parade towards the exit. There's nothing sadder than dejected game-show contestants, who have to go back to their regular lives filled with mounting bills, getting out of debt, unpaid parking tickets, and no quick-and-easy solutions. But America is a land where the strong prevail. In groups of three, the survivors play a simulated round of *Whammy!* at which time I continue to work the entire room with my playing style of screaming all answers, high-fiving, and jumping when excited.

"Okay, if I call your name," announces Harv at the conclusion, "you're booked for this Tuesday's show."

I prepare myself to be one of their game-show chosen darlings, the inner circle, if you will. Names are called. More names are called. Disaster—Hank, the part-time bounty hunter's name, isn't on the list. Has my American Dream been rained upon?

Only eight people made the cut. Did I not jump high enough? Was my *big personality* too small!?

Greatly dejected, I go drown my sorrows in a big bowl of udon noodles and contemplate moving to Canada where they have an entirely different set of socialized game-show contestants who vie to win over four hundred in cash. But it was not yet my time to be Whammied out. When the last udon noodle is slurped, there's a phone message from Harv.

"Hank, you took off too soon," states an apologetic Harv. "I'd like to book you as a contestant on next Wednesday's show!"

Big-money-no-Whammy, here I come! Blazing with guns drawn, I'm ready to hit the American airwaves, whilst combining the perfect marriage between game-show contestant and professional wrestling, doing everything short of hitting the other contestants in the face with a metal folding chair.

Game Day

I report for game-show duty at 8:15, Wednesday morning. Around twenty of us, from various days of auditions, have made it to the next level; all have taken that step closer to game-show infamy and the American Dream. If this were the Tom Cruise movie *Top Gun*, we would be the elite, but cocky, squadron preparing for fighter-pilot battle.

Did You Know?

Did you know due to the game show scandals of the fifties, no one is allowed to bring a cell phone into the waiting area in fear they might use it to call an insider and get the answers for to-day's *Whammy!* questions? Also, you can actually go to jail—you know, *jail*—for cheating on a game show!

> "What are you in for?"
> "Murder!"
> "What are you in for?"
> "I cheated on Whammy!"

"Be ready to be called!" yells the perky contestant coordinator. With that preliminary battle warning, all women in the room simultaneously start putting on their makeup, though we learn that some of us might end up waiting around all day and not even make it on today's taping. (Damn you, Whammy!) Then, the *Whammy!* rules and strategies are explained. We're told to use the words *big bucks* and to specify exactly what we want to win from the large prize board. (Will there be a jetpack?)

Strategy dictates to pass spins to make the other players hit a Whammy and *lose* everything! If you hit a *Double Whammy*, something will be dropped on your head. (Will it be an anvil?) When this occurs, we're told to keep it on our head for comic effect. Whoever accumulates the most prizes and cash in the end, wins. (The others lose.)

Piping in after every comment is the obligatory loud "funny" guy among the contestant group, who has something "funny" to say after anything is said.

"I got a bottle of whiskey in the car I wish I could drink!" says the obligatory "funny" guy.

"You're too much," says his sidekick, who laughs at everything he says. The obligatory "funny" guy gets old fast.

Three people are called for their *Whammy!* tour of duty. Then another group. Relentless, the obligatory "funny" guy still tries to be "funny," but in a much louder voice. ("You're too much!") The lucky wheel then takes a spin, landing on my number.

"Can we have Hank, Kevin, and Jewell in the next group!"

"WHAMMY! WHAMMY! WHAMMY!" I scream, arms in the air, prepping myself to be beloved by America. "WHAMMY! WHAMMY! WHAMMY!"

Like astronauts in *The Right Stuff*, the three of us make our way towards the launching pad of game show-dom. With each step I'm just that much closer to my American Dream.

"WHAMMY! WHAMMY!"

Kevin and Jewell, two peppy, clean-cut contestants with smiles brimming up to their eyeballs, are filled with nervous energy, as we're greeted by Harv, who pooh-poohs the last group for being too low-key.

"Remember, big personalities!" stresses Harv. "A lot of energy!"

"YOU GOT IT, HARV!" I shout. "I WON'T LET YOU DOWN!"

A studio audience stirs restlessly waiting for our show to be taped. They get paid roughly thirty dollars to sit here all day and pretend to be really excited about *Whammy!* Before taking our places, for a psychological competitive edge, I unbutton my shirt, revealing underneath my ace in the hole; a T-shirt I had printed that says I'M # 1!

"You two are going down!" I tell Kevin and Jewell. Perhaps a bit sensitive, Jewell makes a sad face. "That's bad karma," she says, not getting the whole competitive, American Dream aspect of winning the game. Come on, this is no time for a tea party to make friends; this is Whammy-time! I should metaphorically want to crush Jewell's head into the metaphorical game-show set and *take no prisoners*! But I look over at her, and somehow I feel bad. My quest for the American Dream is raining on her American Dream, and her pursuit of happiness. I could easily alter my American Dream, not because she's cute, but because if I truly try to win, I'd be buying into the whole game show Americana ideology that pollutes our airwaves. Instead, why not make my American Dream to subvert the whole game machine from the inside, in the American tradition of such radicals as Abbie Hoffman (if he were on game shows). Yes, I'm going to lose, and I'm going to lose *big!* Oh, fair Jewell, I shall not diminish thy noble woman's pursuit of cash and thy fabulous prizes. Yes, my goal now is to be the worst contestant in the history of the game—that's now my American Dream!

We take our places on the podium and prepare ourselves to make game show history. Drawing spots, I'm third in the order.

"It's time to play *Whammy!*" bellows the announcer. The podium rotates. The *Whammy!* board lights up. The audience applauds. In turn, we address the camera.

"I'm Kevin, from Santa Barbara. I'm a Pilates instructor. And I want to win big bucks so I can go to Hawaii for my friend's wedding!" He enthusiastically claps as he speaks.

Audience applauds.

"I'm Jewell, from Boca Raton, Florida. I'm a student. And I want to win big bucks so I can buy a new couch!" For added effect she points to the camera.

More applause. My turn. I rotate towards the camera, bug-eyed, like someone just put something up my butt. I know how to play the crow.

"I'm Hank, from San Francisco. I'm a part-time bounty hunter. And I want to win big bucks so I can throw a party and YOU'RE ALL INVITED!"

The crowd goes wild. Instead of pointing to the camera, I point directly to my right and slightly up. For good measure, I throw in a few *woo*'s and pump my fist hard in the air. I find myself jumping.

"Let's get this game started by giving away a little money!" exclaims well-groomed host Todd Newton from his host-questioning area.

Round One

While the other players take their turn, I relax and lean on the podium, resting my hand on my head.

"Come on, big bucks, no Whammy!"

Pilates instructor Kevin hits the buzzer, trying to make the *Whammy!* board stop on big money or a prize, and accumulates hiking gear. Jewell (of Boca Raton, Florida) hits a Whammy right off the bat. (Poor Jewell.)

My turn. Underachieving, I root for the worst prizes, as I begin my dismantlement of the game-show machine. "Woo! Woo! Come on *robotic vacuum cleaner*, no Whammy! WOO! WOO!" I scream, devising a signature buzzer hit (circle my hand above, hit it, then snap my finger and point). Smashing my hand down with all my might (then snapping my fingers and pointing), the entire board freezes (I think I broke Whammy?).

"You don't have to hit it so hard!" stresses ornery Harv as the taping is stopped and a technician comes out to fix my buzzer.

"Does that mean I'm disqualified?" I ask with concern. Hell, no! Whammy is once again up and running.

"Woo! Woo! Come on, DVD player. I want to watch *Big Momma's House!*" I scream, taking another spin of the board, this time hitting my buzzer much lighter. Well, fuck me sideways; I land on *big money!*

"This question is worth three thousand dollars!" exclaims well-groomed host Todd Newton before reading off a card.

The question is probably going to be something tough, such as, "What is the half-life of uranium?" But it doesn't matter, being that I'm purposely going to blow it for Jewell's sake.

"In 1984, this singer and former Miss America was asked to give up her crown for posing nude."

Before I have time to throw the answer and yell, "Harry Potter!" I find myself screaming, "Vanessa Williams!"

"That's the correct answer!"

"Woo! Woo!" I find myself jumping again.

I've immediately taken a huge lead. That's not right.

"Are you going to spin or pass?" host Todd Newton asks.

"PASS! PASS!" screams the crowd.

Though I wanted to spin out in hopes of getting a Whammy, I hear myself screaming, "PASS!"

Kevin of Santa Barbara gets my turn. The poor little fella Double Whammies. He loses his hiking gear. (Damn you, Whammy!) For some reason, wads of fake hair drop on his head.

"That's the end of the first round, with Hank in the lead."

"WOO! WOO! WOO!" I shriek, red in the face, pointing to my I'm #1! shirt.

Well, fuck me sideways, I'm winning by three thousand dollars. Abbie Hoffman wouldn't allow that if he were on *Whammy!* This is going horribly wrong.

Harv comes over, looking like a pleased father. "This is going to be the show that will be used as an example for other contestants to follow!"

Coming back from the break, it's the "let's get to know the contestants" portion of the show.

"So Hank, you're a part-time bounty hunter," says the host.

"Well, Todd, lets put it this way: if you were a fugitive, I would know several ways to hogtie you and transport you across state lines!" I state. More "WOO! WOO!" More pumping of fists in the air.

"One question, Hank, if you throw a party, and everyone's invited, who's going to clean up?"

"I'm going to clean up! I'm going to clean up on *WHAMMY!*" Judging by the studio audience's reaction, I've clearly become the crowd favorite, proving that any part-time bounty hunter can be adored on a game show. *"WHAMMY! WHAMMY! WHAMMY!"*

Round two involves more questions of simpleton-like toughness, in an attempt to accumulate spins for the final round. A new style tactic for me: buzzing in and screaming the answer as loud as I can.

"Angelina Jolie starred as Laura Croft in the movie version of what video game?"

"*TOMB RAIDER*! IT'S *TOMB RAIDER*! *TOMB RAIDER*!"

Turning towards the audience, I raise my arms in the air. "IT'S PARTY TIME!" wondering why I didn't shout, "*BING CROSBY!*"

Small children wouldn't have trouble answering these questions correctly. Then it hits me; I just might win this game. Sure, I've decided to mock the entire social convention of game shows (and all it stands for), because I felt empathy for poor Jewell and her pursuit of a new couch, but there's a damn good chance I could truly go home with *big cash prizes!* (I really don't mind big cash prizes.)

Moving into the final round, part-time bounty hunter Hank is still violently ahead. Each of us must use up our spins and avoid the dreaded Whammy. Kevin (of Santa Barbara) comes out of the gates like a madman, and starts accumulating cash and prizes left and right. He Whammys once, but like a skilled prizefighter, shakes off the punch, gathering more cash, and passes three mandatory spins to me. I shake my fist at him for doing so.

Poor Jewell. It's obvious her American Dream of a new couch will not be realized. She gets two Whammys in a row. For some reason, dozens of letters drop on her head.

This is it. All I have to do is avoid the Whammy on my three mandatory spins.

The studio audience starts chanting my fake name (they're actually chanting!)

"Hank! Hank! Hank!"

I accumulate golf clubs, golf balls, and a few thousand more dollars in my bank (sadly, no robotic vacuum).

"Come on, big bucks. No Whammy!"

Boom! More cash.

"YES! YES! YES!"

The crowd is going wild. I'm going wild. I throw Jewell's let-ters in the air.

"Come on, big bucks. No Whammy!"

"Hank! Hank! Hank!"

Boom! I win a snowboard. This is too ridiculous. I'm not sup-posed to be winning on a nationally televised game show (air-ing on the Game Show Network).

"Okay, Hank, you have one last spin," reminds host Todd Newton.

"Come on, big bucks. No Whammy!"

"Hank! Hank! Hank!"

Like in slow motion, I close my eyes. The board spins. My hand hits the buzzer, and . . . and . . . and . . . CHILL-OUT ROOM! (Whatever the hell a chill-out room is.)

"OH, MY GOD! OH, MY GOD! OH, MY GOD!" I hear myself re-peating, finding myself truly excited as a schoolgirl winning a spelling bee. The crowd goes ape shit. I go ape shit.

"This is *sooooo* sweet!" I hear myself screaming, doing an im-provised samba.

My total winnings are over twelve thousand dollars in cash and prizes! This is fucking ridiculous. I truly am jumping around like an idiot. I truly am hugging the host! I truly am excited. But worse, I truly have bought into the whole game-show machine. I have achieved the American Dream. I have won on a game show. Hank the part-time bounty hunter is the grand-prize win-ner! It only took a few thousand dollars for me to totally sell out on national television (okay, cable television). And you know what? It's fucking sweet!

Blind Date, Lederhosen, and Me

Blind Date is the granddaddy of all reality dating shows. The concept is simple; two strangers go on a date filled with inane activities, accompanied by idiotic bubbles providing commentary on their potentially amorous adventure. Finding true love on television, while the audience watches, sounds like the American Dream!

Unfortunately, people don't tune in to see true romance, but to see people *fail* and/or look *stupid!* (And occasionally "get busy.") Reality dating shows aren't about true romance; they're about making *good television*, and it's agreed that I make good television. And making *good television* is the American Dream, that's why I must infiltrate the world of reality dating shows and get on television's *Blind Date*.

FIRST, SOME "REALITY" DATING PREPARATION:

- 1 thong Speedo (that displays ample butt crack)
- 1 unzipped blue track-suit top (with no shirt underneath, of course)
- 1 large, gold "bling-bling" dollar-sign chain
- 1 pair of really high-cut jean shorts
- 1 visor
- 1 pair of aviator sunglasses (to be worn at all times)
- 1 set of really cheap-looking rings, one for each finger

I'm dressed like an Armenian landlord. I vow to not tell a single piece of true information the entire date. I'll go by the name Hank Bartholomew III. Hank has trouble remembering the names of those he dates.

My Blind Date *Filming Day Is Set*

I head to the *Blind Date* production office in L.A. The place is bustling with a swarm of men filling out applications to be potential Blind Daters.

"I'm here to date!" I announce to the room, signing a waiver stating they have the right to air anything (and can make me seem as stupid as) they want. And if I happen to get naked (it could happen), they can show it unscrambled on the *Blind Date: Too Hot for TV* DVD. I sign Hank's name.

The casting director, an older-sister type, escorts me into a small room for my video interview in front of a large *Blind Date* logo.

"Don't hold back, I've heard it all," she says with a wry smile, and begins her onslaught of personal dating questions.

"What kind of women are you attracted to?" I'm asked.

"I like women with a big ol' J. Lo booty," I stress. "You know, something you can grip on to." I grip my hands, adding, *"Grrrrrrr!"*

"Do you want to date a wide variety of women?"

"Yes. Just as long as they have a big ol' J. Lo booty. You know, with something to grip on to. *Grrrrrrr!"*

"How do most of your dates go?"

"I would say, I end up having sex with 92 percent of the women I go out with. The other 8 percent usually ends with second base . . . *if not more!"* (Pause.) Especially if they have a big, ol' J. Lo booty!"

The casting director presses further, "What's your sexual turn-on?"

"I like to do it *German-style!"*

"What's *German-style*?" she asks. (I thought she's heard it all?)

"All I can say is, it makes you scream *achtung*!"

Then I throw in a few kickboxing maneuvers and once again state my affirmation for big ol' J. Lo booties (*Grrrrrrrr!*).

Two p.m.: My Date Begins

Did you know it takes two large SUVs to film a *Blind Date* date? Each day, several four-person crews film three different dates for syndicated immortality. Our SUV is fully rigged with cameras to capture all dating action as it unravels.

The rules of filming are explained as I vigorously nod my head. (It goes without saying, don't use the word *motherfucker* as an adjective.)

"Try not to talk about movies and music," says the field producer. "Don't make any reference to the show. Just let the cameras be a fly on the wall."

"A fly on the wall," I repeat.

"And try not to talk to each other when we're not filming."

The field producer expounds as we make our way to the future Mrs. Hank Bartholomew III's apartment, "The majority of people who come on *Blind Date* are wannabe actors. And not very good ones at that." He then goes on to tell a story about a girl from the previous week, who ended her date by peeing standing up.

"Where was she from?" I ask, thinking I might know her.

"From hell," adds the bitter PA (who tells sordid tales of couples breaking into the bone-dance while filming in the SUV).

We pull up to my blind date's apartment. She lives in what can best be described as "a Hollywood dump." (My blind date is poor!) The crew sets up their cameras.

For a suave first impression, I've brought a few gifts: a $6.99 jug of blush wine (creating the inconvenience of her carrying it all day), a fake flower arrangement, and a picture frame ($3.99) that says I LOVE YOU! (This might be a big claim, but I have a feeling we're going to really hit it off!) Inside the frame, I've inserted a picture of me with an ex-girlfriend. I've put a red X through her head.

My blind date is put into place, to film that all-important first impression. I march toward the building, jug of wine in hand, as the cameras roll. She has long, dark hair. She turns around, revealing that she has massive meat pillows . . . and is working it.

"Whoa! Look at you," I cry. "Woo!"

I present the jumbo jug of blush wine.

"This is for you. It's wine, from wine country!"

Though the container is three times larger than your average bottle of wine, my date is clearly not impressed.

"Oh, $6.99!" she snips, reading the price tag off the twist-off cap.

"Yes, that's the price," I clarify, handing her the fake flowers and the picture frame. "That's a picture of me. Disregard the fact that I'm with another girl."

There's a few beats of awkward silence, broken by her spouting, "Well, are you going to be a gentleman and carry this bottle of wine?" Damn, I hadn't thought about that.

We're already having classic, zany *Blind Date* tension (what will the crazy *Blind Date* bubble say about that?). I make my excuses and grab the jug.

"LET'S DATE!" I exclaim, following with, "Do you like pie?"

"Yes."

"What kind of pie do you like?"

"Apple."

Letting this sink in, I speak directly to the camera. "The date is already going really, really well," much to the annoyance of the field director, who once again explains the filming rules.

Here's a Task

The field producer makes me drive the camera-rigged SUV (through L.A. traffic), follow the other SUV, and charm my date—*all at the same time!* Several times I lose the van, and we have to stop filming as someone from the crew tells me to turn around.

I find out my date (I don't know her name yet) wants to be an actress (how surprising!) and works as a bartender. She, in turn, learns that I work as a motivational speaker who recently quit his job to pursue his dream of becoming a professional mime (studying in France under the master, Miou-Miou).

Then come the hard questions.

"Have you ever had to file a restraining order on any past boyfriends?"

"No."

"When was the last date you went on?"

"Two days ago," she perks. This upsets me.

"Oh, great! What's his name? *What's his name?!*"

"Josh."

"So this so-called Josh is my rival, huh?!" I spew with disgust, getting a bit possessive. My date (I still don't know her name) refuses to give me his phone number so I can call him right now.

"Do you want to see how fast I can drive this SUV?" I ask her, punching the accelerator. The camera crew seems nervous. "Do you think Josh could drive this fast? Huh?!"

Our First Zany Blind Date Activity

Not to knock the creative juices (and production budget) behind *Blind Date*, but our first big dating activity involves going to a park in Burbank and drinking from my large bottle of $6.99 blush wine.

"Okay, every time you drink, you have to tell a deep, dark secret about yourself," I suggest.

My date (I have now learned she is called Emma) takes a swig of blush, and then reveals, "Back in high school, I used to go dumpster diving." (That's *craaaazy!*)

We share a laugh. It's my turn. I take a big slug of white zin, then look off into the distance.

"I once gouged a man's eye out with my thumb!"

I immediately take another slug of wine. Game over.

More Zany Activities

Thank God we started drinking, because now I no longer have to drive the damn SUV; we get chauffeured around! I take time to swear a lot, so they'll have to bleep it out. And then comes the bragging. "I do competitive eating contests," I boast out of nowhere, as we sit in the back. "I can eat eight sticks of butter!"

We pull into a massage place in Burbank (I hate Burbank).

"Did you know [*Blind Date* host] Roger Lodge is only four foot nine?" I add. "He's a mere wisp of a man!"

The cameraman looks pissed.

"Okay, you guys were having great conversation, but we can't use it, because you started to *talk about the show*."

We go inside the massage place.

"I'm Peter, and the two of you will be getting massages today!" exclaims Peter, who will be giving us massages today.

I put down my large jug of vino and give Peter a big hug. He hugs back. I still hug Peter. He let's out a nervous laugh and lets go. I keep hugging him.

"This is Brenda," I say introducing my date.

"That's *Emma*."

"What-*ever!*"

In a room separated by a curtain, we get naked under individual sheets and prepare for side-by-side massages. I make sure a good portion of my butt crack is showing, so it will need to be scrambled out.

They pull open the curtain and the massages begin. I use the time to impress Emma (I now know her name) with my extreme intellect.

"I used to study philosophy in college." She's intrigued. She sees a new side to me.

"I mostly studied Manwellian Discourses. Are you familiar with the philosopher Manwell?"

"No, I'm not."

"The philosopher Manwell said, 'Those that can't, shall,'" I expound. "And those that shall, shan't!"

She takes this in. We grow silent. The silence is broken by me accidentally seeing date Emma's naked butt and telling her so.

"Well, that's the only time you're going to get to see it naked," she huffs in a you-go-girl fashion. (It's more zany *Blind Date* tension.)

Man, America's going to think she is such a bitch (while I'll come across as lovable).

Dress to Impress!

Did you know that a men's bathroom stall is what's used as the changing room for the "dress to impress" portion of *Blind Date.*

I brought along a pair of traditional German lederhosen and a mountaineering hat. They said "dress to impress," but did they specify *which* country (or era in history)?! I think I succeeded.

I pull up my knee-length socks and fasten the last few straps of my lederhosen while giving a hard look into the mirror. (I resemble one of the Von Trapp children from *Sound of Music*.)

The field producer has a problem with my lederhosen.

"Are you putting me on? I think you're just playing for the cameras."

"No, this is how I 'dress to impress,'" I explain. "I used to work for a German fashion designer in Struddlesburg, Germany. In fact, I designed these!"

He goes off to make a call and get lederhosen approval.

Just then, an old man in a cowboy hat comes into the bathroom. We stare at each other. Explaining is in order.

"Don't worry, this is all a part of a TV show," I say, realizing the two of us (man in cowboy hat, guy in lederhosen, standing by urinal) looks like a Village People video from another dimension. The producer comes back. Lederhosen: *approved!*

With cameras in place, I jump the gate in front of the restaurant, spring in front of my date like Peter Pan, making my big lederhosen entrance.

"*Mien Frau! Ich bin* hungry. Let us go dine!"

There's confusion.

"Why are you wearing lederhosen?"

"They're really comfortable!" I stress, showing my range of motion.

We're herded into a backroom of the restaurant (again, located in freakin' Burbank). As a stationary camera rolls, and I fully utilize the drink tab at *Blind Date*'s expense (it's fun to get drunk on television!) and get down to some serious dinner conversation.

"I'm not wearing anything under my lederhosen, you know," I proclaim as date Emma bites into her vegetarian taco salad. "Would Josh wear lederhosen for you?"

Sadly, she said he would. (I hate Josh.)

Suddenly, the tables turn. The waiter snickers, bringing out a plate containing many sticks of butter.

"Well, you said you could eat eight sticks of butter," snaps my blind date. "So, let's see you do it!"

I look down at the sticks of butter. She's called my bluff right here on national, syndicated late-night television! What can I do but jam an entire stick of butter into my mouth (then quickly spit it on the floor).

"I'm just warming up!"

I jam another whole stick of butter in my mouth and start talking politics.

"*MMMmmmmmm!*"

"Do you ever get out in public?" she sneers, as I spit that stick of butter on the carpet, as well.

"There's a serious side to me, too," I try explaining, my face caked in butter.

"Oh, yeah? Well, then let's see it!"

I clear my throat. I look into her eyes. My expression changes.

> *I never struck before that hour,*
> *With love, so sudden and sweet!*
> *Her face, it bloomed like a sweet flower,*
> *And stole my heart complete!*

Date Emma's complete demeanor changes. For the first time on this whole entire date, she sees a serious side to Hank Bartholomew III.

She's truly surprised.

"That was really sweet. Really, really sweet."

She grabs my hand. We hold our gaze. Then I jam another whole stick of butter in my mouth.

The Cowboy Crowd

It's a goddamn cowboy bar! A country band will be playing soon. Before they do, my blind date has become my muse. I jump onstage and grab one of the mics.

"Ladies and gentlemen, I am here from syndicated television's *Blind Date*," I explain, trying to pimp some applause. The redneck crowd mildly responds. "I'd like to take this opportunity to sing a very special song I wrote in honor of my date."

Again, more light applause. The cameras roll. I clear my throat. Date Emma looks up with admiration. I hold the mic very close to my mouth. I start loudly screaming her name over and over again, like I'm in horrific pain.

"EMMA! EMMA! EMMA! EMMA!"

Confusion, then anger spreads across the crowd.

"EMMA! EMMA! EMMA! EMMA!"

I keep doing this until, I shit you not, the PA system blows out. It's on late-night television if you don't believe me.

Sadly, Our Date Is Over by Ten pm

Now what would being on *Blind Date* be without securing the good night kiss at the door (accompanied by a crazy bubble summing up our entire dating experience)? Even though I've mentally tormented this poor woman the entire evening, I still bet I can turn the tables (for the sake of good TV).

"I had a really good time, blah, blah, blah, etc. . . ."

Victory is mine! We share a close-mouthed kiss for the entire *five-second duration.* (In your face, Josh!) Then I pipe up for better TV.

"I have a confession to make. I'm not really a millionaire with a yacht."

Before she can respond, I lick her face and run away. The camera follows me for the famous postdate solo shot. (What *will* the stupid bubble say?).

Suddenly, dozens of little Latino children come running out of nowhere; we're surrounded. We have become minor celebrities of the entire cul-de-sac.

"They're on *Blind Date!* They're on *Blind Date!* Are you going to marry her? Are you going to marry her?!"

Because of the fanfare, we have to move to a different neighborhood for our one-on-one with the camera, and most important, sharing with the *Blind Date* viewing audience whether there'll be *a second date!*

"Hank was a lot of fun! Yes, I would definitely go out with him again!" my date tells the camera.

It's my turn. The camera rolls.

"I'd rather be hit in the back of the head with a *shovel* than go out with her again!"

Whether it's true or not, it makes for good TV, and good TV is the American Dream!

CHAPTER NINE

MARIJUANA AMERICAN DREAM

THE AMERICAN DREAM:
IN THEIR OWN WORDS
Ed Rosenthal, author and marijuana
activist, who was arrested in 2002 for
growing medical marijuana, and in a
landmark case, served one day in prison

If I weren't a political person, I would be living the American Dream in many ways. I live in a spacious house; I have a great office; I write what I want; I take time off; I have health insurance; I'm happily married; I have two healthy kids; and yet I'm probably one of the people who is saying the most that this isn't it!

The propaganda that the government and the corporations have fostered about the American Dream has changed over the years, but really it's a false one. It's based on wealth and convenience and not on meaning of life. To me, the American Dream would be a 180-degree reversal of policy. It starts off at home, that people should be treated equally, and extends to our foreign policy and how we interact with the world. I see the American Dream as a more equal distribution of the wealth and total change in American foreign policy, so we act as a member of the world, not the ruler of it.

I see the whole issue of marijuana as one of a group of progressive issues, in the same way as environmentalism or equality or civil rights or human rights.

I think it's really un-American to tell farmers what plants they can or can't grow. They do that not only with hemp but with different farm restrictions. I think farmers should be able to grow what they want to grow. You really need an authoritarian mindset to tell a farmer what they need to grow.

Marijuana growers in Northern California think they are living their American Dream; I think it's going to come crashing down. Society has taken some of those people, who in other circumstances would probably be living a more urban life or a more social life, and forced them for the pursuit of happiness to go into a more remote area where the government has not as much authority. If what they were doing wasn't illegal or persecuted as much, they might actually choose to live a different life—they are forced into that life. Society has forced them to that extreme. It's not their fault. They didn't do anything wrong. That lifestyle may very well work for them, but society created this problem that they had to find a solution. In order to find their freedoms they had to go to a remote area and live on the fringes.

I wouldn't be the first writer to say the American Dream is an illusion. Will we ever reach it or get near it? We thought we had it. Was that really the Dream, when people look back to the fifties and say that was the American Dream?

In the early eighties a group of Russians came over to the United States. As they were leaving they made these remarks: "It's remarkable, because in order to keep order in the Soviet Union we need the KGB and all these harsh things, in order for people to think alike. And here in the United States, you do it without any of that! How do you do it?" So the Dream that most people think they're living, and I'm not putting people down, but they've been so propagandized that they are living in a fog.

Permanent 4:20

The low hum of the fan reverberates throughout the drying room. Like Norwegian smoked fish, freshly cut stalks drip in abundance from wire, segregated by different strains. Trainwreck hangs everywhere. The confined space is thick with a distinct sweet smell.

"If you do what I say, you'll have more money than you ever had before," the supervisor says to Jake, providing some motherly business advice.

"I'm asking for 30 percent," Jake replies. His serious entrepreneur expression suggests that one day, all this could be his.

"Mad props to you, Jake! You get so fucked up and still get the work done. I'm so proud of you!"

"I did ten hits of acid today and finished off my gallon bottle of rum!" Jake boasts on obstacles overcome to fulfill his work ethic.

Jake loves weed so much he chooses to sleep in the drying room, where he dozes off dreaming of nothing but big, tasty buds.

Marijuana, also known as cannabis (as well as chronic, ganja, gage, bammy, grata, moocah, grifa, Baby bhang, Juan Valdez, etc.) is embedded in our nation's history. The American Historical Reference Society notes that seven of our early presidents were potheads (although not exactly in those words). Their list includes such notary statesman as Washington, Jefferson, Madison, and Monroe! Jefferson smuggled Chinese hemp seeds to America. Washington wrote in his diary that he occasionally savored a nice pipe packed with "the leaves of hemp." Bill Clinton, famously, smoked pot but didn't inhale.

Mexicans and black jazz musicians can be attributed for the illegality of marijuana that swept the country in the early twentieth century, which prior to that time was legal, and in fact sold in shops as an over-the-counter pain reliever (the 1893 World's Columbian Exposition in Chicago included a Turkish booth complete with hashish smoking).

Antidrug campaigners claimed that terrible crimes were a result of Mexicans who used marijuana, while newspapers, especially those run by William Randolph Hearst, in 1934 sensationally editorialized: "Marihuana influences Negroes to look at white people in the eye, step on white men's shadows, and look at a white woman twice!" That's right, marijuana is as American as baseball, apple pie, and racism!

So what can be more American than working on a large pot farm? The man-child fantasy of anyone who has ever looked forward to 4:20 (mythically referring to either a police code for a marijuana bust, or the preferred time for high school kids to meet and light up).

I'll be like a little stoned kid running through a candy shop— with a big case of the munchies. Yes, I'm going to venture off the grid of normal nine to five society, duck beneath the law, not to mention stick it to "the Man," while I live the American Dream!

The Search Begins

I discover early on that it's not exactly easy to find a pot farm to infiltrate. (Maybe because it's kinda illegal?) I had one weed-enhanced locale all lined up in Sebastopol. Except on the night before leaving for my marijuana tour-of-duty I get an e-mail from the grower saying with bitter irony:

> Some losers came last week and stole all my plants . . .
> called themselves the DEA . . . stupid name if you ask
> me . . . bummer . . . oh, well.

Damn, only a mere day prevented me from witnessing the Man bringing down the Marijuana American Dream. Since it's already November and the end of harvest season is rapidly approaching, expedient action is required on my part. I need a plan B.

Fortuna takes a lucky spin. The next weekend, at your typical drug-fueled Burning Man party, I meet a completely insane woman adorned in a tutu. Better yet, she has connections to a grower in Mendocino County who runs a very large pot farm. It gets better. She refers to the man as Papa Smurf. A Hollywood screenwriter couldn't concoct a better name for an old hippie dude running a northern California pot farm. I imagine Papa Smurf like Marlon Brando in *Apocalypse Now*. Except Papa Smurf wears a big Dr. Suess hat and smokes the largest bong known to humanity while spouting, "I watched a snail crawl along the edge of a straight razor. That's my dream. That's my nightmare. Crawling, slithering, along the edge of a straight . . . razor . . . and surviving."

As bad techno blares, the crazy tutu-clad woman says I could meet her at a to-be-announced location up north near the town of Willits, and then follow her to the secret weed-growing destination. She then goes back to dispensing droplets of mysterious liquid on random people's tongues. I quickly determine that this woman would be the ideal female I would never want to marry. Regardless, my American Dream awaits!

Into the Land of the Green

Like Wisconsin is to cheese, northern California is to marijuana. The Emerald Triangle is comprised of three counties, Mendocino, Humboldt, and Sonoma, encompassing the region that grows the best bud on the planet (surpassing runners-up British Columbia and Amsterdam), home also to the Emerald Cup Cannabis Awards.

In order to fit in I decided to adopt the adequate pot-farm persona:

PERSONA: Burnt-out hippie, Harmony
DISGUISE: Hemp clothes, tied dyed shirt, overalls.
Posing as a smelly hippie, no deodorant needed for this trip.
DIETARY HABITS: Strict vegan who finds it ethically wrong to eat animal crackers.

It's still been a chore getting to this point. Several days running I kept calling my tutu-wearing pot-farm connection, ready to depart. Either she'd return my calls at four A.M., or I'd get the response, "Whoa, was today the day we were supposed to go?!" (I guess aspects of flakiness have to be weighed into the equation within the weed community.)

Finally, with much diligence, I set sail, entering the type of backwoods northern California territory where you stop at gas stations and drifters with backpacks approach and ask, "Are you going north?" Either they want a ride or want to bury you in a shallow grave out near the redwoods. Like brave Ulysses, I block out their roadside siren songs and avoid crashing into the rocks (or shallow grave). I drive on.

Lumber trucks haul newly cut remnants of massive, ancient trees. Old men in plaid who drive pickups gather outside the local store. Off the main highway, near Laytonville, I veer onto a gravel road leading into the thick woods, trying to keep up with crazy woman's truck now dangerously speeding ahead of me. Traversing up a hill, past a giant multicolored-lightbulb peace sign, we swerve off to an even more remote gravel road, twisting down the mountainside, deeper into the foliage—hidden farther from civilization. We round a sharp turn near a water tank: scattered in the woods are several tents, random vehicles, and faint human activity obstructed by the massive trees. I've reached my marijuana Shangri-La.

This a rare occasion where my dreadlocks will assist in being undercover. Parking behind an RV with a dolphin painted on the back window, I wonder if this will be the last time I see my vehicle before the DEA sweeps in as part of "the big raid."

My connection gets out of her car, with pot stems stuck all over her back from the drive, and immediately says, "I'm going to leave you here and go work on another farm."

(Pause.) "Okay." I'm confused; she'll be living her American Dream elsewhere.

I'm led down a dirt path, past an old trailer covered in a blue tarp, where trash and empty beer bottles spill out of garbage bags, along with junk and old stove piping. Numerous peacocks roam the grounds almost acting as watchdogs, as we navigate towards a newly built wood-framed structure covered with Tyvek HomeWrap. A group of workers perched on the porch next to an obligatory hippie drum seem to be product testing.

"Tell Sheryl she's a little thief," snaps a skinny guy named Zeke, eyes bugged out of his emaciated skull and shirt pulled over his head to block the sun, upon our arrival to my connection. "She said she trimmed two pounds, and her bags were empty!"

My connection produces several paper packets filled with an unknown substance. A quick, whispered discussion is conducted with Zeke. Money is exchanged. Others follow suit. When all the packets are gone, my connection takes off again in her car, leaving me, on my own, in the woods . . . with reefer addicts!! Is this the beginning to the sequel of *The Wicker Man?* Will I soon be sacrificed to some pagan god while Zeke dances around naked wearing an animal head?

"Anyone up for Hacky Sack?" I declare to the room in order to show some communal bonding after I'm dropped off by my connection to play in their marijuana sandbox.

The majority of the weed is drying today, so there's not much trimming going on. Zeke informs, as we enter the makeshift structure.

Roughly two dozen young, transient hippie workers are in the midst of various forms of weed production. Hairy-armpitted girls abound. More dreadlocks than a Bob Marley tribute concert. A bearded, shaggy-haired guy, who looks like the Dude from *The Big Lebowski,* paces the room, wearing a bathrobe, shorts, sandals with socks, and smoking from a pipe constructed out of a Gatorade bottle.

"For two weeks up here we had no weed to smoke," Zeke laughs. "That's the irony. People would say, 'But look at all these plants, all this weed.' Yeah, but they're not ready to harvest!"

All I see is a shitload of weed. Buds and stems litter the wooden floor. Full brown-paper grocery bags labeled STRAW-BERRY COUGH. Large coolers filled to capacity with fresh-cut marijuana are stacked everywhere, emitting that strong, pungent, sweet weed smell that permeates the air in the sparsely furnished room.

"Three weeks ago this building was filled to the roof with weed hanging from the rafters for trimming," Zeke adds. Rachel, a smiling woman with a matronly shape, who acts as the den mother of marijuana, picks up some cut greenage from a trimmer's tray. "There's monetary value in the leafy stuff. There's small buds, and you can make bubble hash," she explains, providing some motherly marijuana advice on pruning the buds with scissors in order to get them into salable shape. "It takes twice as long to trim undercarriage, and you make half as much!"

True. Trimmers are paid by weight; most average about a pound a day and net two hundred dollars. (A pound of Mendocino weed fills almost an entire large turkey bag, and sells for roughly $2,500 to $3,700.)

Mendo Blendo is the umbrella name for all the weed strains that grow here. Trainwreck is the most popular. Strawberry Cough is really trendy this year. Like mainstream product placement, when a gangsta rapper sings about a specific strain of weed, say Diesel or Purple Coochie, that will drive up market prices. Same if it wins the prestigious High Times Cup. Pot nerds sit around like wine snobs, focusing almost all their conversations around, well, pot. ("Sensimilla is the best weed." "The kona strains are sooooo good.") They reference weed-growing books by title and author. Names of various strains (Melti Cola, Silver Haze, Afghan Rootaraliss, Septiva, X-Mas

Tree, etc.) are recited with ease. As always, the purple strains still stand strong in popularity.

"We got hippies coming through here all season," smirks Rachel.

"Some guys have been up here for six months."

"Like who?" I ask.

"Zeke."

"I've been here since February," he smiles (looking like he's been awake that long as well).

Zeke leases land from Papa Smurf, rather than just throwing up a greenhouse, like the naïve fools busted by the DEA in Sebastopol (who perhaps needed to fill a yearly quota of busts, and new farms are the first to go). The best way to work your way into the grower community is by proving yourself. "People look at all the bud and think you make hella lot of money," Zeke says. "You're paying for everything, trimmers, equipment, lights. You're paying for the lifestyle!" he clarifies. "It's the freedom and to live off the grid. This is what I got to work towards!"

Rachel, a former chemistry major grew up with Zeke in Portland and came out when he asked her to help out. She confesses, "We scrape by the rest of the year!" Regardless, she still has her rent back home paid for the next two months while living in a tent free of charge on the Papa Smurf homestead.

Zeke, on the other hand, owns a house in Sebastopol and is looking to buy some winter property in Mexico. "I have some business there," he confirms with a smirk. Zeke hires people to live their American Dream. "You got to support your family," he says, regarding the transient trimmers, who've come from such far-reaching places as Israel, England, and South Africa, usually meeting someone at a party who hooks them up. (That's what I did!) Apparently, though, my pot connection wasn't well received.

"She's the only one who's been asked to leave," Rachel states, eyeing me with mellow suspicion. (I'm associated with the only person asked to leave!) During her reign of terror, my connection freaked out and started bossing people around while erratically screaming, "You're not giving me enough attention as a person!" much in the same manner someone would scream, "The bees! The bees! Get the bees off me!" when no bees are present.

"That's not the way it works," Rachel makes clear. "We're trying to be like family here. You got to adjust to many vibes. One person can throw it off!"

"How did she start working here?"

"She gave Zeke a blowjob."

Nodding his skinny, bugged-eye head, Zeke confirms this information.

"Eeeew!" I say to myself. (Thankfully, that's not how I got the job!)

The sun shines down. The clouds part. The marijuana smoke momentarily clears. It's him! Situated in the room's center, a gray-haired old hippie dude with an ultrarelaxed demeanor and obligatory sandals with socks reclines in a chair tallying figures in a notebook. There besets the mythical and legendary Papa Smurf. Though not spouting the "The Horror! The Horror!" he's in the midst of holding stoner court. Instead he spouts, "The cops are just soldiers of the State. Think about it!"

I think about it. Then, kissing up to Papa Smurf, I interject, "Bush and Hitler—same shit, different asshole!" (Pause.) "Think about it!"

A conformist old-school handshake is offered to "the new guy." In turn, I pull Papa Smurf in for a big, drawn-out hug ("Come here, you!")—complete with back patting.

"This is a Kona cross," Papa Smurf says like a proud parent, holding up a large, dried, stinky bud from an enormous filled bag, "I've been cultivating this strain for twenty-three years!" As if it were a fine Beaujolais, he points out the characteristics. "See how it's woven with dashes of purple and emits a strong, sweet smell."

"It smells like sticking it to the Man!" I exclaim, to show my loathing of authority. (Cool-guy handshaking follows.)

Due to our shared animosity toward the Man, Papa Smurf has me follow at his heel for his morning inspection. First the greenhouse. My eyes widen. Inside are roughly twenty-eight to thirty marijuana plants.

Some hover around eleven feet high, practically touching the greenhouse's plastic roof, and weigh in at roughly two hundred pounds. I have a strong desire to pop out from behind stalks and tell corny jokes, like a stoner version of *Hee Haw*.

Papa Smurf eyes his abundant vegetation. "There's a culture war between the remaining loggers and values," he says. Since the logging industry is dying, local redneck loggers have now taken to raising a few pot plants to make extra money. "But it doesn't reflect their inner spiritual understanding," Mr. Smurf adds, with his Zen outlook on mass cannabis production. "Even law enforcement has a schizophrenic view about it," he insists. "They don't think growing marijuana is the most pertinent thing in their lives."

Johnny Law could crack down on pot production in Mendocino, but it would financially ruin the local economy. The government also looks the other way in order to keep the wealth level booming in northern California, fueled by agriculture, wine, and weed—fostering the true American way! In 2004, raw timber brought an income of $66.6 million, wine grapes brought in $60.1 million, while marijuana in Mendocino bought in $1.5 billion.

"It's not just a truce, but there is openness and coexistence. Because it's productive, it creates jobs and hard workers. This area focuses more on the law and integration, than confrontation."

Papa Smurf lives his American Dream.

It has always been a smooth, hemp-hued road during his twenty-five years as a grower at this locale. In 1998, Papa Smurf was busted for having 837 pot plants. For the copious amount of cannabis, he spent a grand total of one night in jail and was sentenced to sixty days of community service. (You get more jail time in NYC for smoking one joint.) "The county's concern was money," Papa Smurf explains. "They didn't want to put me in jail because they didn't want to spend California money."

Some local county supervisors see the war on marijuana as lost and think it's time to legalize, regulate, and tax the multibillion-dollar illicit crop. The most severe action taken on a local grower was three years' prison sentence, "He didn't keep a secure place," Papa Smurf reasons.

With a license, now you can legally grow twenty-five plants, which yield ten to twelve pounds, to sell to medical-marijuana clubs. (Though he has a license, Papa Smurf still sells to the highest bidder willing to fork over hard cash.)

"In Humboldt the culture war is more obvious," relays Papa Smurf. More money is spent by the DEA to crack down on growers, and because of it, Humboldt growers are generally much scarier dudes, compared to the mellow Mendocino hippie vibe.

DEA busts are more frequent; in turn, growers often come heavily armed. (I can't see Papa Smurf—or anyone named Papa Smurf—brandishing an AK47.) Growing weed is a multibillion-dollar cash-crop business that works primarily under the radar. It brings in more money than milk farming (with a lot less cow shit to deal with)—so don't fuck with them!

Pointing to his house, which looks haphazardly thrown together like the whole operation could be moved in a second's notice, Papa Smurf shares, "I lived in a teepee, I lived in a tent, and now I live in this cardboard box."

"Who is the Man to tell us where to live!" I add with passion.

Inside, additional garbage lies in heaps. Stacked dirty dishes. Everywhere large bins of trimmed weed are piled up. It's like for two decades someone's had a really big stoner roommate (which is the case). Papa Smurf raised two children in this abode, who are now in their twenties. "They're conservative, cuz their values are based on Judeo-Christian values." Not sure what that means, I nod my head.

Papa Smurf reasons that being raised around weed growing causes one to be a self-starter: his daughter created her own clothing label (more sandals with socks?). "It's all about taking charge of your life," Papa Smurf summarizes about the pot farm vocation. "It's to say, 'This is what I want in my life, and you know, Mr. Corporate America, you can't provide it!'"

"Fuck Corporate America!" I state, looking at his garbage-filled house in the woods. (Hug-instigating commences.)

Papa Smurf stops in his tracks among the bins of trimmed weed, forgetting why we came to his house in the first place. "Let's try the circuit one more time," he says trying to jog his memory. We double back.

Let's Work!

Zeke is slumped on the couch, with body constructed like he was just hit by a truck. Zeke shares, "I was projectile vomiting last night." Zeke adds, "I did some coke." Zeke elaborates, "I think I got sick because I used to do a lot of crack."

Head nodding on my part. As much food production is going on (sandwiches, etc.) as weed trimming, punctuated by quiet moments when all you hear is chewing. Frequently, someone throws out the question, "Does anyone have a lighter?" which is followed by a discussion of lighters, followed by the sound of lighters clicking, followed by the sound of coughing spasms. Some follow the progression by lumbering like a zombie outside to loudly spit.

I sit next to Brian. He works a day job in Santa Rosa printing T-shirts, and deejays on the weekends. Meticulously, Brian trims in silence like a Soviet-bloc factory worker doing the job for the Motherland.

Snipitty-snip-snip.

While we work, hippie music plays (surprisingly, mostly songs about weed). My clothes and hair smell of pungent herb. Bob Marley has to come into the music mix at some point—and he does!

"Does this ever get monotonous?" I throw out to the group.

"Not when I get paid," replies a Russian girl clad in a stocking cap.

Brian speaks for the first time. "I close my eyes at night and still see buds." He then falls silent.

"I did a hit of ecstasy yesterday just to keep me awake," Rachel contributes.

"Sometimes it helps if you get really good and blazed first," recommends Russian girl. (True, this is work only a stoner would enjoy.) "It's like a quilting circle," she adds.

Snipitty-snip-snip.

Counting roughly thirty 20-gallon tubs filled with untrimmed weed, I pull huge, baby-arm-size buds of Trainwreck from a grocery bag on the floor. I'm getting a green thumb—literally. The surgical glove on my left hand is caked with green residue; my fingers stink. Stems and pieces of small buds are stuck to my clothes, behind my ears, in my hair, enough to make a drug-sniffing dog froth at the mouth and vigorously hump my leg.

Unafraid to mask her true body odor, crossed between BO and weed, Russian girl comes over to evaluate my trimming. "With the Trainwreck, you should really shave it," she instructs. "It's the heaviest of all buds, so it will work out for you when you weigh it." She hands me a more efficient pair of trimming scissors. "Here, try these. They're spring-loaded."

"What's the policy on smoking while working?" I ask (not for self-indulgence, but for the pursuit of journalistic excellence).

"You can smoke the little pieces."

Journalistic excellence is pursued!

Snipitty-snip-snip.

People come in out of breath from walking up the hill carrying more containers of dried weed to be trimmed. A group of glaze-eyed guys from Los Angeles show up, wanting to get paid by Papa Smurf. Jovial at first, they end up leaving with stoned, unhappy faces.

"I guess everyone is bummed out about the weight of their trim," Rachel concludes. "I even caught them cutting off the tops and putting them in bags!" (I hope, no retaliation.)

More women criticize my trimming (but in a nonconfrontational way, not to "harsh my mellow").

"Clean it up, so it has a little more form and a nice, consistent shape. Make it look like weed you'd want to buy."

I look at her and respond, "I'm high!"

She picks up a bud. "Can you make this tighter?"

(Pause.) "I'm really high!"

Twenty minutes into trimming, I quickly determine that trimming pot is a completely mindless activity. If this were totally legal, sanctioned by the government, I'm sure this work would pay roughly seven dollars per hour. (Good thing it's not legal.) Instead, there's talk of legendary trimming masters who have netted up to five hundred dollars in a day.

Russian girl shares, "You can make the same kind of money or better as you would a job where you need an education or work nine to five." Comparing herself to her mom (who is educated and works nine to five), she follows a similar credo as strippers:"The money is just so good." Russian girl is being paid in weed instead of cash, "In order to show what I got," so she can sell, yielding even more money than her educated mom.

"Stupid educated mom!" I contribute.

"There's a whole generation of kids raised in the culture," Rachel shares, as the trimming drags on, mentioning from experience how the psychological stress of growing up outside the law warps their relationship with drugs and money. "Their value system is different. They always have so much and don't have the checks and balances of someone working at Burger King for eight dollars per hour." Instead of flipping burgers, they can simply go to music festivals every weekend and make a living selling their wares.

"I'm going to Santa Barbara next week. It's going to be for both business and pleasure!" remarks Jake, whose T-shirt says AMSTERDAM. Taking a break from trimming to fill his pipe with a nug of weed from his tray, he also opts to be paid in buds in order to sell to rich college kids for a healthy profit.

"I sold to the High Times guy," Zeke interjects, adding with a sense of minor pot-celebrity pride, "He wrote about how good the Super Silver Haze is in Sebastopol."

You know when you buy weed and feel obligated to hang out with the dealer afterwards, stuck hearing about their band or life philosophy? This is a whole room full of those guys! These are the weed dealers who'll go back to their respective communities to enrich them with northern Cali's finest ganja.

"A hockey bag can fit seventy to one hundred pounds of weed," Zeke says, regarding the magnitude of a recent transaction of B-grade British Columbia weed. The only drawback: "You're working with a syndicate when you deal with B.C. weed. The industry up there is run by the Vietnamese mob."

"Zeke will sell to the biggest gangsta thugs in San Francisco," throws out the Dude, now cooking and oblivious that he's splattering food on his bathrobe. "He'll sell to the kind of guys who, when you walk in, you can see the guns in the room!"

"I got homies in the Mission and homies in the Fillmore," Zeke boastfully confirms.

Somehow, I get the feeling that one day Zeke might end up in a wood chipper.

Once, the Dude tried to sell twenty-one pounds of Trainwreck in town to a guy—a big guy (if in a motorcycle gang, maybe he'd be nicknamed Tiny). He took the Dude's megabag of marijuana, looked him dead in the eye, and snarled, "What are you going to do about it!" The guy walked away with free weed. "He knows you can't call the cops." (Pause.) "For every ten to twenty pounds you sell, you are going to lose a pound or two!" The Dude clarifies, "It's not that it's illegal. It's theft. You don't have any legal system to fall back on."

"I lost sixty pounds one year, and I trusted the guy," Zeke confirms, referring to a guy who lied about having a large potential sale, then split town. Speaking from experience, Rachel professes, "The people you think you can trust the most will fuck you over the hardest!"

I assure her by saying, "If it helps matters any, I'm someone you can't trust!"

Suddenly, we're interrupted by a short, shirtless guy who comes storming in from outside. With a wild look in his eye, he frantically huffs and puffs like someone who just ran a 10k. Collapsing into a chair, he tilts his head up toward the ceiling and doesn't move. His huffing stops (so does his puffing). A few concerned people momentarily put down their pipes and trimming equipment to investigate the situation.

"Waco! Waco!" cries the Dude, shaking him. (I guess his name is Waco.) "Waco! Waco!"

Is Waco dead? Will Waco ever get up again?

The Dude explains, "Waco just did four hits of ecstasy." Eyes still closed, Waco suddenly mumbles, "It tastes just like Nutra-Sweet." (So that's what was in the paper packets.)

Hilarious story about Waco: on the way to a music festival in L.A., Waco rolled a UHaul trailer filled with nitrous oxide tanks, which were to be sold to festival-goers by the balloonful.

"Funny he was the driver. He's on probation in Nevada!"

(Laughs.)

"I'm glad I wasn't driving, I always have acid on me!"

(Laughs.)

"I was doing ecstasy for a while, cuz it makes the acid trip seem pretty awesome."

(Laughs.)

"It tastes just like NutraSweet," once again Waco mumbles.

Everyone lets out an "Oh, Waco!" laugh and a sigh of relief. Pot trimming and weed smoking is resumed. More silence. More sounds of lighters. More food loudly being chewed.

I'm no nuclear scientist. But I'm starting to get the feeling that people who work on pot farms really, really, really like drugs. They've found their nirvana; they've found their American Dream. Could it be more ideal?

A Growers School

Two guys work vigorously by their tent like a pair of entrepreneurial machines of bubble-hash production. They're fixated on the task at hand, and their concentration is unbroken. A lanky kid, with a suburban-shopping-mall white-gangsta vibe, dips a large bagful of stems and leaves ("shake," if you will) into a bucket of water.

"You got to wash it down and get the green out with constant rinsing," he explains, like a farmer producing a superior lima bean—that gets you really high! The gangsta kid gestures wildly with his hands, clarifying that a fifty-pound bag should be used for mass hash production. More water is drained from the bags into the buckets. His partner in bubble-hash-production crime—a guy with long dreads and a Jamaican-flag tattoo—utilizes a power drill to mix a bucket of the dark green substance. "You don't want any leaf. The bag will get fewer plants and keep all the THC crystals. Then it changes to a nice golden brown when dry," he says, like Mr. Miyagi coaching a bong-wielding Karate Kid.

Back inside, we're ready for the next stage of bubble-hash production. The small stove is turned on. "You heat it up in a plastic bag in boiling water, then mold it," gangsta kid says, shaping the hash like Play-Doh. He then displays the final rectangular result, showing it to Papa Smurf for his approval. Then, "Since we're up here, might as well take a little rip break!" He madly grins, lighting up the house bong emblazoned with flames running down the sides, "No harm in testing the product!"

A huge bong hit is taken. Coughing. More coughing. Coughing subsides. Then, "Damn, that's why I love hash," he remarks, in a wincing voice, illustrating by holding his hands near his lung area. "All the THC gets in there." Further coughing follows. Gangsta kid shares between coughing spasms, "I used to be a straightedge kid. I played baseball and all, till I broke my foot. Then, my family moved from Seattle. (Pause.) You can say I got California-ized!"

Like tasting Guinness at Dublin's Guinness factory, this is the pure thing. Gangsta kid offers me a sample of some fresh bubble hash. For the further pursuit of journalistic excellence, I accept. More journalistic excellence follows. My body feeling encased in cement, follows after. Now too stoned to work, I stare at the shape of the clouds. One cloud resembles Abe Lincoln. Except Abe Lincoln without a beard (or stovepipe hat). Hey, my blue Gatorade looks just like Windex. How can I be sure it isn't? What if I am drinking Windex?! Will everyone be too baked to help me? The peacocks are really starting to freak me out. If I'm this high from two hits of hash, should I worry? Everyone else must be muuuuuuch higher. They won't notice my slack-jawed staring as anything unusual. Nothing to worry about. . . . Damn, there're a lot of peacocks! Is this how the Manson Family started?

Two dreadlocked trimmers lay outside, on top of a woodpile, also too stoned to work. Not to be judgmental, but their conversation verges on asinine. It goes something like:

"I ordered barbeque chicken in Willits, and that shit was covered in teriyaki sauce. It's called barbeque chicken."

"It's called barbeque chicken cuz it's cooked on a barbeque."

"It said 'barbeque.' It didn't say 'teriyaki'; that's my point."

"Barbeque is just a cooking technique."

(This debate goes on for another good ten minutes.)

They both suddenly stop talking midsentence and immediately fall asleep.

The Day Burns On

The Dude stands outside staring at his automobile. Illuminated on the front bumper is a large dent. "I got my car stuck in a ditch last night." Surely nothing to do with driving stoned, the Dude drove fifteen miles past the turnoff to the farm. He then tried to quickly double back, resulting in his car shooting off the road. "I had to pay four hundred dollars to get it towed."

"It's all good!" I say with faux hippie optimism.

I've turned into a stupid stoner. Having lost my way back to the makeshift wooden building, I follow at the Dude's heel for direction.

Inside, Waco now stumbles around, mumbling, "Where the fuck's my wallet? Where the fuck's my wallet!"

"You're a bastard for giving him those bad drugs," Rachel, turning to the Dude, says.

"You got Zeke fucked up and now Waco."

"That's what I'm here for," the Dude replies, then recaps, "You missed when Waco took four hits of E. 'Droplets,' he called it."

"It tastes just like NutraSweet!"

Waco's far from the craziest person Rachel's encountered from her years on pot farms. "There were these hippie boys from Bodega Bay. We were staying in this tree house. It was pouring rain, and there were all these guns and coke around and hard alcohol," she recalls, regarding that volatile combination and the possibilities of mishap thereof.

Rachel has just returned from a run to the town store in Laytonville, with such essentials as a gallon of rubbing alcohol, a case of turkey bags, and trimming scissors. Rachel says, "One of the features of the local stores is they have all the supplies we need. I asked if they had a bottle of alcohol. They said, 'Do you want one like this or one like this?'" she laughs, outstretching her arms in imitation of the all-knowing store clerk, familiar with the key elements in bubble-hash production. "In town, there're four billboards for hydroponics stores. That says something about the community and where the money is!"

"You can see it all around you, if you know what you're looking for," Zeke moans, referring to the two out of three people in Mendocino who grow marijuana. Water coolers, greenhouses, and camouflage to hide the plants are big Scooby Doo clues. "There was an acre of weed right off the freeway," he adds. "The weed was so tall you could actually see it over the fence!"

The Dude recalls a local newspaper article: "The local sheriff said, 'I'm so sick of hearing about marijuana. They can give me the same money to fight coke and meth any day!'"

"Last week the UPS guy came by. He was tripping when he saw the greenhouses," Zeke adds, picking a scab.

Adjusting his bathrobe, the Dude takes another rip from his Gatorade bong. "Honestly, when the PG&E guy comes out here to check the meters, he looks at our plants and waves at us!"

The Dude surely knows weed. He's been a grower for the last twelve years. The basement of his Santa Rosa home houses a ten-light hydroponic operation large enough to have four square feet of room per plant. "I'm his suburban counterpart," he says, gesturing towards Zeke. "Generation Y-Not!" he smiles, taking another rip from his Gatorade bong.

The ignorant tend to pooh-pooh the Dude's American Dream. "When people find out you're a grower, they have certain connotations attached to that. You're raised a certain way to think about drugs; that's it's illegal, that it's an inhibitor. They have no idea what they're talking about." Hydroponic—the most chronic of weed—requires much greater skill to grow, because you have to control the nutrients, elements, and growing conditions indoors (compared to growing weed outdoors, where it will grow anywhere, because it's, well, a weed). "If you do it, you want to be really good at it. You got to be gutsy!"

Yes, one has to face such obstacles as susceptibility to armed robbery (from gutsy, disgruntled customers) and the constant fearful umbrella of being busted over high electric bills, which prompt police to look through your trash for evidence. Why the risk? "You don't have to go to a job every day, and you work in drugs," the Dude says. (That, along with the potential of making $10,000 some weeks.) In a moment of seriousness, he adds, "If something happens to me, I don't have a job to fall back on. This is all I know how to do!"

"You slit your toe," Jake interrupts, noting a big bloody gash on the Dude's foot. "How did you do it?"

"I don't know," the Dude replies, unfazed. "Maybe it was on the trailer?" Another rip from the Gatorade bong.

Fields of Dreams

A fence on the hillside. The latch opened. A clearing hidden from the road. Inside one of the four large pot fields.

"Be sure to close the gate, otherwise deer will get in here and chew the plants," Jake says, embarking on an afternoon inspection.

"What happens to the deer?" I ask.

"They get real high!" Jake replies. "They'll lay down and not want to move." (Sounds like Zeke.)

Jake loves weed. He's been both a grower and seller for the last four years. "I started smoking weed at age twelve. I started selling to my friends. First it was a quarter, then a half, then a pound, and it escalated from there!"

Passing a huge marijuana plant fallen over into a large clump, bearing a multitude of buds glistening with various shades of purple, Jake gleefully exclaims like a kid on Christmas morning, "I never seen outdoor so good! The weather in this area is real perfect for growing." His face lights up, "Two weeks ago I was picking nugs as big as my arm! When I tell people, they don't believe me!"

The female plants produce the sweet-smelling buds, attracting the male plants with the seeds to provide pollen. Like a fine wine, if you get a really good strain of weed, the thing to do is highly cultivate it for cloning; you put leaf in water, add some growth hormones, and you get a new plant of that strain.

"You get to know the Trainwreck smell. It's real sweet compared to the Purple strains," Jake says, holding up a large bud to his nose and sniffing.

Time for the Pepsi Challenge.

I'm told to get down on my knees, close my eyes, and sniff two separate stinky buds. (Worst-case scenario: I'm about to be shot execution-style for knowing too much!) Sniffing commences.

Opening my eyes, I blurt, "That's Trainwreck!" pointing to the bud on the left.

"You're right. It's much sweeter." Other differences: "Trainwreck gives you a head high. Purple Indica is more of a body high; it makes you slump on the couch."

Taking another blessed sniff of sweet Trainwreck, Jake looks off into the canvas of wilderness, smiling with a twinkle in his eye. "This is my American Dream. You get to grow weed and hang out with like-minded people. It raises opportunities both financially and socially." Elaboration: "My dream is to have a huge hydroponic basement in Tahoe. There's no theft up there, and there's always new customers." Tahoe tourists will gladly pay high prices and freak out at the quality ("Those got orange hairs, dude!"), which, in turn, finances Jake's snowboarding lifestyle.

"My dream is to open a muffin shop," I throw out with a dreamy look. "Then I can eat muffins all day!"

Rachel appears. Trekking up the hill through the woods, smiling, she makes her way to where Jake and I stand near a tree. Three peacocks have navigated to the highest branch of a tree, now emitting otherworldly noises from high above.

"The birds really freak out when the helicopters fly over," Rachel states, sitting down on the side of the hill. Fortunately for peacocks (and weed growers), there's no money from the Bureau of Narcotic Enforcement this year for CAMP (Campaign Against Marijuana Planting). Funds have been cut for helicopters to patrol Mendocino pot farms. "It's created this boomtown of growers and changed the market," she says, smiling. "People have gone crazy, and it's much more relaxed cuz the threat is gone!"

In the distance, the fog slowly rolls over the hills from the coastline. Like a slinking ghost, it gradually overtakes the expanse of forest. The sun starts setting, giving off incandescent orange and Halloween red over the canopy of nature. "This is what it's all about," Rachel, who's been up here every fall since she was seventeen, relishes the scene. "Being able to support yourself and being able to be here!"

The sun makes one last flicker, like a lighter that's suddenly stopped working, then disappears in the horizon. Darkness.

Dinner

A loss of time seems to occur with workers on the pot farm.

"Is today Thursday or Friday!?" questions Waco, rolling around in a chair. "I forgot what day it is!"

"It's Thursday," I inform him.

"No way!"

"Yeah. It was just daylight savings time, so you need to turn your clock forward."

Heavy thought is put into my logic. A flaw is seen. Then the retort: "You can't do that."

I now can have full moronic conversations in pot-speak:

"Is that the Trainwreck?" I ask.

"Yes."

"Do you prefer the Trainwreck bubble hash or the weed?" is my inquiry.

(With a look like someone solving a ridiculously hard math problem.) "It's just different."

"It's a head high, right?"

"Yeah, but I like more of the purple after dinner."

"So do I!" I agree, adding, "Because it's more of a body high!"

A heater is haphazardly hooked up to a propane tank by the Dude, who's fumbling with the device. It feels like something could easily blow up accidentally. Zeke looks at his shirt, which was scorched from a falling ash. "It's funny, cuz I used to be into crack," he says of the wacky reminder of simpler times. Waco falls out of his chair. It's only seven PM.

Dinnertime creates a dysfunctional stoner-family feel, as a meal is prepared for everyone. And a typical stoner dinner it is. Utilizing whatever eating utensils they can find; a knife, a stick, a very large spoon, hands, etc., people consume stir-fried vegetables. When eating is involved, on a pot farm, it gets very, very quiet.

"There's no meat in here?" I whine like a pain-in-the-ass pointing at the vegetables. "I don't eat meat!" (Pause.) "Or soup!"

I imagine hundreds of pot farms right now in this area having the exact same dining scenario (involving other people just like these, only with different names).

Becoming increasingly aggressive, Waco now keeps repeating, "I have to turn myself in tomorrow!" "I have to turn myself in tomorrow!"

His situation is restated: "Waco flipped a UHaul trailer with the nitrous oxide tanks, while driving to L.A.!" (Laughs.) An update: "Tomorrow he has to turn himself in to the court." (More laughs.) "He blew all his money on legal fees!" (Huge laughs.)

This might be the last we see of Waco for a while. Good thing he's tripping his nuts off hours before turning himself in to authorities. Zeke and the Dude are driving him back to Santa Rosa tonight, along, of course, with a massive amount of weed.

"Make sure you have a medical marijuana card," Rachel recommends.

"I'll be the decoy," the Dude assures, still clad in his bathrobe. "If the cops pull us over, I'll say I don't have a license and take off running into the woods." (Again, the making for the best episode of *Cops* ever!)

Before leaving us on our own, the Dude provides some advice. If a confrontation should arise, he insists that the local sheriff recommends, "Hide the bodies!"

Rachel reassures, "You read about dead bodies in newspaper."

Further reassurance from Zeke, confirming that in the past L.A. gang members armed with AK47s have come to this area to rob farms. Loveable hippies have been killed in their sleep, because the weed is so profitable and abundant. It's the dark side of the Marijuana American Dream.

The Dude gets worked up. "They think they can come up here and rob us? You're in our territory! It just takes one phone call," he says, in order to round up the local posse. "We take care of our own!"

Looking around, just in this room alone there must be tens of thousands of dollars worth of weed. Looking at those minding the weed—an elite squadron of misfit superheroes of another dimension—I realize how comically easy that would be!

Late Night

The barren, makeshift structure is freezing, fucking, cold, warmed only by the small, improperly connected propane heater. In complete, utter silence, four of us sit, huddled together, stoned out of our heads, watching a DVD of *Borat* on a tiny television situated on top of a crate of freshly cut marijuana. The others have left, gone to sell weed and hash back in their respective communities, where the premium, bodacious quality will be highly praised! I'd love to get the hell out of here, but I'm far too stoned to drive on these remote, hilly, gravel roads. Instead, I'm stuck like a man trapped in thick quicksand. Still noncommunicative, DJ Brian sits in the exact same spot he's been the entire day, trimming relentlessly, like a mechanized windup toy who dreams dollar signs.

"This movie is really funny if you're high!" I say, pointing to the TV. No reaction whatsoever. Outside, it's pitch black, haunted-house foggy. You can barely see your pipe-holding hand in front of you. This would be the opportune time for the gangs with AK47s to rob the entire place—leaving no witnesses! All they would have to do is ward off the four of us— completely stoned out of our heads, watching *Borat*, deep in the middle of marijuana-enriched, isolated nowhere. I think you could rob this place with a penknife and affected raspy voice.

"Did you bring any Chewie?" breaking the silence, Dean, a seventeen-year-old kid with dreads, wearing a baseball cap with a pot leaf on it (he must like pot), asks me.

"What's that?"

"Blow!"

"Hey, I just do the green not the white," I say, trying to sound like the cool guy. (I guess in the land of the weed, the one-eyed man with Chewie is king.)

Dean disappears. (Where the fuck did he go?!) He then reappears. Dean is now high above us climbing on the thin, wooden ceiling beams, fucked up out off his head. "You got to think like a spider," Dean says, traversing spiderlike across the sketchy rafters. Dean is really freaking me out. "I once climbed a 250 foot redwood tree!" he states.

A loud noise suddenly erupts from the foggy outside, sharply cutting through the deafening silence. We look at each other. Another noise. *Borat* is put on pause.

"That's not your everyday sound," concerned Dean remarks, descending spider-like from the rafters.

It must be the guys with AK47s! Hurrah! What protection do we have? I could create some sort of explosive weapon with the hazardous propane tank. Utilizing the element of surprise, Dean could jump spiderlike on them from the rafters. Another loud noise!

Dean shoots a serious look. "I just heard two car doors slam!"

I'm too stoned to move. DJ Brian can't be bothered to stop trimming. Grabbing a hammer, Dean goes outside to investigate. Returning moments later, he looks worried and pale.

"What was it?" I ask, eyeing the propane tank (and leftover stir-fry, yum!)

"I heard laughing and saw people walking with flashlights!"

"Was it an L.A. gang–type laugh?" I question.

Dean goes outside again. Is this the last we'll see of Dean? Are drug barons going to kidnap us then eat our brains as part of a ritual to ward off evil law-enforcement spirits?

No gunfire, only leftover chow mein. Dean comes back holding two takeout cartons. "Does anyone want Chinese food?"

The noise, it turns out, was a couple of trimmers returning from dinner in Laytonville. Too baked to react, we resume watching *Borat*. I can only imagine nightly being afraid of unknown noises. Stoned and paranoid about armed L.A. gangs is not the ideal combination.

Too much shenanigans for one evening, I decide to call it a night before *Borat* concludes and head towards the foggy haunted-house abyss outside.

"There's a tent you can sleep in with a mattress," Rachel informs, leaving me wondering how much smelly hippie sex has been had on that mattress? There are no showers. The toilet is a dug hole surrounded by poison oak. Once again, hello, scabies!

I instead opt to sleep in my jeep. With the heater blasting, I immediately fall into a cramped, blissful, panic-induced slumber, wondering, when the L.A. gangs come in the middle of the night, will I be the first one shot? Realistically, they'll probably slit my throat as to not wake the others—they're pros after all. And then again, there's always the DEA!

More Trim

In the morning—awake with noneaten brains—much like watching *Borat* in complete silence, the six of us now trim buds in complete silence.

Snippity-snip-snip.

DJ Brian still sits in the same chair from last night (and the entire day before), only taking periodical breaks to light up and smoke. Dean's wide awake ("He was up all night on crystal.")

Two girls from San Diego have joined us—both three-year, experienced zen masters of trimming, who've been up here since April. By their side, a huge finished bag of trimmed weed (mine, not so much). The zen masters trim buds with the proficiency of old southern gentlemen whittling a George Washington head out of a good piece of hickory. I, on the other hand, spend a lot of time hovered over the heater, just staring at individual buds, thinking they resemble thick pinecones (and occasionally verbalizing this).

More insightful conversations centered around pot:

"What did you smoke this morning?"

"Trainwreck."

"That gets you really high!"

"Do you ever notice how these look like pine cones?" I contribute.

The dreadlocked one of the zen masters mentions her upcoming birthday, "I'm going to be thirty, but I feel like seventeen." (Could it be cuz you trim weed for a living?)

"What else do you do besides this?" I ask and wonder.

"Not much else," she says, then falls into zen-trimming silence.

Somehow I can easily picture her living room. Bong on the table. Burns on the couch. Plates of half-eaten food lying everywhere, constantly misplaced car keys, etc. . . . Once the season's over, though, she's moving out of her apartment. "It hasn't been the same since my boyfriend got out of jail," she confesses.

Dean, taking a hash-smoking break, dreams outside on the porch by the hippie drum. He pontificates, "I'd like to sample the pure strains of hash. Like the Trainwreck hash, the Purple Indica hash, the Strawberry Cough hash."

"Did you watch the end of *Borat*?" I interrupt.

Almost with an angry tone, he replies, "I don't know, I didn't watch the movie!"

I refresh: "Remember we were all watching it last night?"

A moment of thought. The wrinkling of the brow. Then, "Oh, yeah." He takes a long rip.

Dean worked on a fishing boat near Bodega Bay before coming to Papa Smurf's pot farm. He quit just a few months back. "My skipper accused me of stealing his weed and selling it. So I said, 'You know what? I'm out of here!'"

When he was fifteen, Dean moved to California from Texas. "I came out with my sister to live with my mom and her boyfriend. I thought it would be cool, but it wasn't," he relays without emotion. So I said, 'You know what? I'm out of here!'" He's been on his own since.

After he quit the fishing boat, Dean was homeless for a while until a friend told him about Papa Smurf's farm. "My homie hooked me up," Dean says. This has now become Dean's extended, yet very high, family.

The fog starts rolling in over the hills from the Coast. The peacocks resume watchdog duties. It will soon be another sunset.

Inside, one of the masters needs to call her mom and legitimize her whereabouts for the past few months. "She still has dreams of me being in the corporate world," she mentions, and then asks her dreadlocked friend, "Can you tell me some names of festivals? I just need names!"

The day moves at a slow stoners' pace. I could see how one day blends into the stoned next, which blends into weeks, which blends into months. I see purple buds when I blink. Somehow my shoulder hurts. The strong smell of weed is making me nauseous. It's like a little kid who loves candy until he's allowed to eat all the candy he wants, and ends up vomiting.

While you don't want to work for the Man, working on a pot farm must be one of the most mindless jobs known to humanity. Those who rationalize that the "money is soooo good," perhaps would do the same if jacking monkeys off paid just as well. ("The money is soooo good!") There's the dream of working on a pot farm, mixed with the reality of being stuck in the middle of the woods with a bunch of stoners.

More transient hippies come through. Those trying to be so "off the curve" somehow end up seeming contrived from the same mold as each other.

"I'm not sure what to do after the season," the dreadlocked girl says. "I'm sure I'll be back here in January, knocking on Papa Smurf's door when I run out of money."

Looking at the time, I can't believe the irony. Expecting a huge reaction, I announce, "Hey everyone, it's 4:20!" No one cares. No one looks up. On a pot farm, it's always 4:20.

ACKNOWLEDGMENTS

The author would like to thank his wonderful family and friends, his agent Caroline Greevan, his editor Ruth Baldwin, the support of the Investigative Fund of The Nation Institute, and everyone else who had a hand with putting this book together.

On a lesser scale, the author would like to thank Madame Curie, character actor Hal Holbrook, Mrs. Butterworth, the people of the great state of New Jersey, redheads, the shy, anyone who has ever played the oboe, and President Grover Cleveland, for all their influence.

Harmon Leon is an award-winning journalist/filmmaker, and author of *The Harmon Chronicles* (ECW Press), *Republican Like Me* (Prometheus Books), *The Infiltrator* (Prometheus Books), and *National Lampoon's Road Trip USA*. His first fiction book is the *Brother's Rjukerooka*.

His articles have appeared in *Esquire, Stuff, Salon, NPR's This American Life, Details, Maxim, High Times, Hustler, Penthouse, Black Book, Cosmopolitan,* and *Wired*.

Leon has appeared on *The Howard Stern Show, Penn & Teller's Bullshit, The Jamie Kennedy Experiment, VH1, Court TV,* and *Blind Date*, as well as the BBC. He has also costarred with the infamous OJ Simpson on a hidden camera reality show called *Juiced!* and performed comedy around the world, including the Montreal, Edinburgh, Dublin, Galway, Vancouver, Adelaide, and Melbourne Comedy Festivals.

Harmon is low in sodium and perfect for the elderly.